CHICAGO'S BEEFIEST S

JUICEMAN

STORY & ART
SCOTT JAMES

COLOURS
NIKOS KOUTSIS
& SCOTT JAMES

LETTERS
FERRAN
DELGADO

EDITOR
GAVIN
HIGGINBOTHAM

COVER
ART: JOHN ROMITA JR & SCOTT JAMES
COLOURS: NIKOS KOUTSIS

FOR MARKOSIA ENTERPRISES LTD

HARRY MARKOS
PUBLISHER & MANAGING PARTNER

GM JORDAN
SPECIAL PROJECTS CO-ORDINATOR

ANDY BRIGGS
CREATIVE CONSULTANT

IAN SHARMAN
EDITOR IN CHIEF

 PUBLISHED BY MARKOSIA ENTERPRISES, PO BOX 3477, BARNET, HERTFORDSHIRE, EN5 9HN. FIRST PRINTING, JANUARY 2023. HARRY MARKOS, DIRECTOR.

ISBN 978-1-915387-93-6

WWW.MARKOSIA.COM

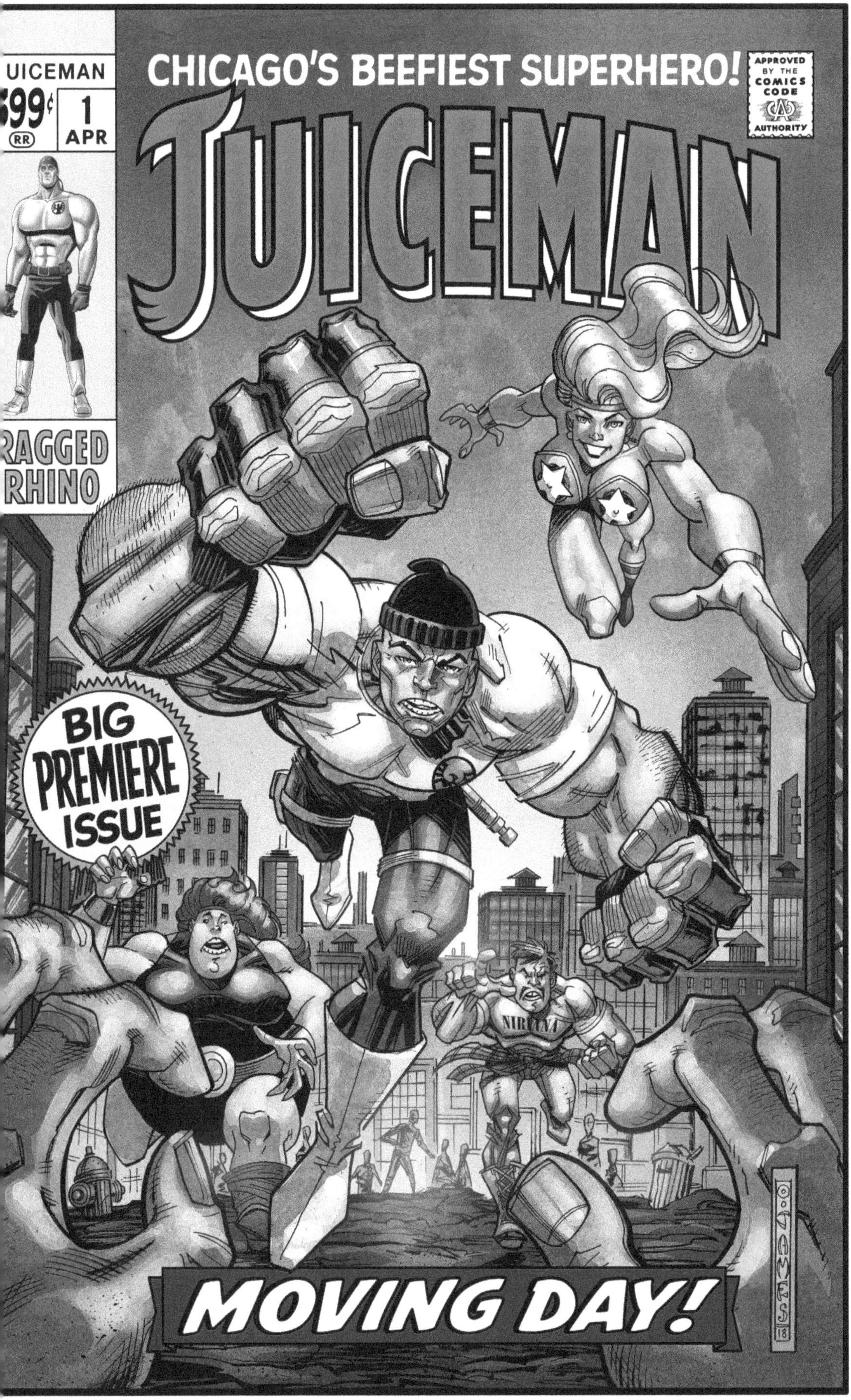

UICEMAN
99¢
RR
1
APR
RAGGED RHINO
CHICAGO'S BEEFIEST SUPERHERO!
APPROVED BY THE COMICS CODE AUTHORITY
JUICEMAN
BIG PREMIERE ISSUE
MOVING DAY!
O. JAMES 18

RAGGED RHINO PRESENTS: JUICEMAN!

SWEET HOME, CHICAGO!

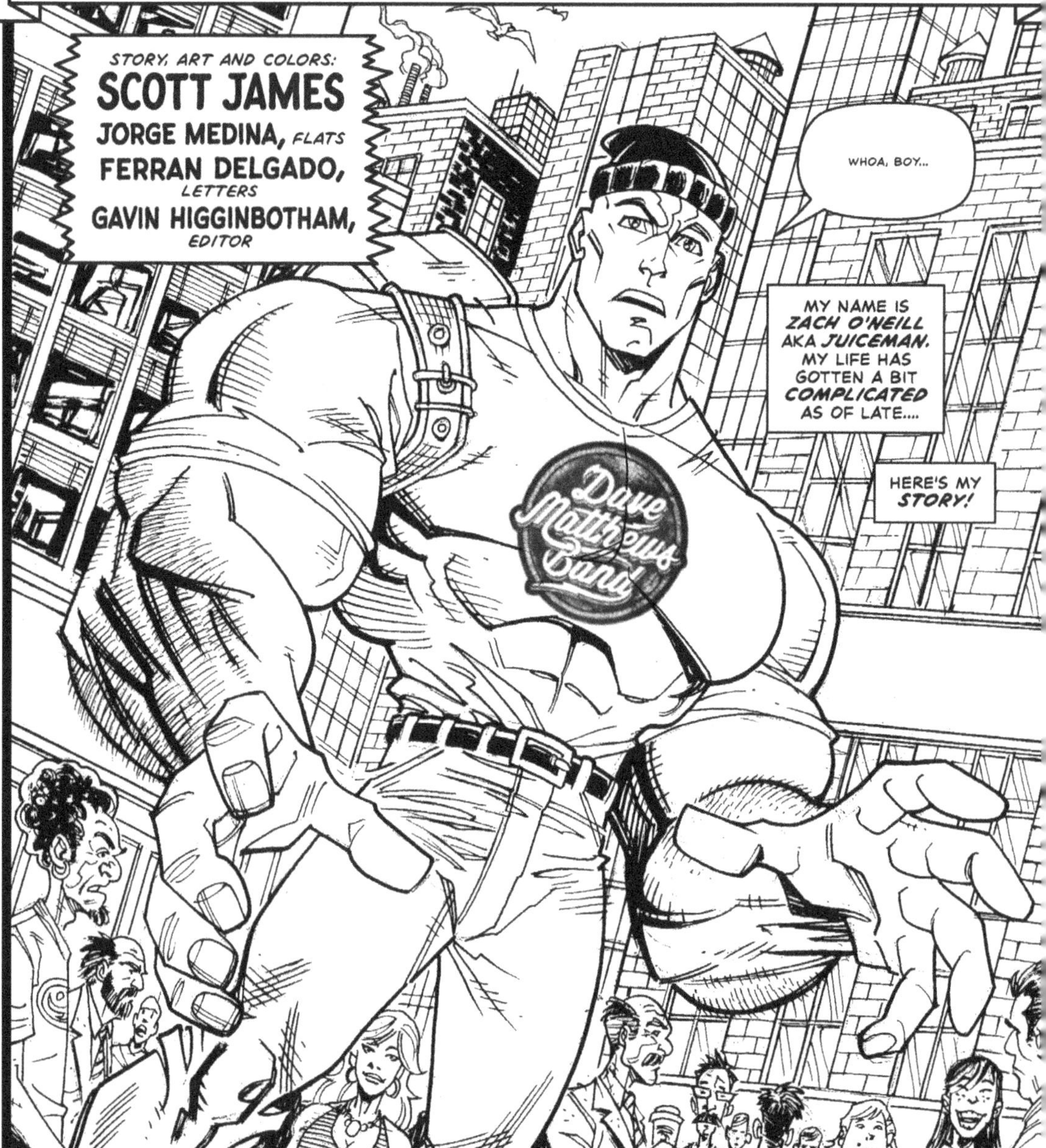
STORY, ART AND COLORS:
SCOTT JAMES
JORGE MEDINA, FLATS
FERRAN DELGADO, LETTERS
GAVIN HIGGINBOTHAM, EDITOR
WHOA, BOY...
MY NAME IS ZACH O'NEILL AKA JUICEMAN. MY LIFE HAS GOTTEN A BIT COMPLICATED AS OF LATE....
HERE'S MY STORY!
Dave Matthews Band

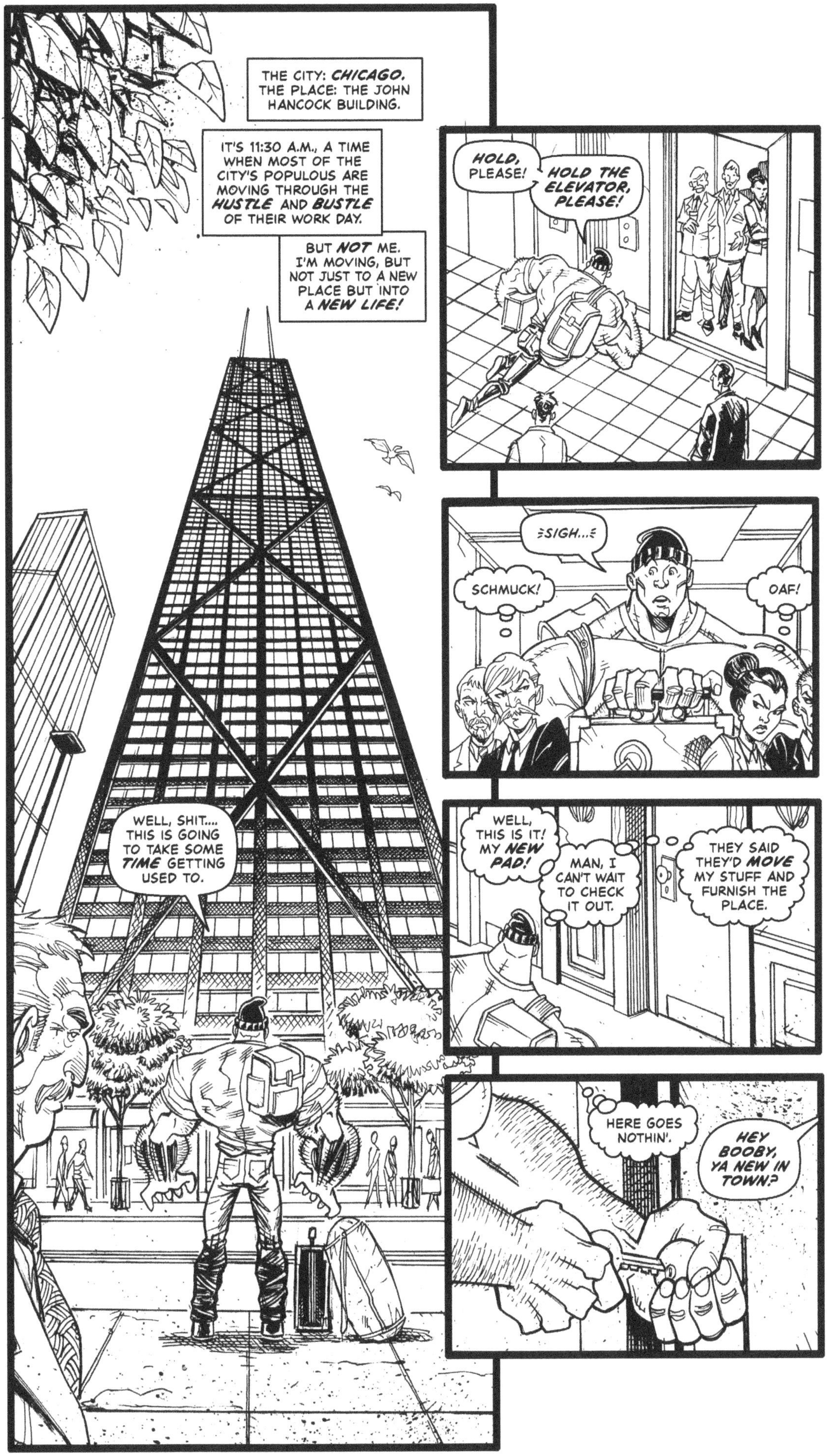
THE CITY: CHICAGO. THE PLACE: THE JOHN HANCOCK BUILDING.
IT'S 11:30 A.M., A TIME WHEN MOST OF THE CITY'S POPULOUS ARE MOVING THROUGH THE HUSTLE AND BUSTLE OF THEIR WORK DAY.
BUT NOT ME. I'M MOVING, BUT NOT JUST TO A NEW PLACE BUT INTO A NEW LIFE!
WELL, SHIT.... THIS IS GOING TO TAKE SOME TIME GETTING USED TO.
HOLD, PLEASE!
HOLD THE ELEVATOR, PLEASE!
SIGH...
SCHMUCK!
OAF!
WELL, THIS IS IT! MY NEW PAD!
MAN, I CAN'T WAIT TO CHECK IT OUT.
THEY SAID THEY'D MOVE MY STUFF AND FURNISH THE PLACE.
HERE GOES NOTHIN'.
HEY BOOBY, YA NEW IN TOWN?

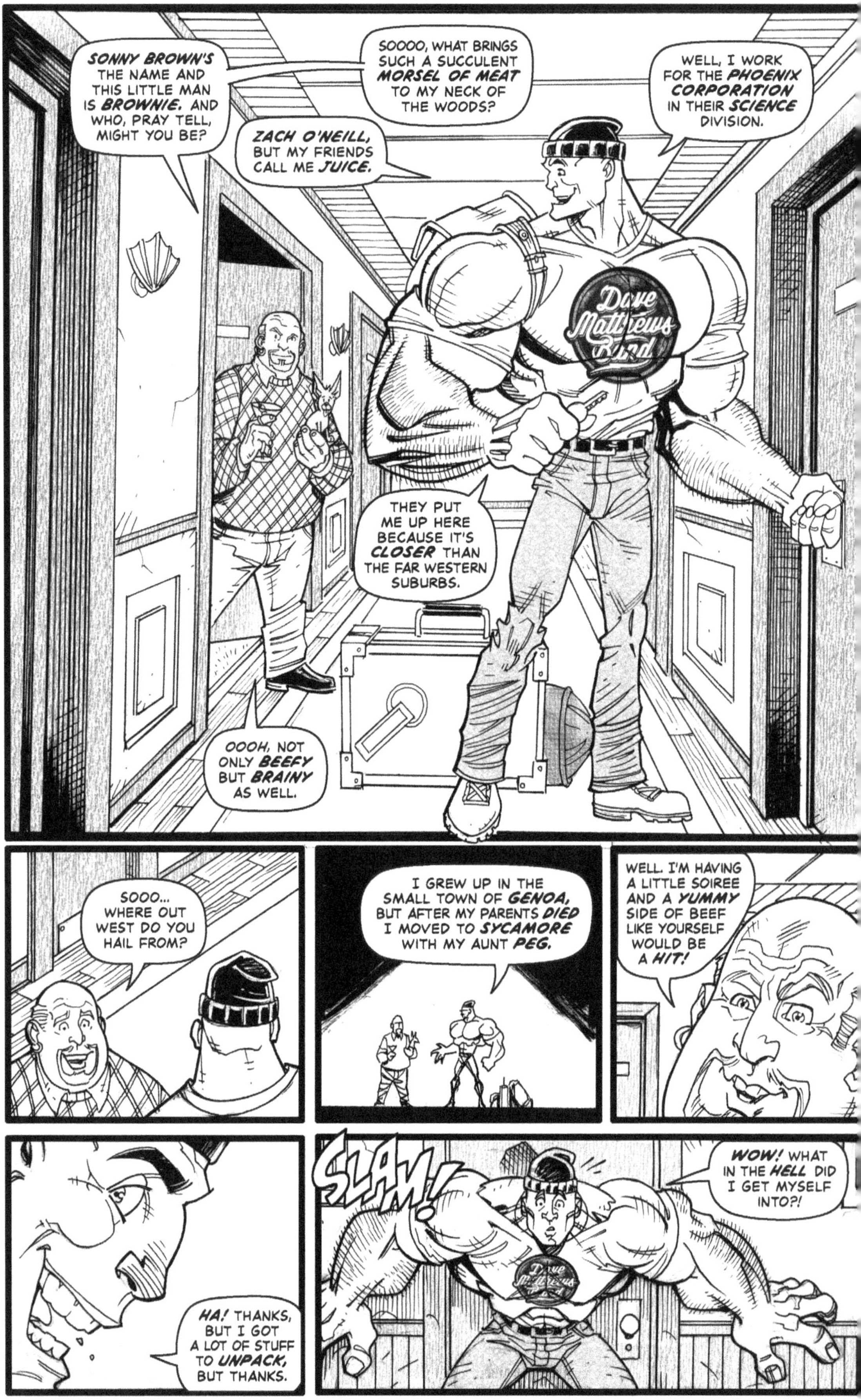
SONNY BROWN'S THE NAME AND THIS LITTLE MAN IS BROWNIE. AND WHO, PRAY TELL, MIGHT YOU BE?
ZACH O'NEILL, BUT MY FRIENDS CALL ME JUICE.
SOOOO, WHAT BRINGS SUCH A SUCCULENT MORSEL OF MEAT TO MY NECK OF THE WOODS?
WELL, I WORK FOR THE PHOENIX CORPORATION IN THEIR SCIENCE DIVISION.
Dave Matthews Band
THEY PUT ME UP HERE BECAUSE IT'S CLOSER THAN THE FAR WESTERN SUBURBS.
OOOH, NOT ONLY BEEFY BUT BRAINY AS WELL.
SOOO... WHERE OUT WEST DO YOU HAIL FROM?
I GREW UP IN THE SMALL TOWN OF GENOA, BUT AFTER MY PARENTS DIED I MOVED TO SYCAMORE WITH MY AUNT PEG.
WELL. I'M HAVING A LITTLE SOIREE AND A YUMMY SIDE OF BEEF LIKE YOURSELF WOULD BE A HIT!
HA! THANKS, BUT I GOT A LOT OF STUFF TO UNPACK, BUT THANKS.
SLAM!
WOW! WHAT IN THE HELL DID I GET MYSELF INTO?!

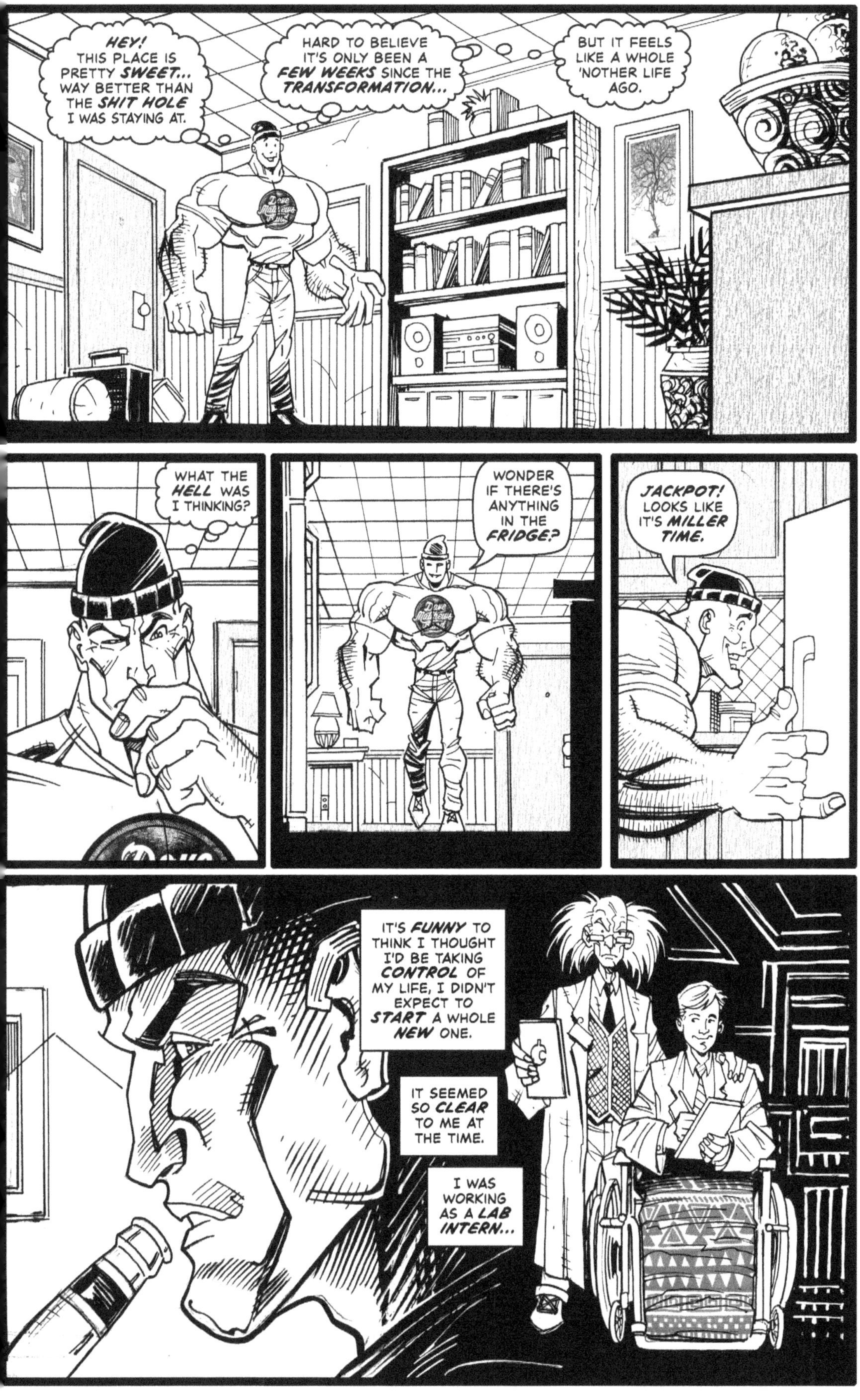
HEY! THIS PLACE IS PRETTY SWEET... WAY BETTER THAN THE SHIT HOLE I WAS STAYING AT.
HARD TO BELIEVE IT'S ONLY BEEN A FEW WEEKS SINCE THE TRANSFORMATION...
BUT IT FEELS LIKE A WHOLE 'NOTHER LIFE AGO.
Dave Matthews Band
WHAT THE HELL WAS I THINKING?
WONDER IF THERE'S ANYTHING IN THE FRIDGE?
Dave Matthews Band
JACKPOT! LOOKS LIKE IT'S MILLER TIME.
IT'S FUNNY TO THINK I THOUGHT I'D BE TAKING CONTROL OF MY LIFE, I DIDN'T EXPECT TO START A WHOLE NEW ONE.
IT SEEMED SO CLEAR TO ME AT THE TIME.
I WAS WORKING AS A LAB INTERN...

...AT THE *PHOENIX CORPORATION'S* BIOGENETICS AND APPLIED SCIENCE DIVISION, UNDER THE TUTELAGE OF *DR. JULIUS ADNOID.*

phoEniX CORPORATION

WE WERE FINE-TUNING A NEW *SUPER STEROID* THAT DOCTOR ADNOID HAD *DEVELOPED.*

IT WAS A *SUCCESS!*

THE *EXPERIMENTS* ON LAB ANIMALS SHOWED *RAPID MUSCULAR GROWTH, TISSUE REGENERATION, INCREASED STRENGTH* AND *STAMINA...*

SO ONE DAY I SAW MY *CHANCE,* A WINDOW OF *OPPORTUNITY--*

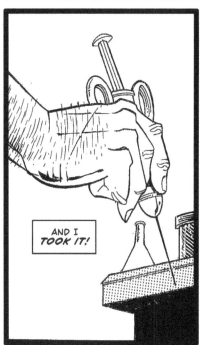

AND I *TOOK IT!*

SOON I WOULD *TRADE* MY DEFINITE FUTURE FOR AN *UNKNOWN* ONE.

BLUB! BLUB!

AND THEN, IN A BLINK OF AN EYE, THE *CHANGE BEGAN.*

WHAT FELT LIKE A DULL BURN, *GREW--*

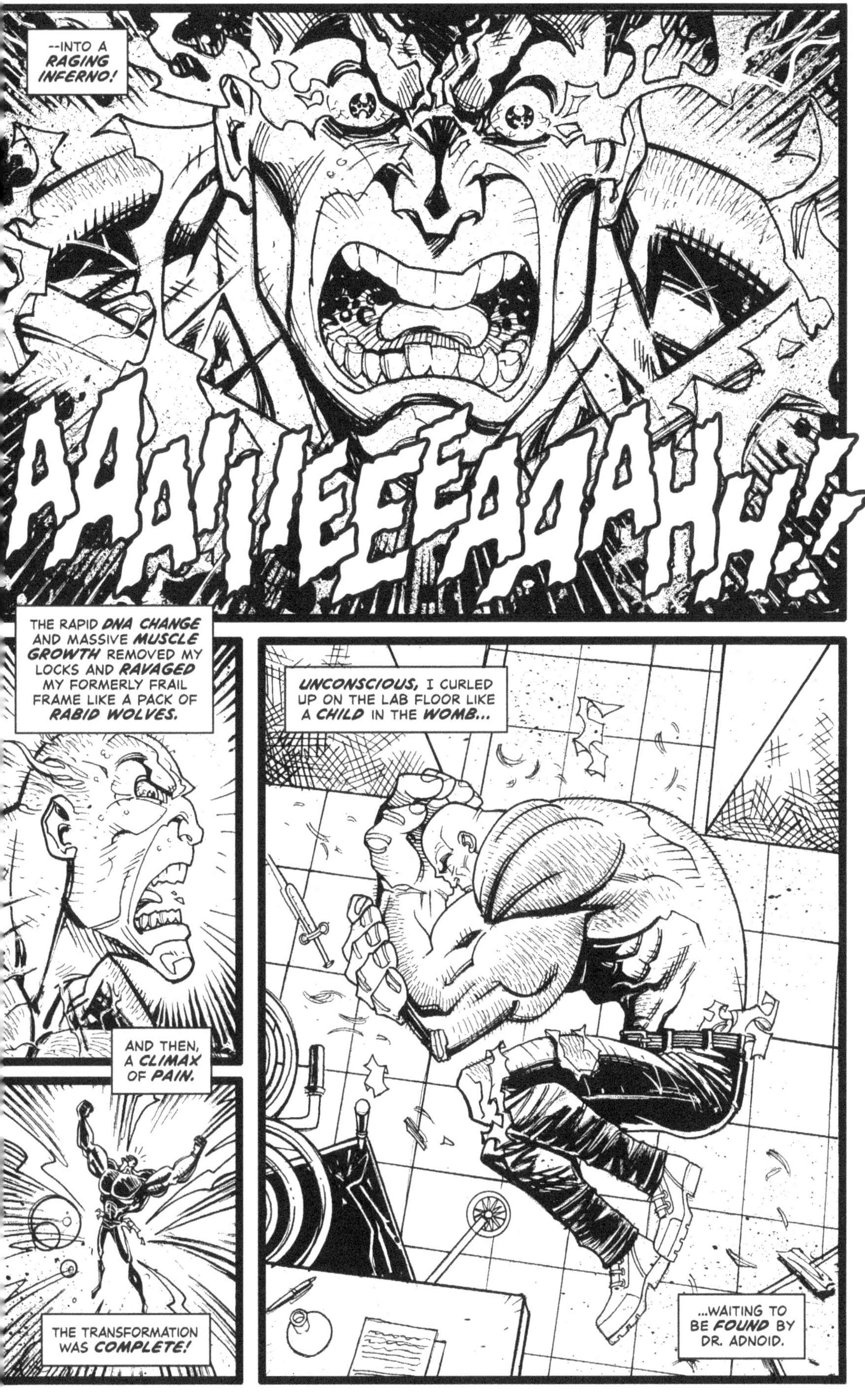
--INTO A RAGING INFERNO!
AAAIIEEEAAAHH!!
THE RAPID DNA CHANGE AND MASSIVE MUSCLE GROWTH REMOVED MY LOCKS AND RAVAGED MY FORMERLY FRAIL FRAME LIKE A PACK OF RABID WOLVES.
AND THEN, A CLIMAX OF PAIN.
THE TRANSFORMATION WAS COMPLETE!
UNCONSCIOUS, I CURLED UP ON THE LAB FLOOR LIKE A CHILD IN THE WOMB...
...WAITING TO BE FOUND BY DR. ADNOID.

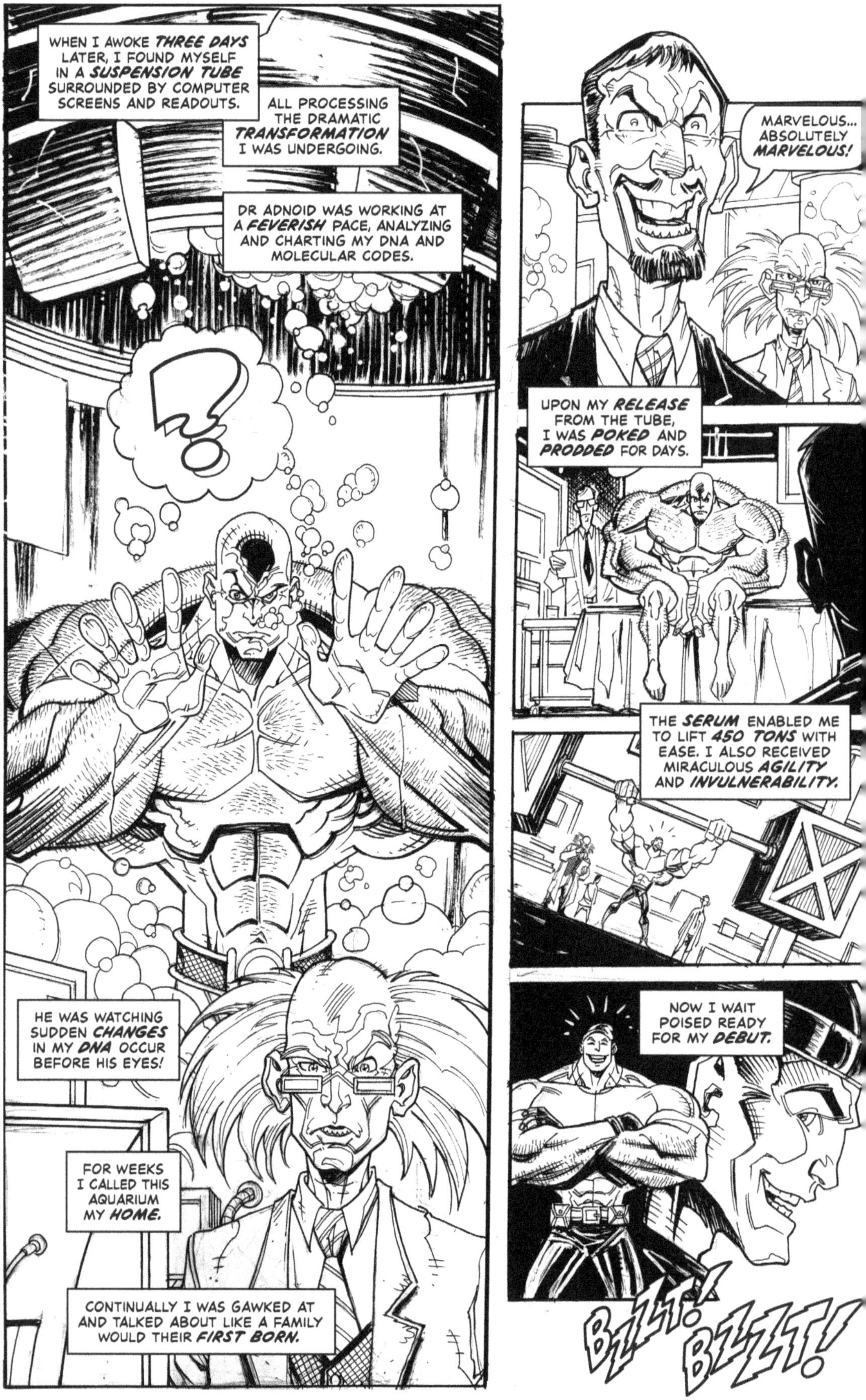
WHEN I AWOKE THREE DAYS LATER, I FOUND MYSELF IN A SUSPENSION TUBE SURROUNDED BY COMPUTER SCREENS AND READOUTS.
ALL PROCESSING THE DRAMATIC TRANSFORMATION I WAS UNDERGOING.
DR ADNOID WAS WORKING AT A FEVERISH PACE, ANALYZING AND CHARTING MY DNA AND MOLECULAR CODES.
?
HE WAS WATCHING SUDDEN CHANGES IN MY DNA OCCUR BEFORE HIS EYES!
FOR WEEKS I CALLED THIS AQUARIUM MY HOME.
CONTINUALLY I WAS GAWKED AT AND TALKED ABOUT LIKE A FAMILY WOULD THEIR FIRST BORN.
MARVELOUS... ABSOLUTELY MARVELOUS!
UPON MY RELEASE FROM THE TUBE, I WAS POKED AND PRODDED FOR DAYS.
THE SERUM ENABLED ME TO LIFT 450 TONS WITH EASE. I ALSO RECEIVED MIRACULOUS AGILITY AND INVULNERABILITY.
NOW I WAIT POISED READY FOR MY DEBUT.
BZZT! BZZT!

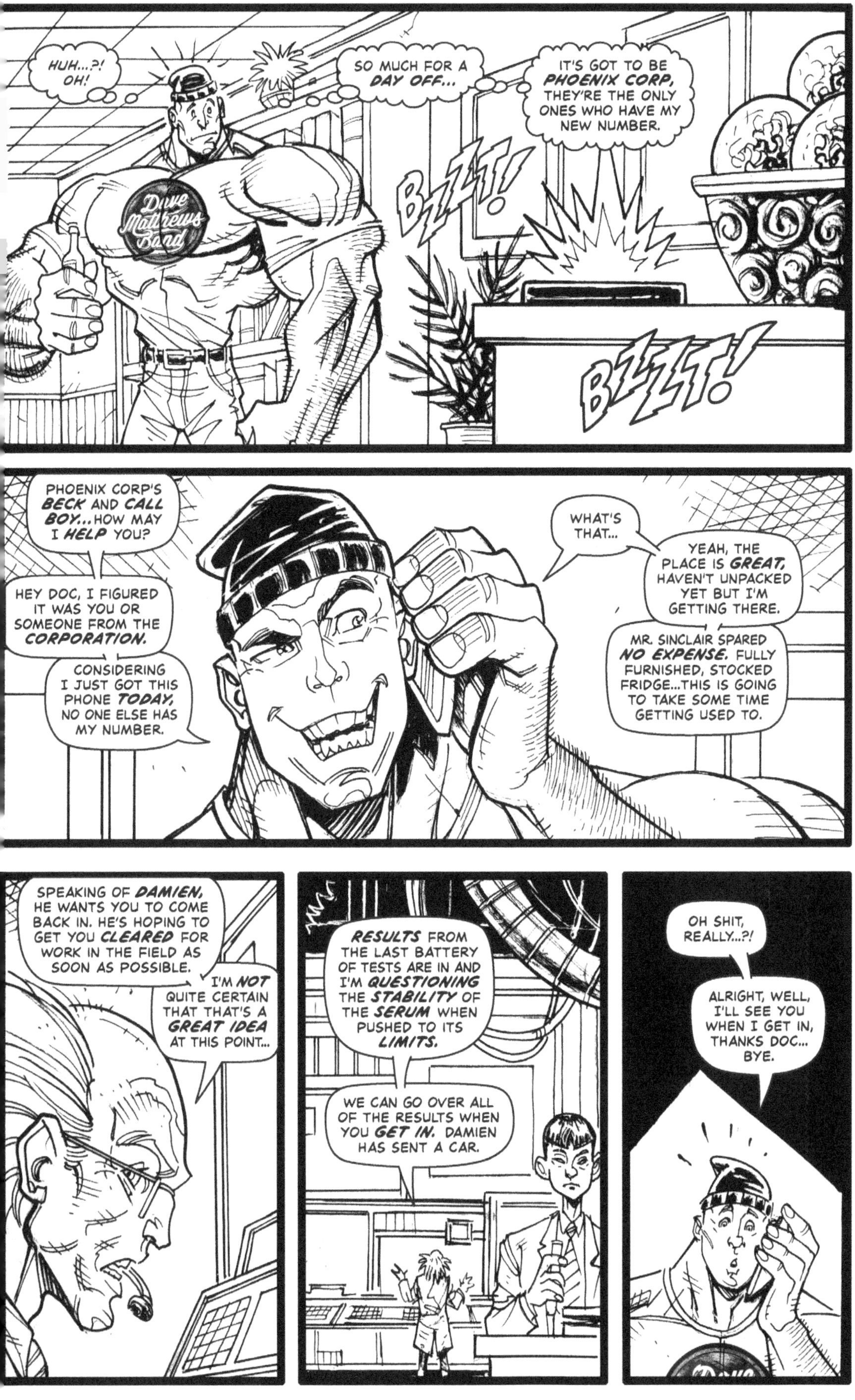
HUH...?! OH!
SO MUCH FOR A DAY OFF...
IT'S GOT TO BE PHOENIX CORP, THEY'RE THE ONLY ONES WHO HAVE MY NEW NUMBER.
Dave Matthews Band
BZZZT!
BZZZT!
PHOENIX CORP'S BECK AND CALL BOY...HOW MAY I HELP YOU?
HEY DOC, I FIGURED IT WAS YOU OR SOMEONE FROM THE CORPORATION.
CONSIDERING I JUST GOT THIS PHONE TODAY, NO ONE ELSE HAS MY NUMBER.
WHAT'S THAT...
YEAH, THE PLACE IS GREAT, HAVEN'T UNPACKED YET BUT I'M GETTING THERE.
MR. SINCLAIR SPARED NO EXPENSE. FULLY FURNISHED, STOCKED FRIDGE...THIS IS GOING TO TAKE SOME TIME GETTING USED TO.
SPEAKING OF DAMIEN, HE WANTS YOU TO COME BACK IN. HE'S HOPING TO GET YOU CLEARED FOR WORK IN THE FIELD AS SOON AS POSSIBLE.
I'M NOT QUITE CERTAIN THAT THAT'S A GREAT IDEA AT THIS POINT...
RESULTS FROM THE LAST BATTERY OF TESTS ARE IN AND I'M QUESTIONING THE STABILITY OF THE SERUM WHEN PUSHED TO ITS LIMITS.
WE CAN GO OVER ALL OF THE RESULTS WHEN YOU GET IN. DAMIEN HAS SENT A CAR.
OH SHIT, REALLY...?!
ALRIGHT, WELL, I'LL SEE YOU WHEN I GET IN, THANKS DOC... BYE.

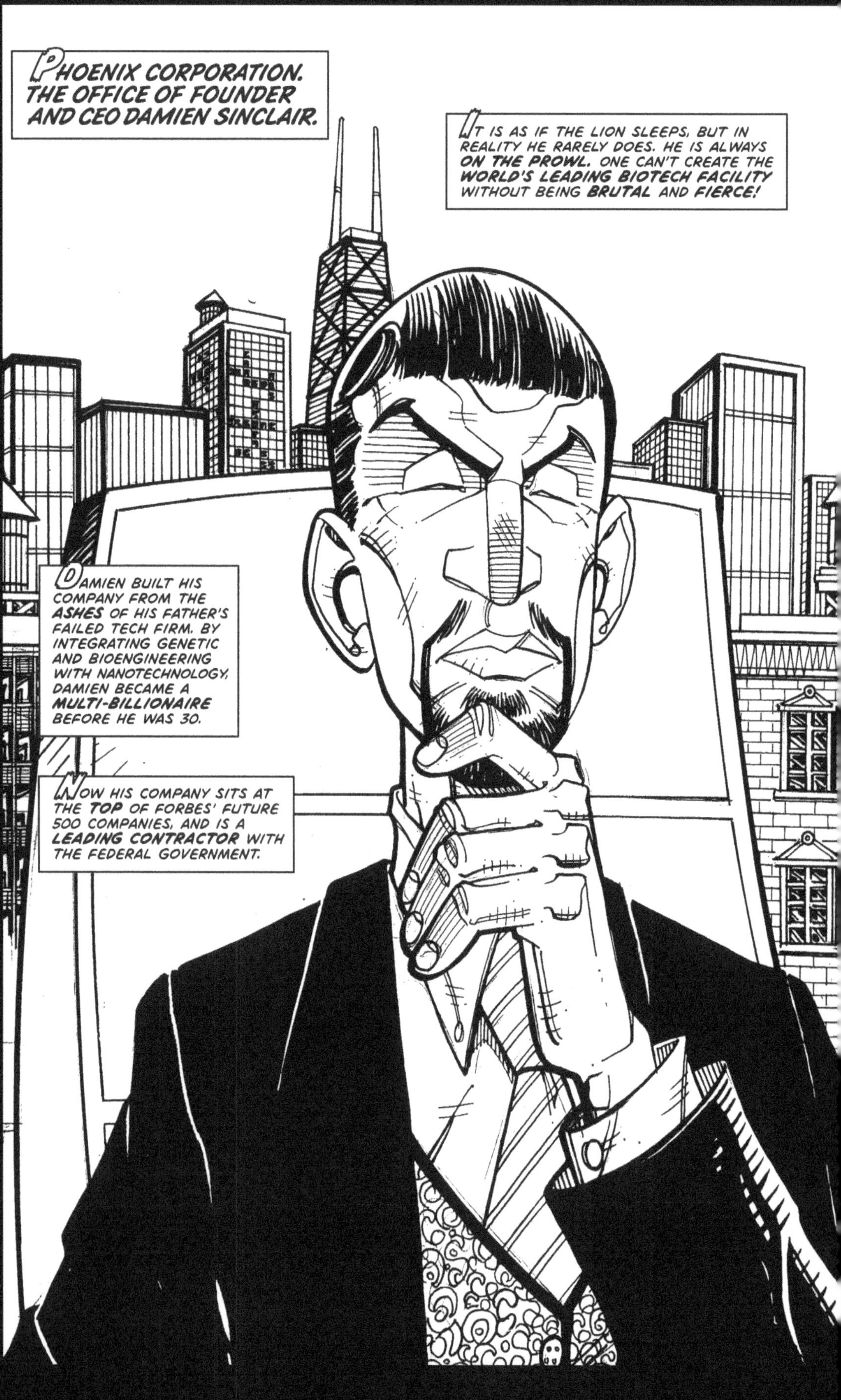
PHOENIX CORPORATION. THE OFFICE OF FOUNDER AND CEO DAMIEN SINCLAIR.
IT IS AS IF THE LION SLEEPS, BUT IN REALITY HE RARELY DOES. HE IS ALWAYS ON THE PROWL. ONE CAN'T CREATE THE WORLD'S LEADING BIOTECH FACILITY WITHOUT BEING BRUTAL AND FIERCE!
DAMIEN BUILT HIS COMPANY FROM THE ASHES OF HIS FATHER'S FAILED TECH FIRM. BY INTEGRATING GENETIC AND BIOENGINEERING WITH NANOTECHNOLOGY, DAMIEN BECAME A MULTI-BILLIONAIRE BEFORE HE WAS 30.
NOW HIS COMPANY SITS AT THE TOP OF FORBES' FUTURE 500 COMPANIES, AND IS A LEADING CONTRACTOR WITH THE FEDERAL GOVERNMENT.

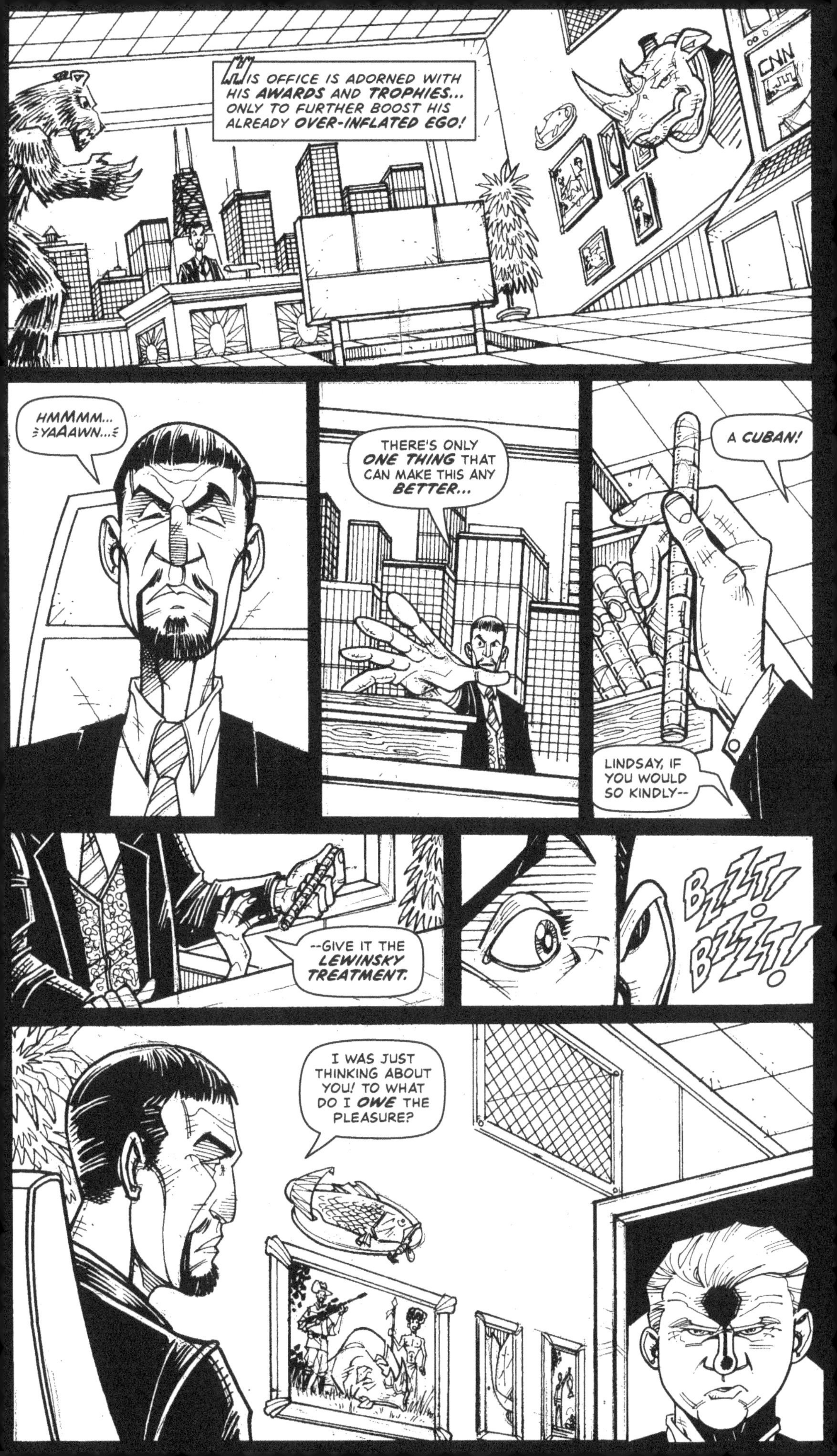
HIS OFFICE IS ADORNED WITH HIS AWARDS AND TROPHIES... ONLY TO FURTHER BOOST HIS ALREADY OVER-INFLATED EGO!
CNN
HMMMM... YAAAWN...
THERE'S ONLY ONE THING THAT CAN MAKE THIS ANY BETTER...
A CUBAN!
LINDSAY, IF YOU WOULD SO KINDLY--
--GIVE IT THE LEWINSKY TREATMENT.
BZZT! BZZT!
I WAS JUST THINKING ABOUT YOU! TO WHAT DO I OWE THE PLEASURE?

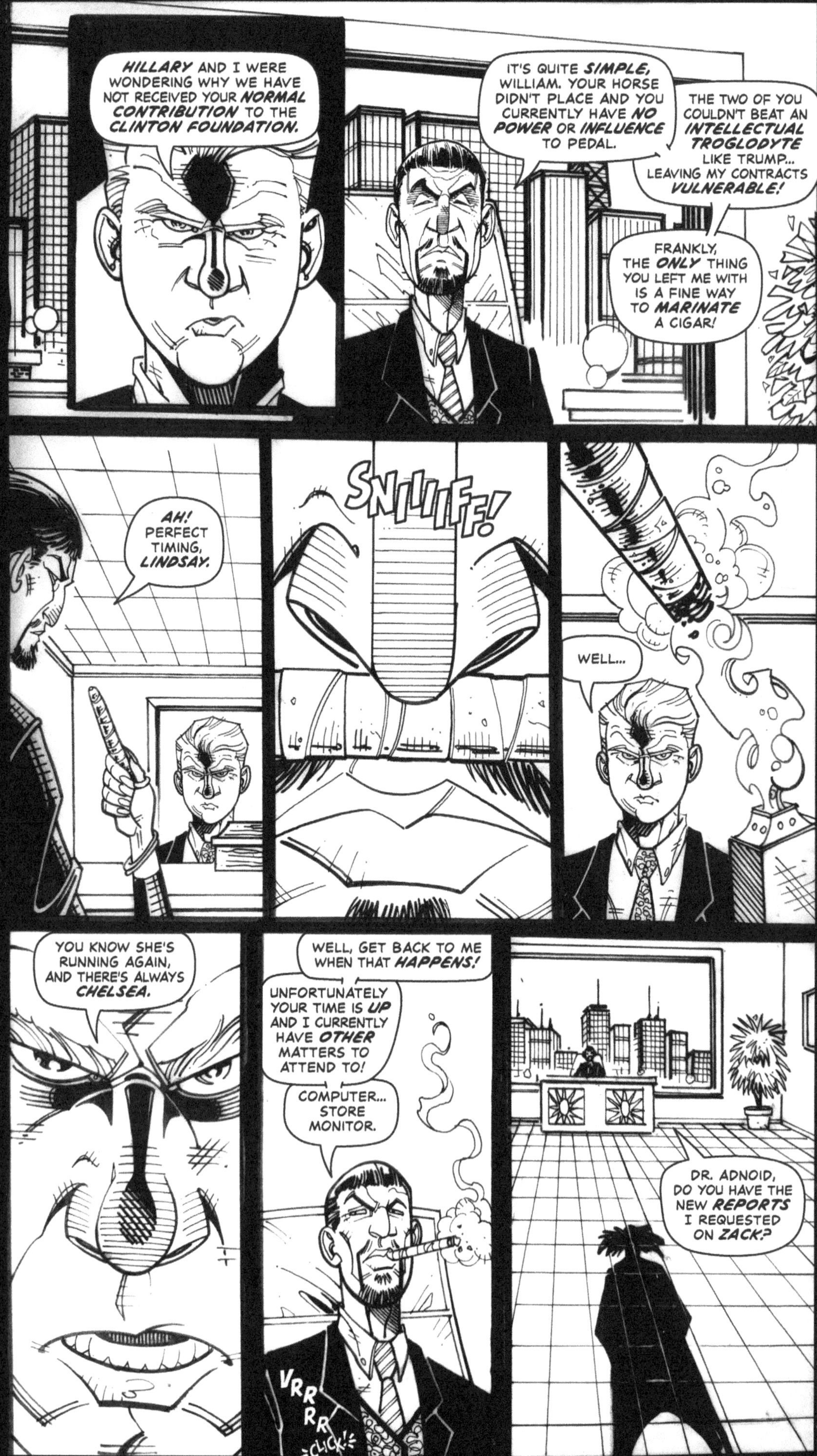
HILLARY AND I WERE WONDERING WHY WE HAVE NOT RECEIVED YOUR NORMAL CONTRIBUTION TO THE CLINTON FOUNDATION.
IT'S QUITE SIMPLE, WILLIAM. YOUR HORSE DIDN'T PLACE AND YOU CURRENTLY HAVE NO POWER OR INFLUENCE TO PEDAL.
THE TWO OF YOU COULDN'T BEAT AN INTELLECTUAL TROGLODYTE LIKE TRUMP... LEAVING MY CONTRACTS VULNERABLE!
FRANKLY, THE ONLY THING YOU LEFT ME WITH IS A FINE WAY TO MARINATE A CIGAR!
AH! PERFECT TIMING, LINDSAY.
SNIIIIFF!
WELL...
YOU KNOW SHE'S RUNNING AGAIN, AND THERE'S ALWAYS CHELSEA.
WELL, GET BACK TO ME WHEN THAT HAPPENS!
UNFORTUNATELY YOUR TIME IS UP AND I CURRENTLY HAVE OTHER MATTERS TO ATTEND TO!
COMPUTER... STORE MONITOR.
VRRRR
CLICK!
DR. ADNOID, DO YOU HAVE THE NEW REPORTS I REQUESTED ON ZACK?

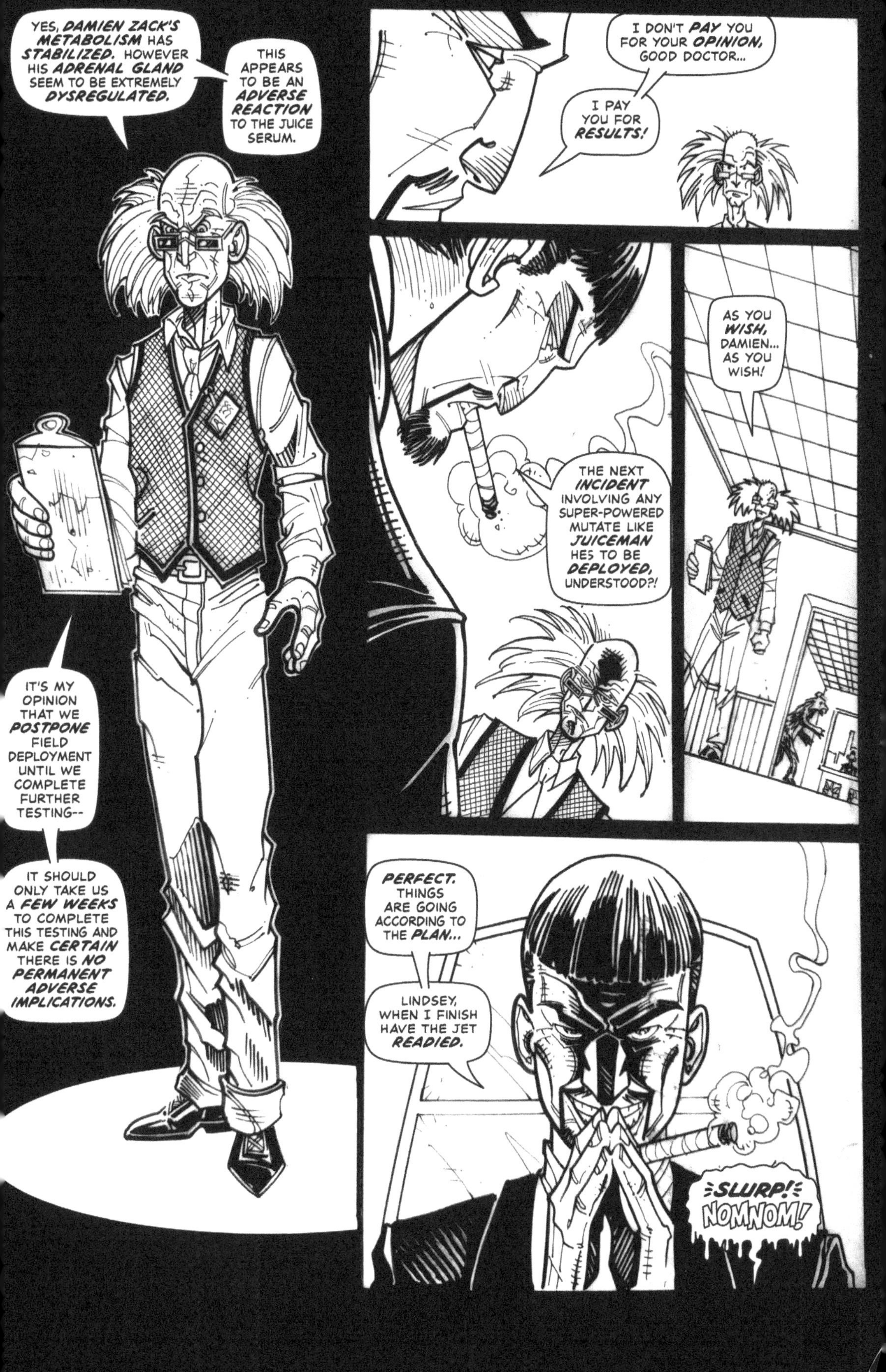

YES, DAMIEN ZACK'S METABOLISM HAS STABILIZED. HOWEVER HIS ADRENAL GLAND SEEM TO BE EXTREMELY DYSREGULATED.
THIS APPEARS TO BE AN ADVERSE REACTION TO THE JUICE SERUM.
IT'S MY OPINION THAT WE POSTPONE FIELD DEPLOYMENT UNTIL WE COMPLETE FURTHER TESTING--
IT SHOULD ONLY TAKE US A FEW WEEKS TO COMPLETE THIS TESTING AND MAKE CERTAIN THERE IS NO PERMANENT ADVERSE IMPLICATIONS.
I DON'T PAY YOU FOR YOUR OPINION, GOOD DOCTOR...
I PAY YOU FOR RESULTS!
THE NEXT INCIDENT INVOLVING ANY SUPER-POWERED MUTATE LIKE JUICEMAN HES TO BE DEPLOYED, UNDERSTOOD?!
AS YOU WISH, DAMIEN... AS YOU WISH!
PERFECT. THINGS ARE GOING ACCORDING TO THE PLAN...
LINDSEY, WHEN I FINISH HAVE THE JET READIED.
SLURP! NOMNOM!

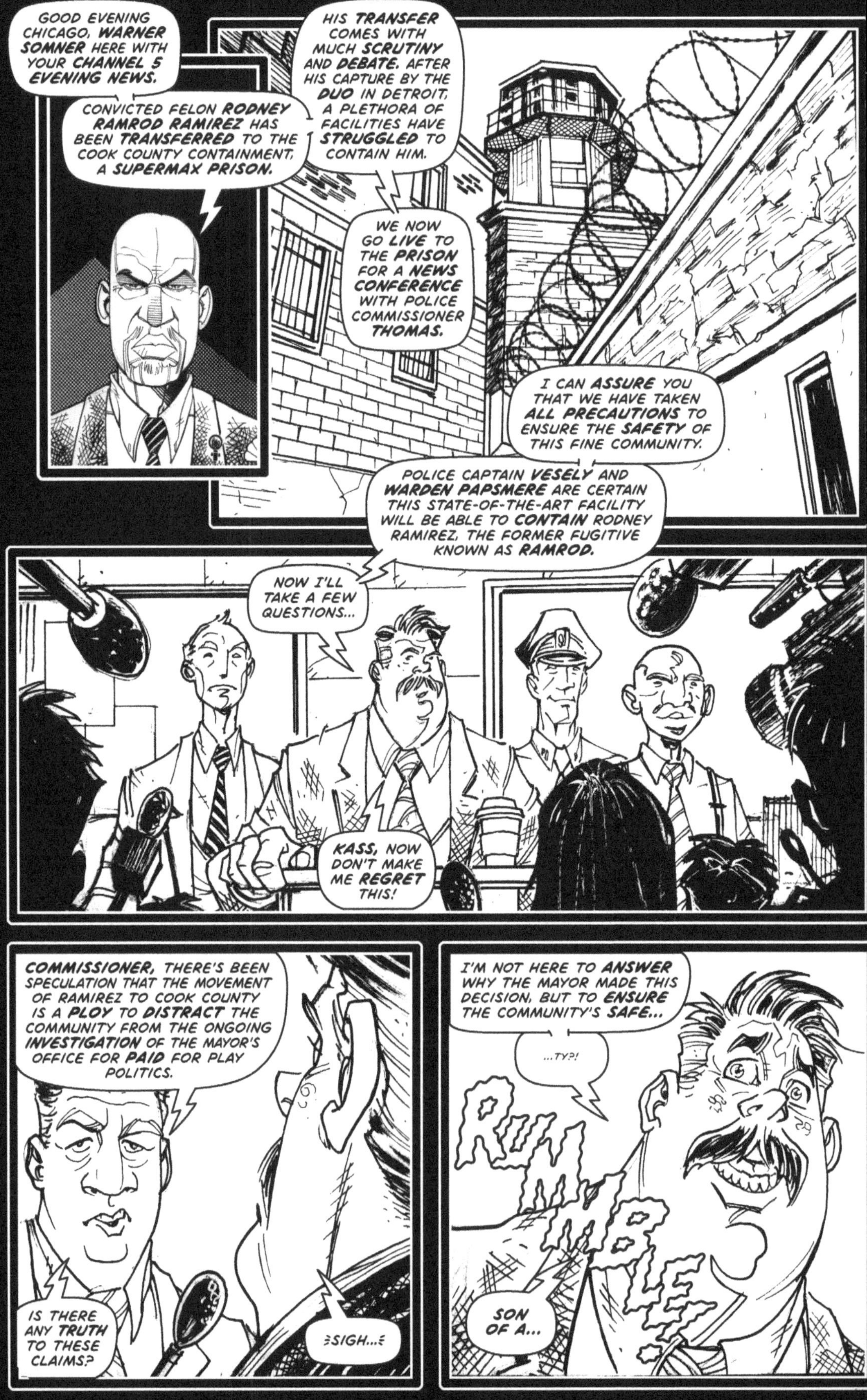
GOOD EVENING CHICAGO, WARNER SOMNER HERE WITH YOUR CHANNEL 5 EVENING NEWS.
CONVICTED FELON RODNEY RAMROD RAMIREZ HAS BEEN TRANSFERRED TO THE COOK COUNTY CONTAINMENT, A SUPERMAX PRISON.
HIS TRANSFER COMES WITH MUCH SCRUTINY AND DEBATE. AFTER HIS CAPTURE BY THE DUO IN DETROIT, A PLETHORA OF FACILITIES HAVE STRUGGLED TO CONTAIN HIM.
WE NOW GO LIVE TO THE PRISON FOR A NEWS CONFERENCE WITH POLICE COMMISSIONER THOMAS.
I CAN ASSURE YOU THAT WE HAVE TAKEN ALL PRECAUTIONS TO ENSURE THE SAFETY OF THIS FINE COMMUNITY.
POLICE CAPTAIN VESELY AND WARDEN PAPSMERE ARE CERTAIN THIS STATE-OF-THE-ART FACILITY WILL BE ABLE TO CONTAIN RODNEY RAMIREZ, THE FORMER FUGITIVE KNOWN AS RAMROD.
NOW I'LL TAKE A FEW QUESTIONS...
KASS, NOW DON'T MAKE ME REGRET THIS!
COMMISSIONER, THERE'S BEEN SPECULATION THAT THE MOVEMENT OF RAMIREZ TO COOK COUNTY IS A PLOY TO DISTRACT THE COMMUNITY FROM THE ONGOING INVESTIGATION OF THE MAYOR'S OFFICE FOR PAID FOR PLAY POLITICS.
IS THERE ANY TRUTH TO THESE CLAIMS?
SIGH...
I'M NOT HERE TO ANSWER WHY THE MAYOR MADE THIS DECISION, BUT TO ENSURE THE COMMUNITY'S SAFE...
...TY?!
RUMMMBLE
SON OF A...

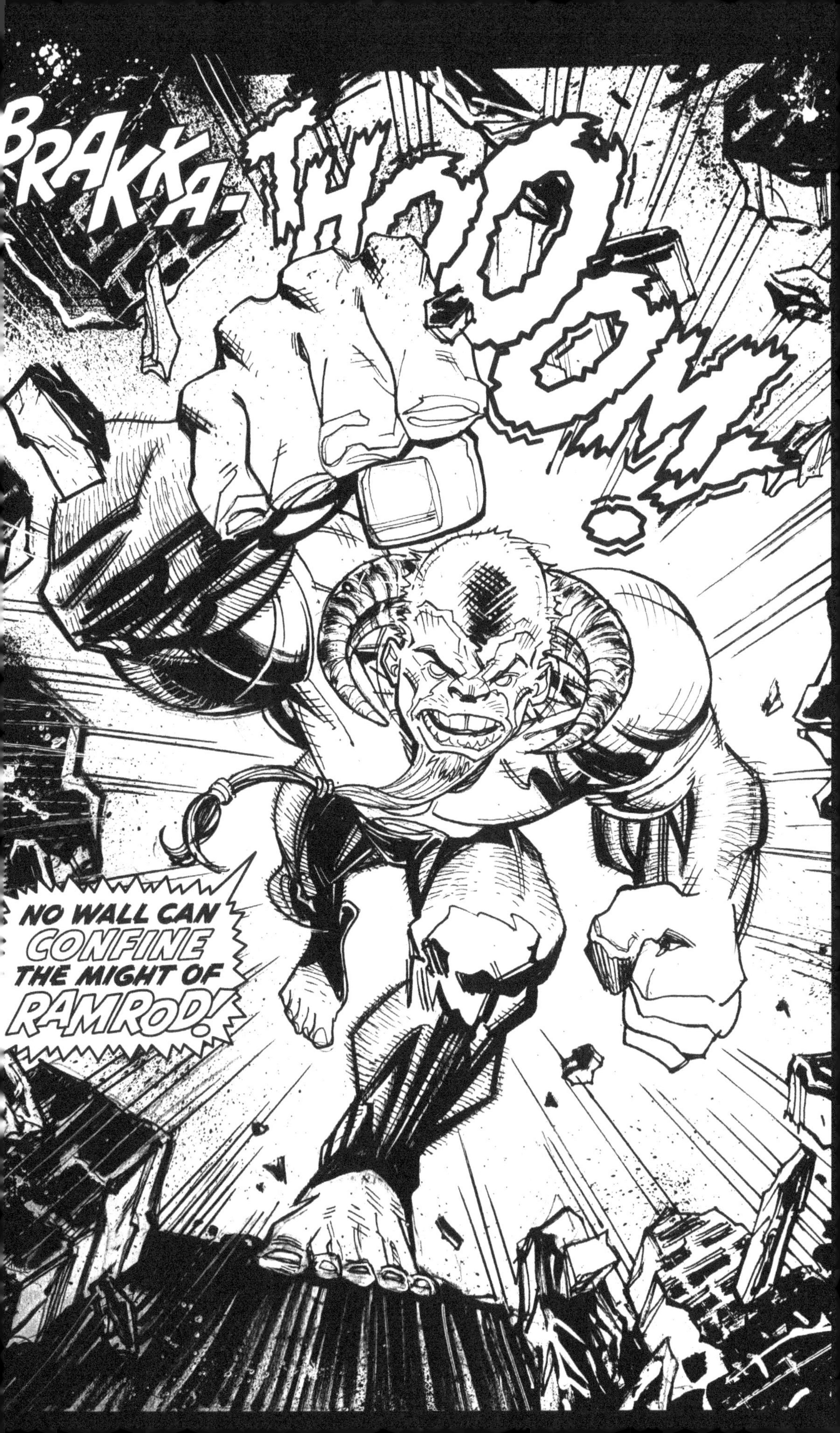
BRAKKA-THOOOM!
NO WALL CAN CONFINE THE MIGHT OF RAMROD!

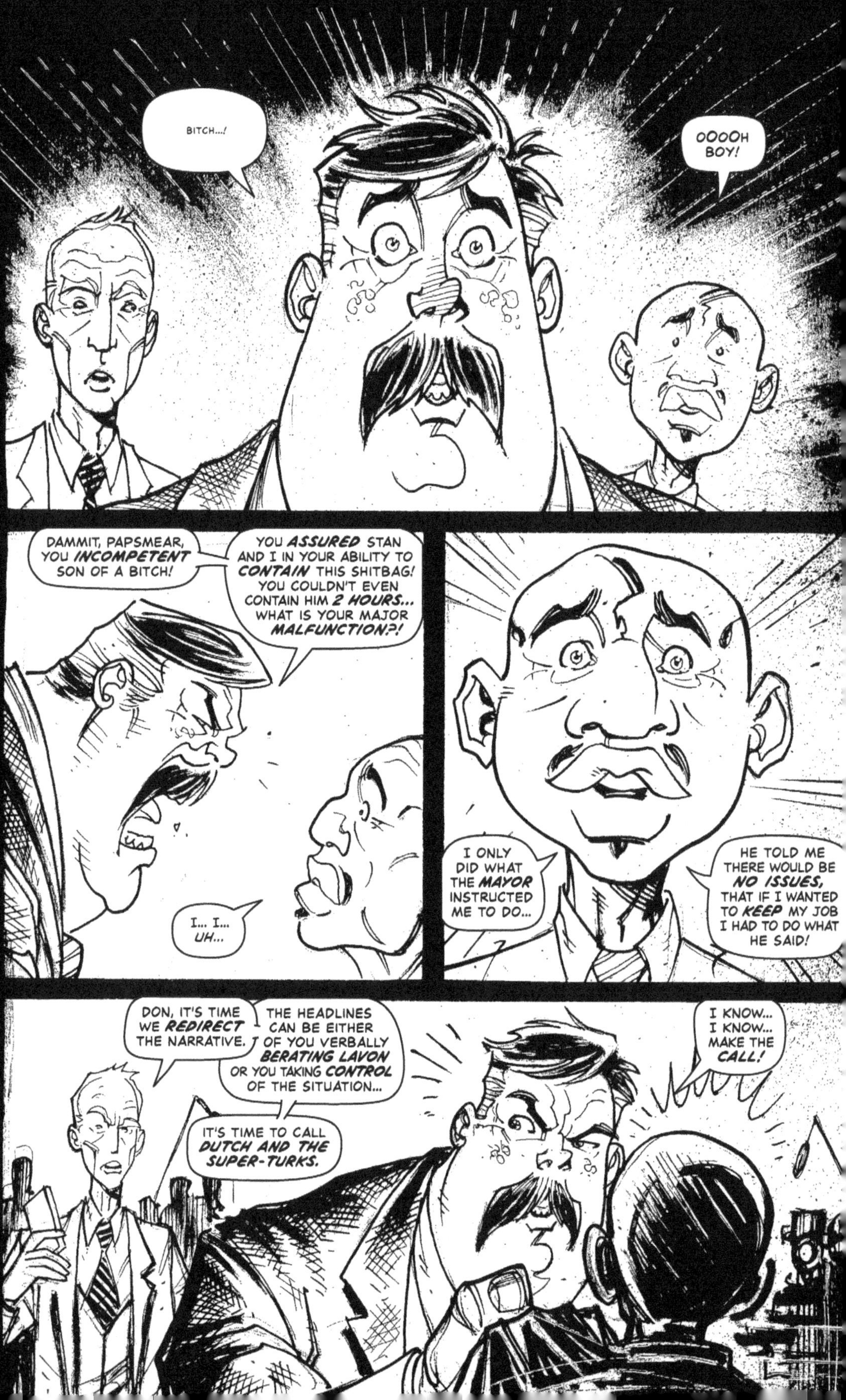
BITCH...!
OOOOH BOY!
DAMMIT, PAPSMEAR, YOU INCOMPETENT SON OF A BITCH!
YOU ASSURED STAN AND I IN YOUR ABILITY TO CONTAIN THIS SHITBAG! YOU COULDN'T EVEN CONTAIN HIM 2 HOURS... WHAT IS YOUR MAJOR MALFUNCTION?!
I... I... UH...
I ONLY DID WHAT THE MAYOR INSTRUCTED ME TO DO...
HE TOLD ME THERE WOULD BE NO ISSUES, THAT IF I WANTED TO KEEP MY JOB I HAD TO DO WHAT HE SAID!
DON, IT'S TIME WE REDIRECT THE NARRATIVE.
THE HEADLINES CAN BE EITHER OF YOU VERBALLY BERATING LAVON OR YOU TAKING CONTROL OF THE SITUATION...
IT'S TIME TO CALL DUTCH AND THE SUPER-TURKS.
I KNOW... I KNOW... MAKE THE CALL!

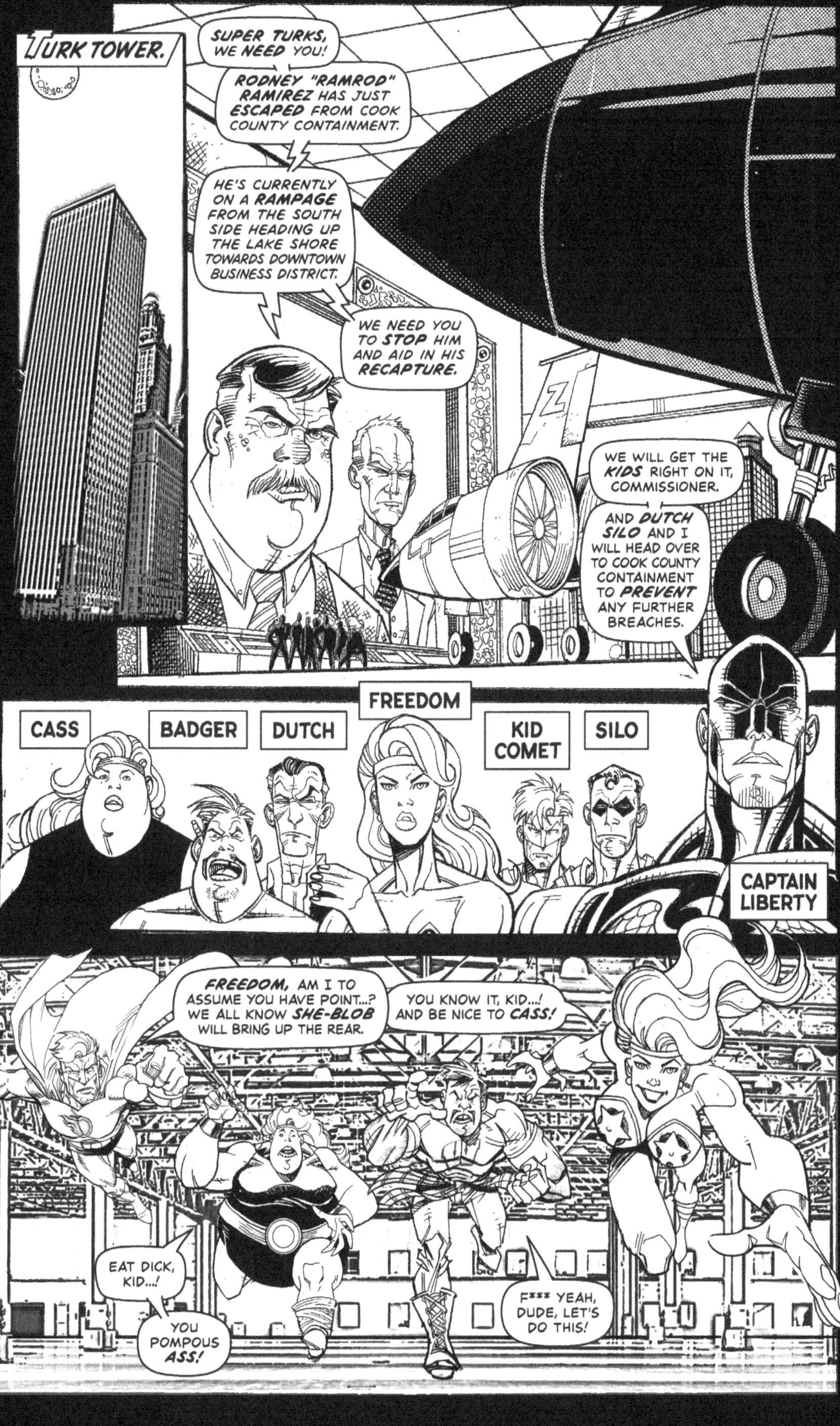
TURK TOWER.
SUPER TURKS, WE NEED YOU!
RODNEY "RAMROD" RAMIREZ HAS JUST ESCAPED FROM COOK COUNTY CONTAINMENT.
HE'S CURRENTLY ON A RAMPAGE FROM THE SOUTH SIDE HEADING UP THE LAKE SHORE TOWARDS DOWNTOWN BUSINESS DISTRICT.
WE NEED YOU TO STOP HIM AND AID IN HIS RECAPTURE.
WE WILL GET THE KIDS RIGHT ON IT, COMMISSIONER.
AND DUTCH SILO AND I WILL HEAD OVER TO COOK COUNTY CONTAINMENT TO PREVENT ANY FURTHER BREACHES.
CASS
BADGER
DUTCH
FREEDOM
KID COMET
SILO
CAPTAIN LIBERTY
FREEDOM, AM I TO ASSUME YOU HAVE POINT...? WE ALL KNOW SHE-BLOB WILL BRING UP THE REAR.
YOU KNOW IT, KID...! AND BE NICE TO CASS!
EAT DICK, KID...!
YOU POMPOUS ASS!
F*** YEAH, DUDE, LET'S DO THIS!

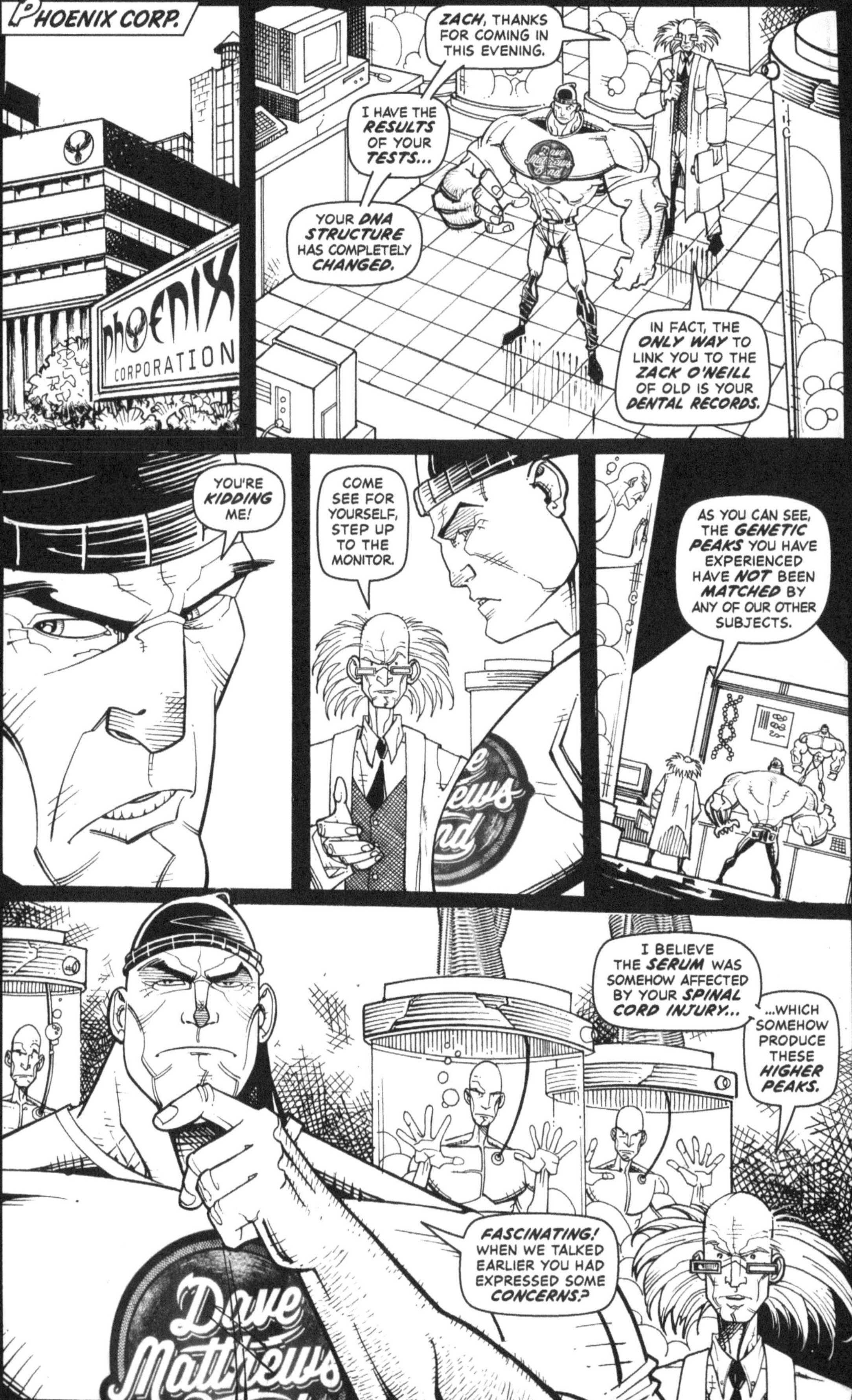
PHOENIX CORP.
PHOENIX CORPORATION
ZACH, THANKS FOR COMING IN THIS EVENING.
I HAVE THE RESULTS OF YOUR TESTS...
YOUR DNA STRUCTURE HAS COMPLETELY CHANGED.
IN FACT, THE ONLY WAY TO LINK YOU TO THE ZACK O'NEILL OF OLD IS YOUR DENTAL RECORDS.
YOU'RE KIDDING ME!
COME SEE FOR YOURSELF, STEP UP TO THE MONITOR.
AS YOU CAN SEE, THE GENETIC PEAKS YOU HAVE EXPERIENCED HAVE NOT BEEN MATCHED BY ANY OF OUR OTHER SUBJECTS.
I BELIEVE THE SERUM WAS SOMEHOW AFFECTED BY YOUR SPINAL CORD INJURY...
...WHICH SOMEHOW PRODUCE THESE HIGHER PEAKS.
FASCINATING! WHEN WE TALKED EARLIER YOU HAD EXPRESSED SOME CONCERNS?
Dave Matthews

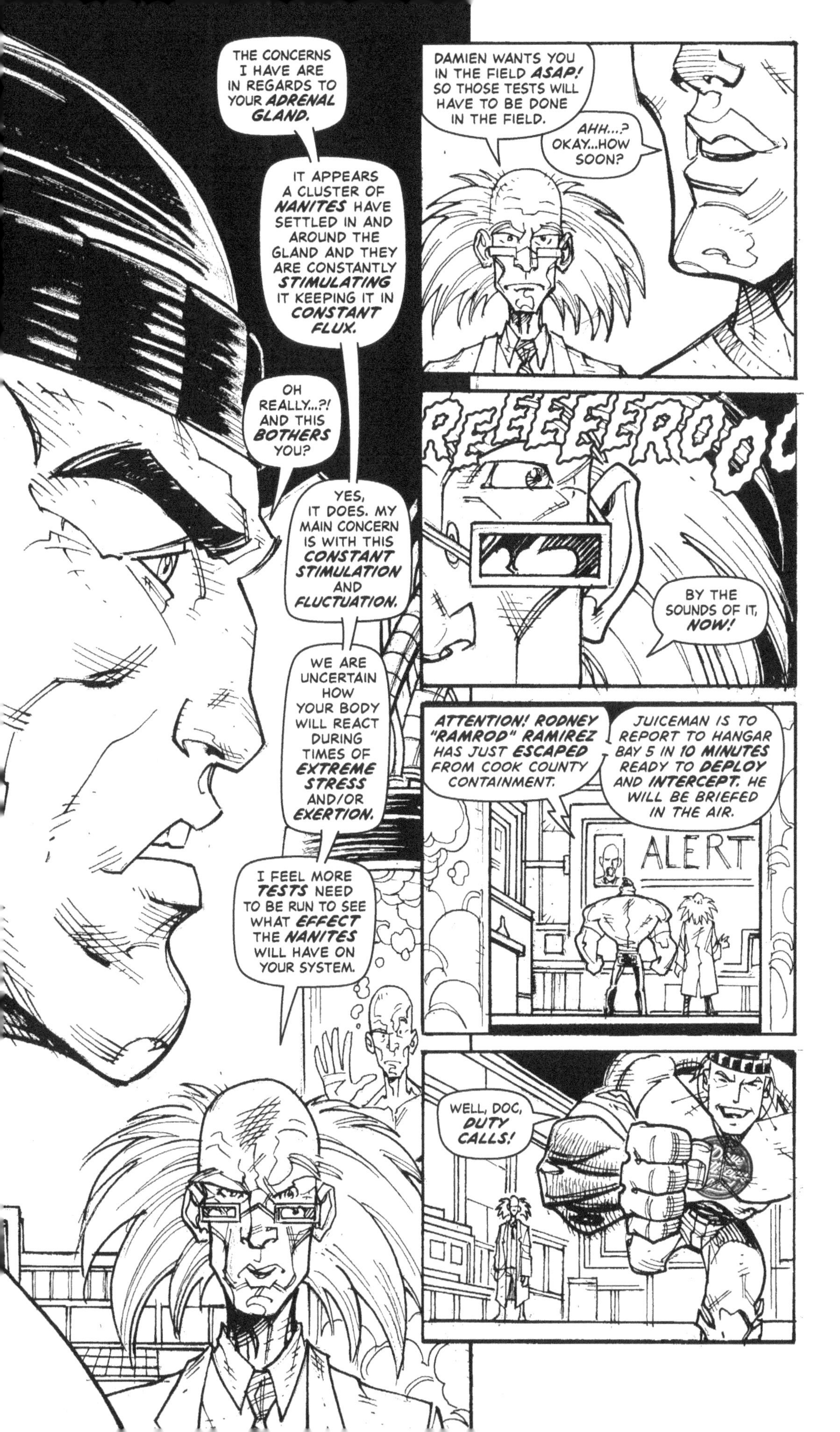
THE CONCERNS I HAVE ARE IN REGARDS TO YOUR ADRENAL GLAND.
IT APPEARS A CLUSTER OF NANITES HAVE SETTLED IN AND AROUND THE GLAND AND THEY ARE CONSTANTLY STIMULATING IT KEEPING IT IN CONSTANT FLUX.
OH REALLY...?! AND THIS BOTHERS YOU?
YES, IT DOES. MY MAIN CONCERN IS WITH THIS CONSTANT STIMULATION AND FLUCTUATION.
WE ARE UNCERTAIN HOW YOUR BODY WILL REACT DURING TIMES OF EXTREME STRESS AND/OR EXERTION.
I FEEL MORE TESTS NEED TO BE RUN TO SEE WHAT EFFECT THE NANITES WILL HAVE ON YOUR SYSTEM.
DAMIEN WANTS YOU IN THE FIELD ASAP! SO THOSE TESTS WILL HAVE TO BE DONE IN THE FIELD.
AHH...? OKAY...HOW SOON?
REEEEEROOO
BY THE SOUNDS OF IT, NOW!
ATTENTION! RODNEY "RAMROD" RAMIREZ HAS JUST ESCAPED FROM COOK COUNTY CONTAINMENT.
JUICEMAN IS TO REPORT TO HANGAR BAY 5 IN 10 MINUTES READY TO DEPLOY AND INTERCEPT. HE WILL BE BRIEFED IN THE AIR.
ALERT
WELL, DOC, DUTY CALLS!

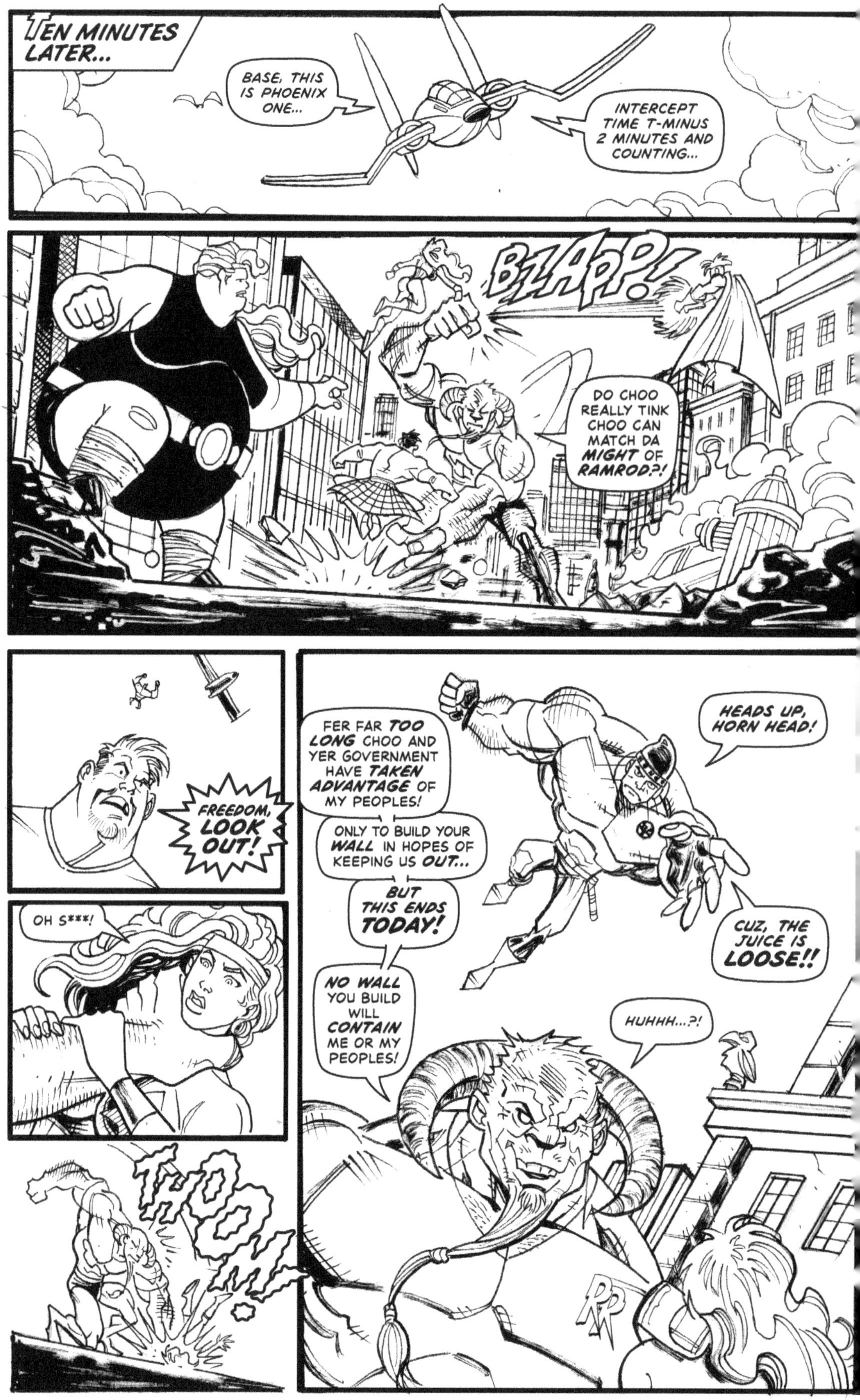
TEN MINUTES LATER...
BASE, THIS IS PHOENIX ONE...
INTERCEPT TIME T-MINUS 2 MINUTES AND COUNTING...
BLZAPP!
DO CHOO REALLY TINK CHOO CAN MATCH DA MIGHT OF RAMROD?!
FREEDOM, LOOK OUT!
OH S***!
THOOM!
FER FAR TOO LONG CHOO AND YER GOVERNMENT HAVE TAKEN ADVANTAGE OF MY PEOPLES!
ONLY TO BUILD YOUR WALL IN HOPES OF KEEPING US OUT...
BUT THIS ENDS TODAY!
NO WALL YOU BUILD WILL CONTAIN ME OR MY PEOPLES!
HEADS UP, HORN HEAD!
CUZ, THE JUICE IS LOOSE!!
HUHHH...?!

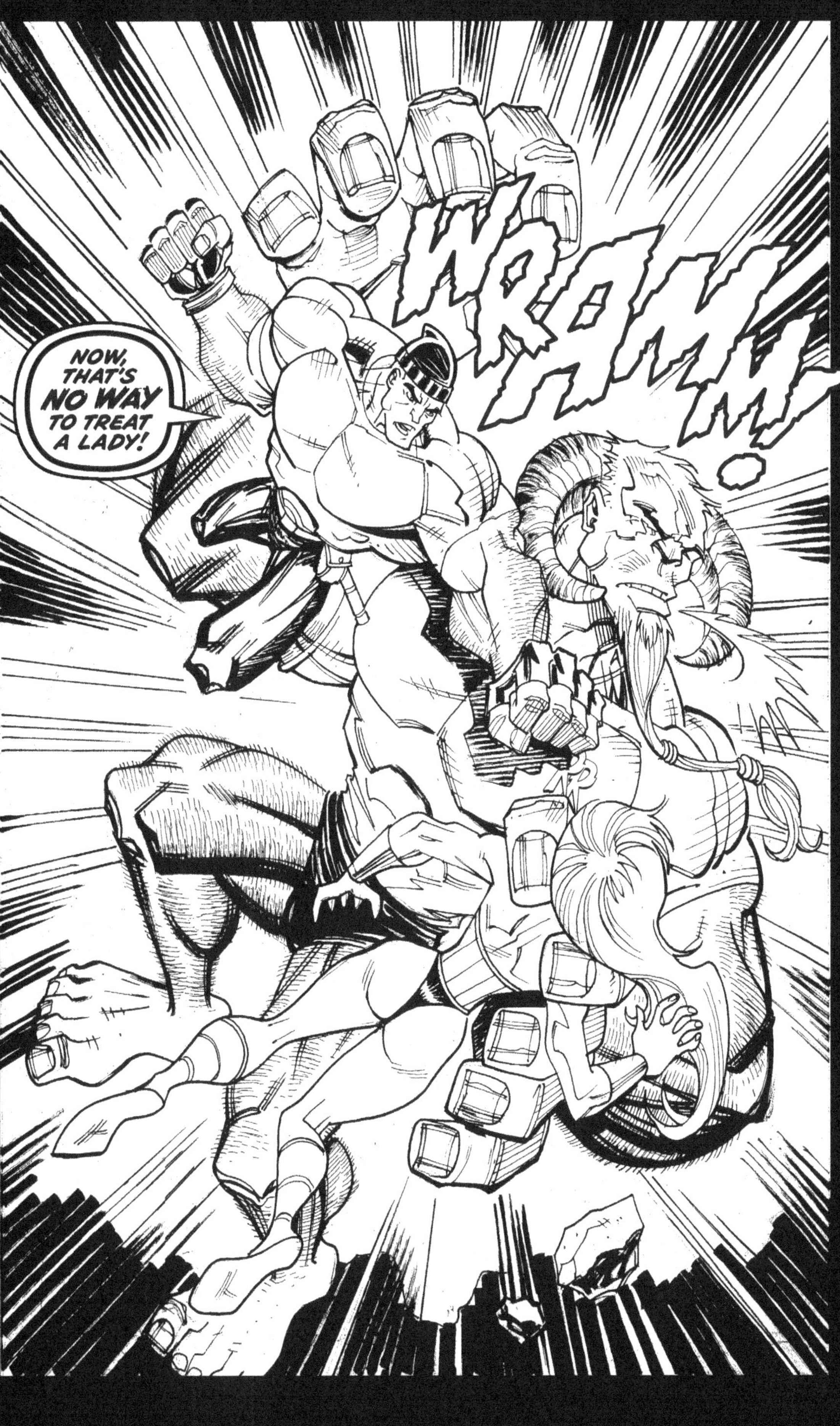
NOW, THAT'S NO WAY TO TREAT A LADY!
WRAAM!

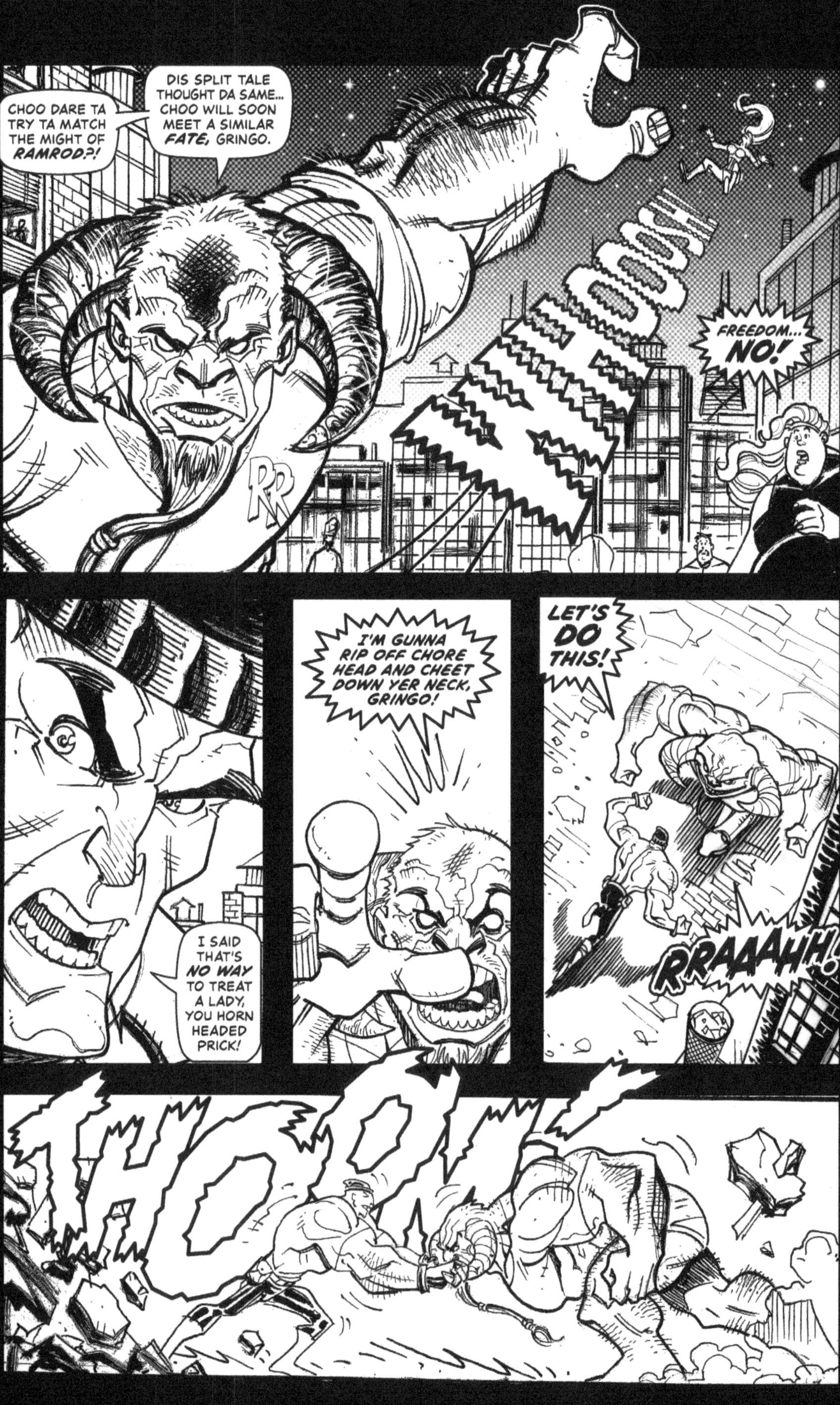
CHOO DARE TA TRY TA MATCH THE MIGHT OF RAMROD?!
DIS SPLIT TALE THOUGHT DA SAME... CHOO WILL SOON MEET A SIMILAR FATE, GRINGO.
WHOOSH!
FREEDOM... NO!
RR
I SAID THAT'S NO WAY TO TREAT A LADY, YOU HORN HEADED PRICK!
I'M GUNNA RIP OFF CHORE HEAD AND CHEET DOWN YER NECK, GRINGO!
LET'S DO THIS!
RRAAAHH!
THOOM!

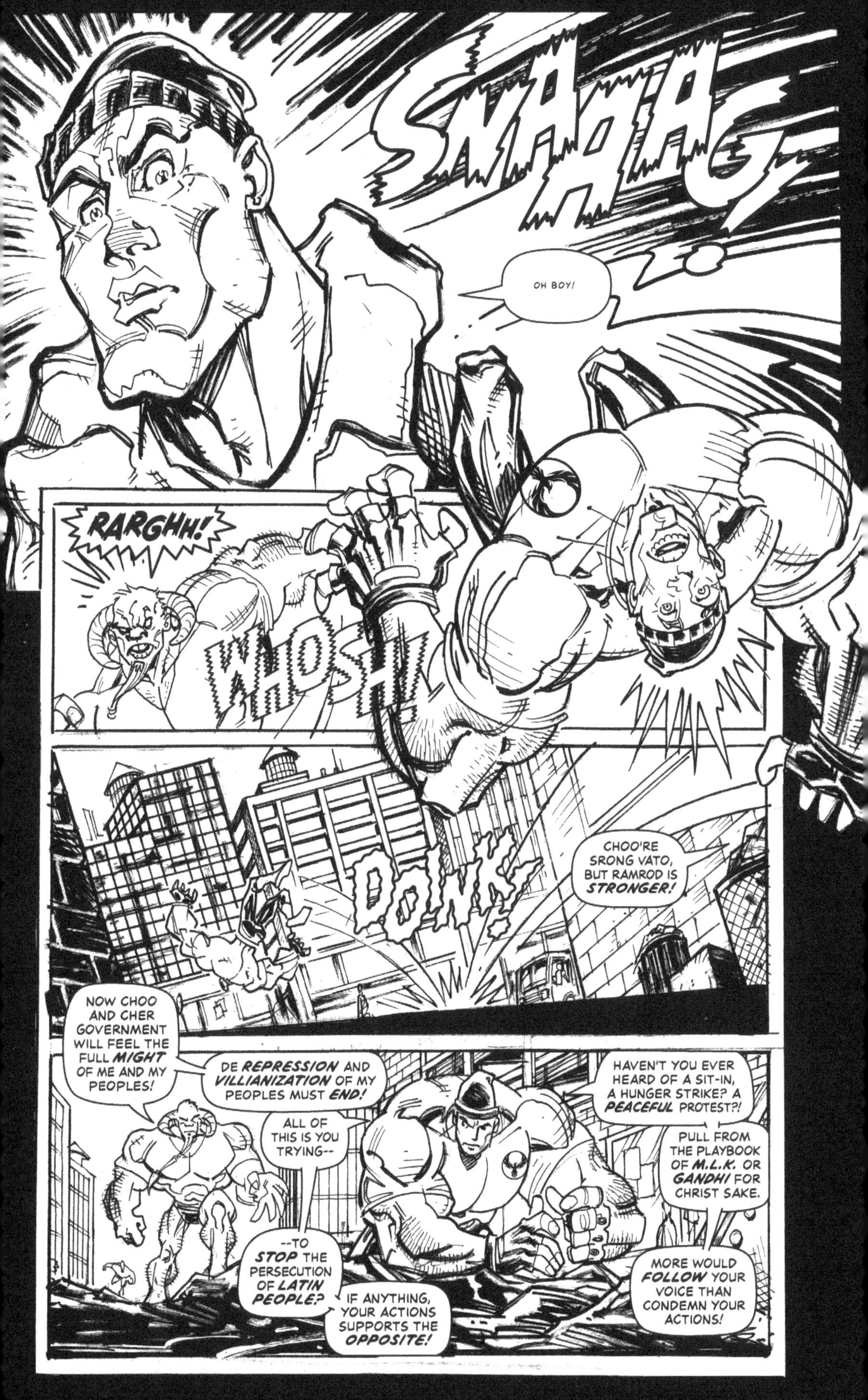
SNAAAG!
OH BOY!
RARGHH!
WHOSH!
DONK!
CHOO'RE SRONG VATO, BUT RAMROD IS STRONGER!
NOW CHOO AND CHER GOVERNMENT WILL FEEL THE FULL MIGHT OF ME AND MY PEOPLES!
DE REPRESSION AND VILLIANIZATION OF MY PEOPLES MUST END!
HAVEN'T YOU EVER HEARD OF A SIT-IN, A HUNGER STRIKE? A PEACEFUL PROTEST?!
ALL OF THIS IS YOU TRYING--
PULL FROM THE PLAYBOOK OF M.L.K. OR GANDHI FOR CHRIST SAKE.
--TO STOP THE PERSECUTION OF LATIN PEOPLE?
IF ANYTHING, YOUR ACTIONS SUPPORTS THE OPPOSITE!
MORE WOULD FOLLOW YOUR VOICE THAN CONDEMN YOUR ACTIONS!

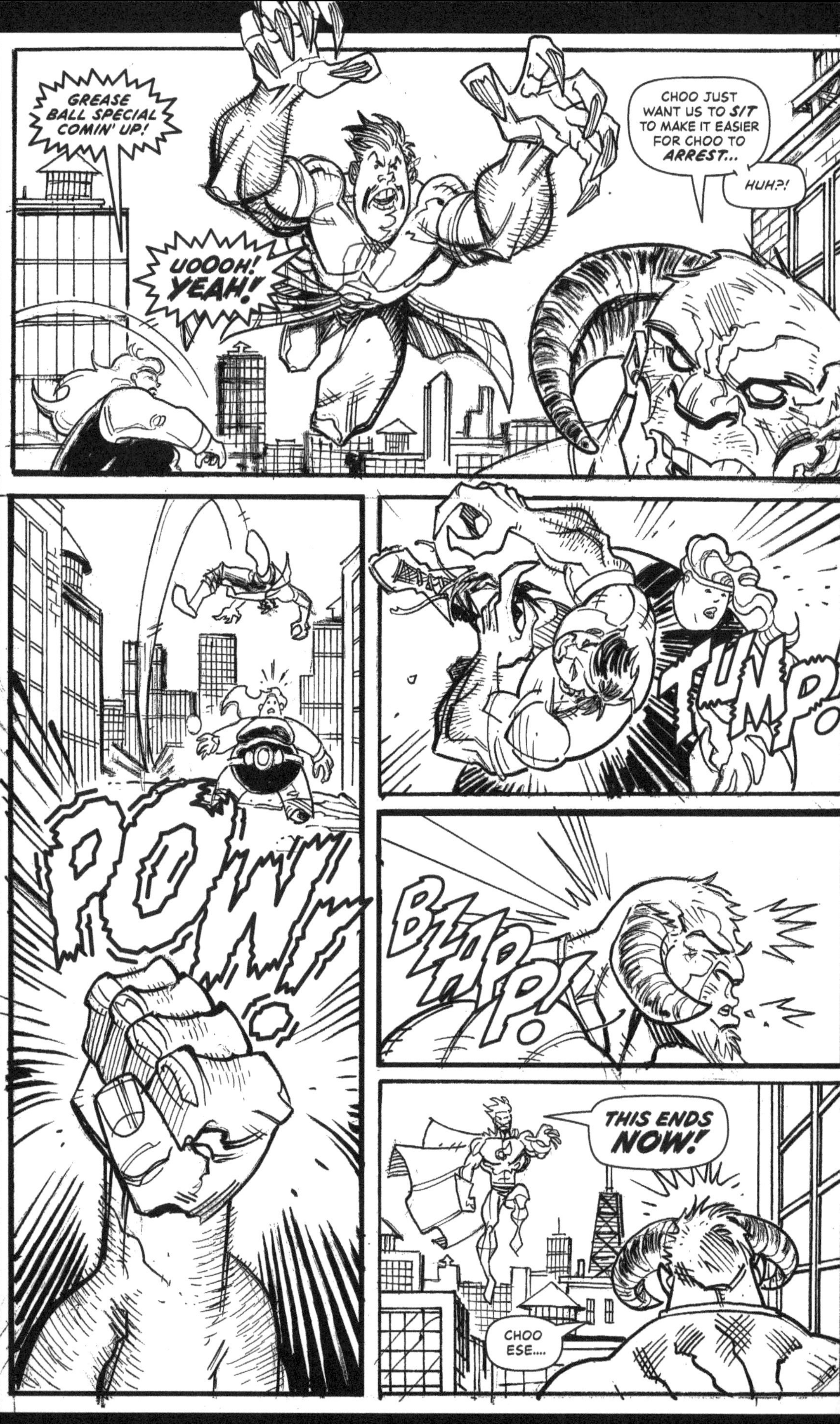
GREASE BALL SPECIAL COMIN' UP!
UOOOH! YEAH!
CHOO JUST WANT US TO SIT TO MAKE IT EASIER FOR CHOO TO ARREST...
HUH?!
POW!
TUMP!
BLAPP!
THIS ENDS NOW!
CHOO ESE....

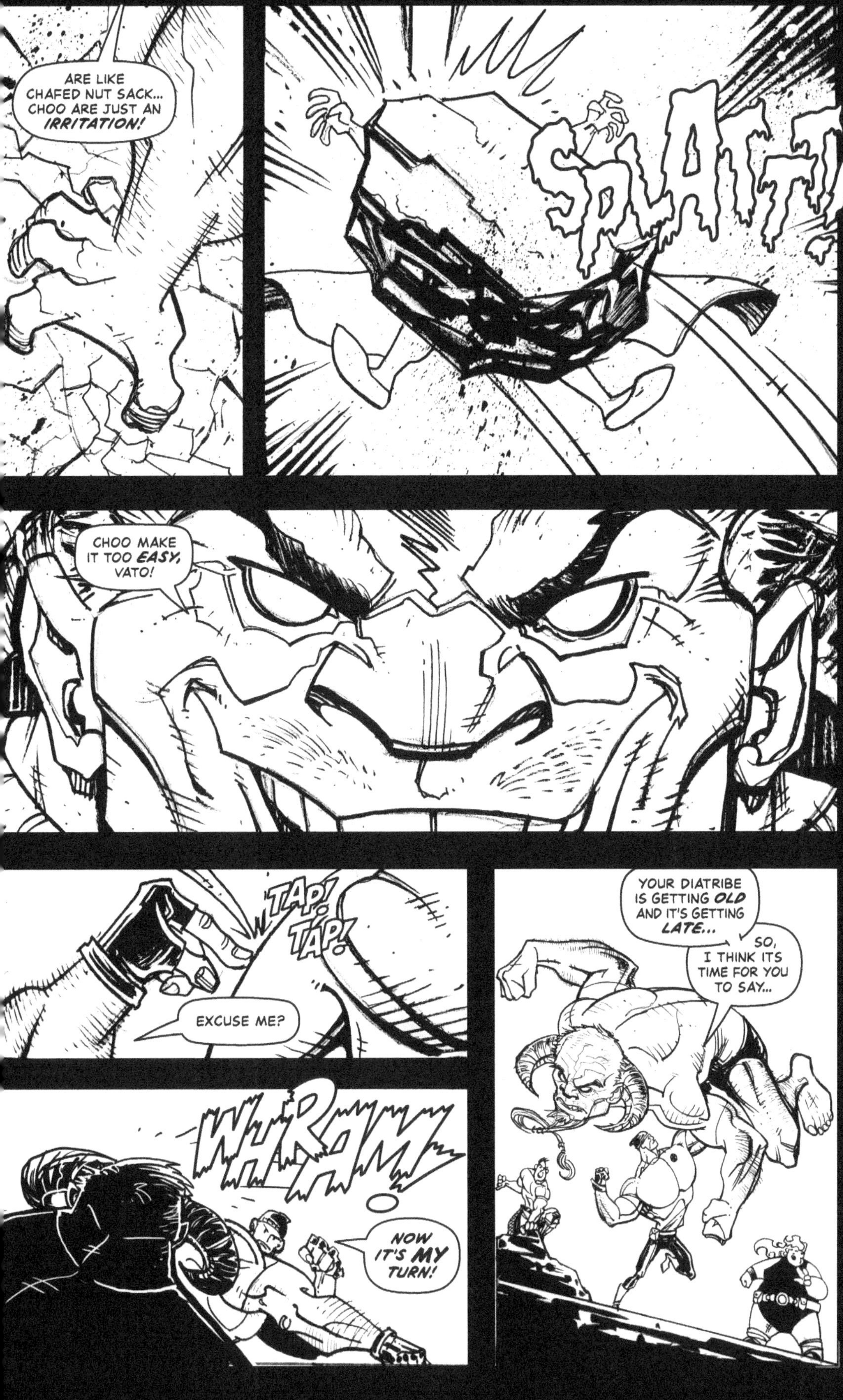

ARE LIKE CHAFED NUT SACK... CHOO ARE JUST AN IRRITATION!
SPLATT!
CHOO MAKE IT TOO EASY, VATO!
TAP! TAP!
EXCUSE ME?
YOUR DIATRIBE IS GETTING OLD AND IT'S GETTING LATE...
SO, I THINK ITS TIME FOR YOU TO SAY...
WHRAM!
NOW IT'S MY TURN!

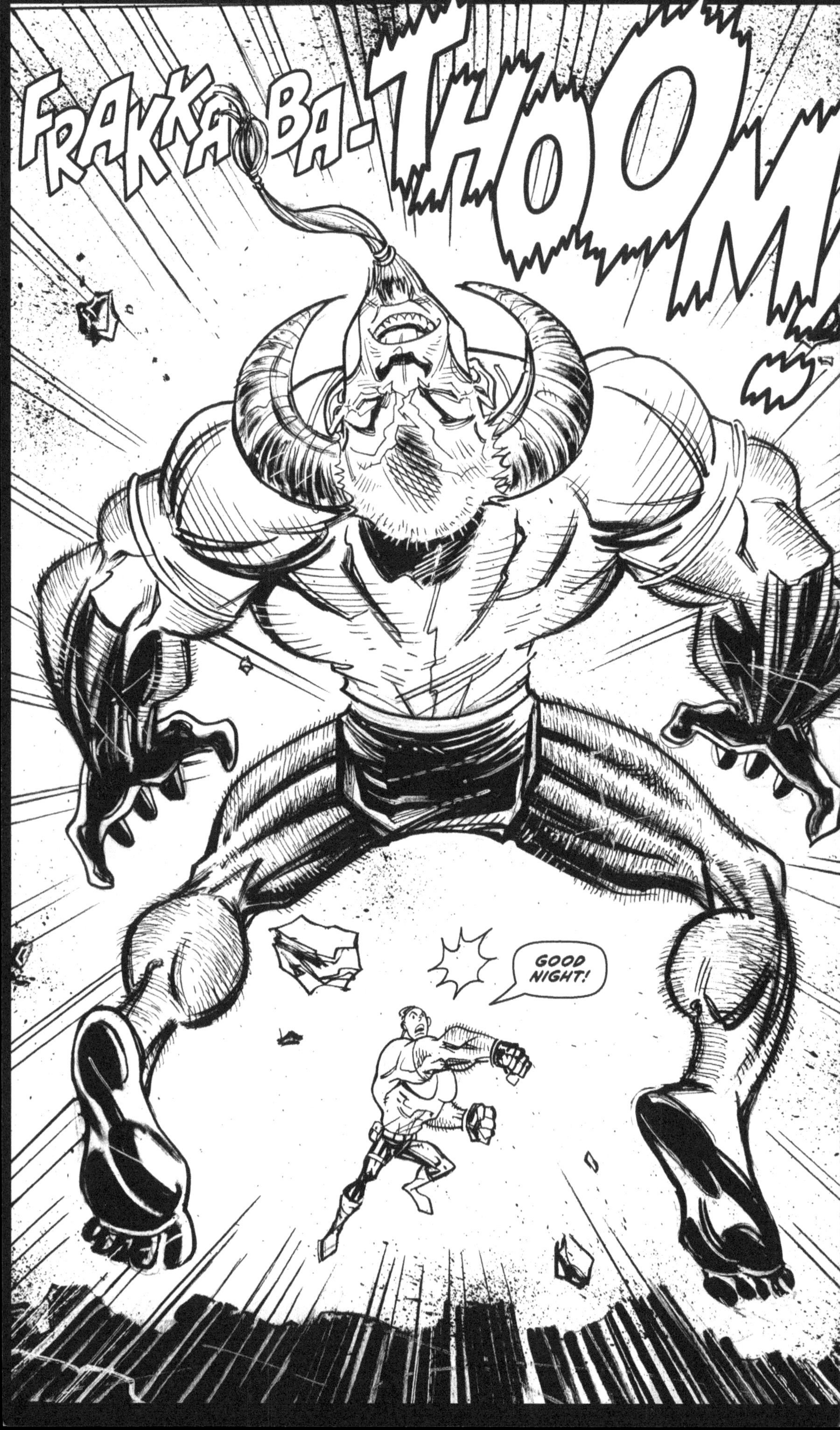
FRAKKA-BA-THOOM
GOOD NIGHT!

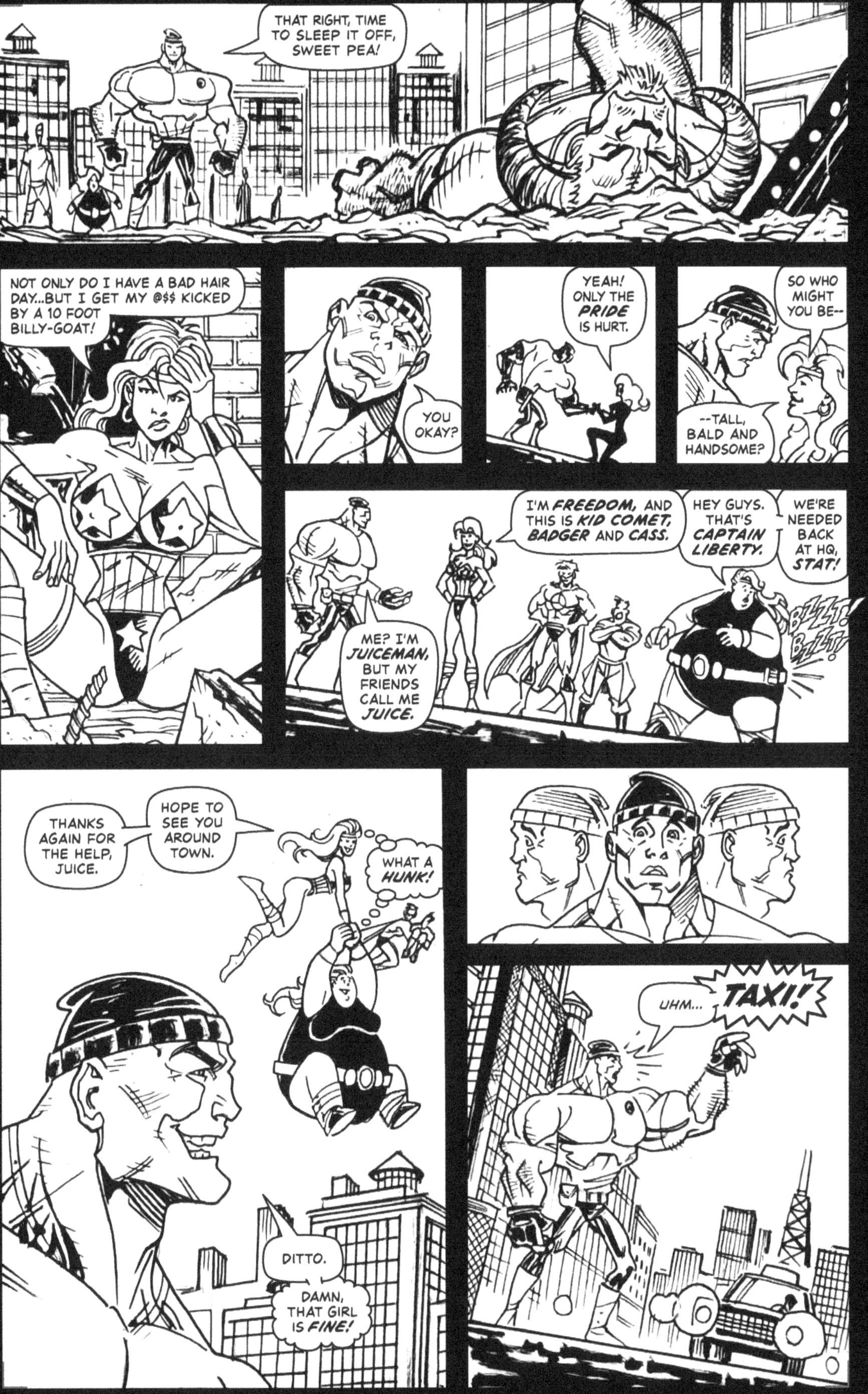
THAT RIGHT, TIME TO SLEEP IT OFF, SWEET PEA!
NOT ONLY DO I HAVE A BAD HAIR DAY...BUT I GET MY @$$ KICKED BY A 10 FOOT BILLY-GOAT!
YOU OKAY?
YEAH! ONLY THE PRIDE IS HURT.
SO WHO MIGHT YOU BE--
--TALL, BALD AND HANDSOME?
ME? I'M JUICEMAN, BUT MY FRIENDS CALL ME JUICE.
I'M FREEDOM, AND THIS IS KID COMET, BADGER AND CASS.
HEY GUYS. THAT'S CAPTAIN LIBERTY.
WE'RE NEEDED BACK AT HQ, STAT!
BZZT! BZZT!
THANKS AGAIN FOR THE HELP, JUICE.
HOPE TO SEE YOU AROUND TOWN.
WHAT A HUNK!
DITTO.
DAMN, THAT GIRL IS FINE!
UHM...
TAXI!

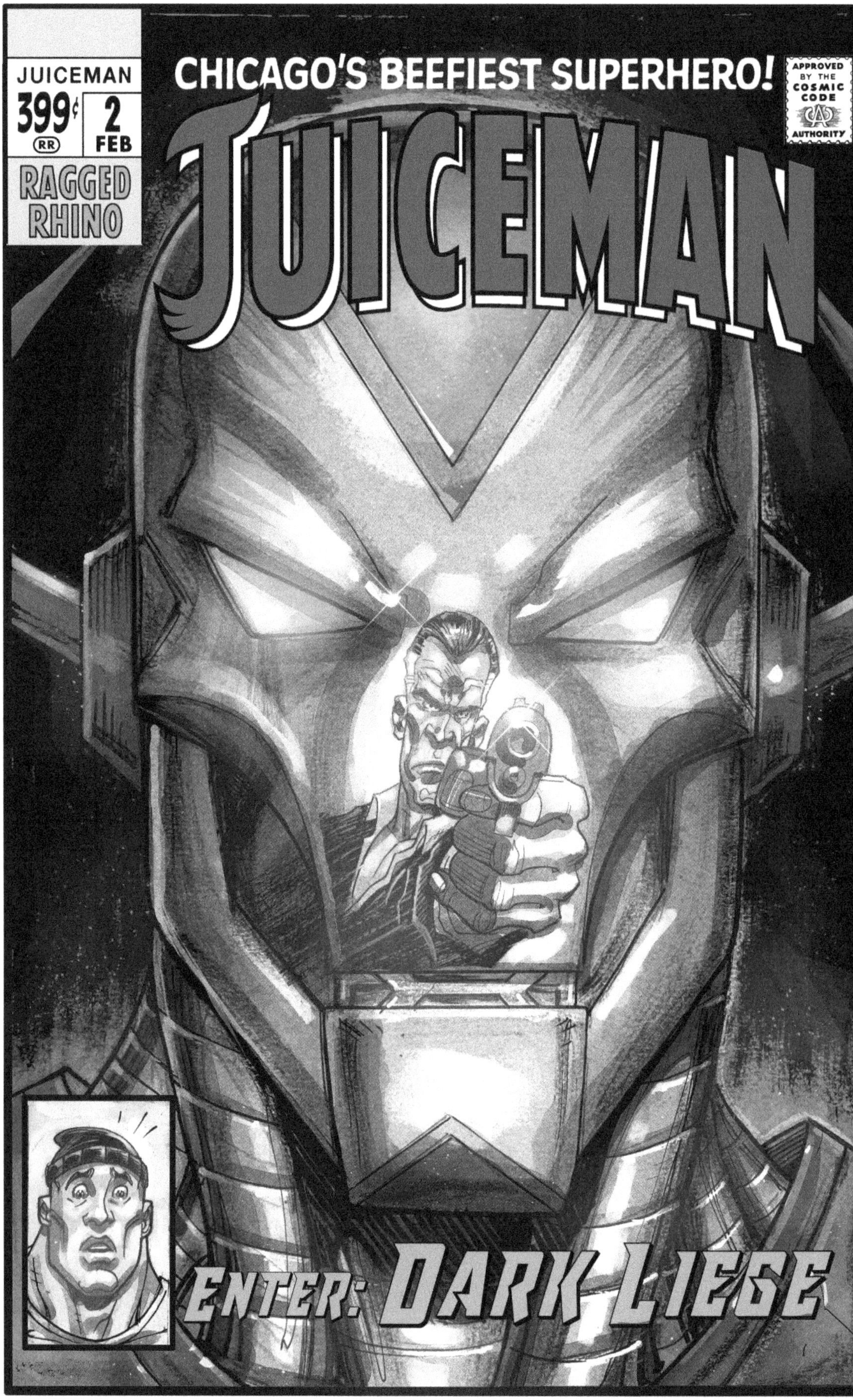

JUICEMAN
399¢
RR
2
FEB
RAGGED RHINO
CHICAGO'S BEEFIEST SUPERHERO!
APPROVED BY THE COSMIC CODE AUTHORITY
JUICEMAN
ENTER: DARK LIEGE

MAN of MYSTERY!

Chicago Tribune

TUESDAY, JULY 16, 2019

NS? CALL 1-800-TRIBUNE

BREAKING NEWS AT CHICAG...

WHO IS JUICEMAN?

Chicago's new superhero makes an instant impact!

The super turks continue... struggle with increased m... ...ulation. Captain Li... ...am seem ill-eq... ...ared to... ...nced hu... ...re const... ...out by... ...ation's Ju...

AFTER MY DEBUT AGAINST *RAMROD*, I WAS THE TALK OF THE TOWN.

IT DIDN'T HELP THAT IN THE WEEKS THAT FOLLOWED I FOUND MYSELF BURIED IN *STOPPING* THE INFLUX OF *MUTATE CRIMINALS*.

THE SUPER TURKS SEEM TO BE *OVERWHELMED.* I WAS EITHER BAILING THEM OUT OR STOPPING OTHER *DISTURBANCES.*

IT WAS DURING THIS TIME WE FORGED A *FRIENDSHIP.*

J. KASS

CHICAGO -- Chicago has a new hero and his name is ...ceman. He is the first of ...posed genetically ...pans. There ...icago's

Photo by Phil McCracken

STORY, ART AND COLORS: **SCOTT JAMES** | **FERRAN DELGADO** LETTERS | **GAVIN HIGGINBOTHAM** EDITOR

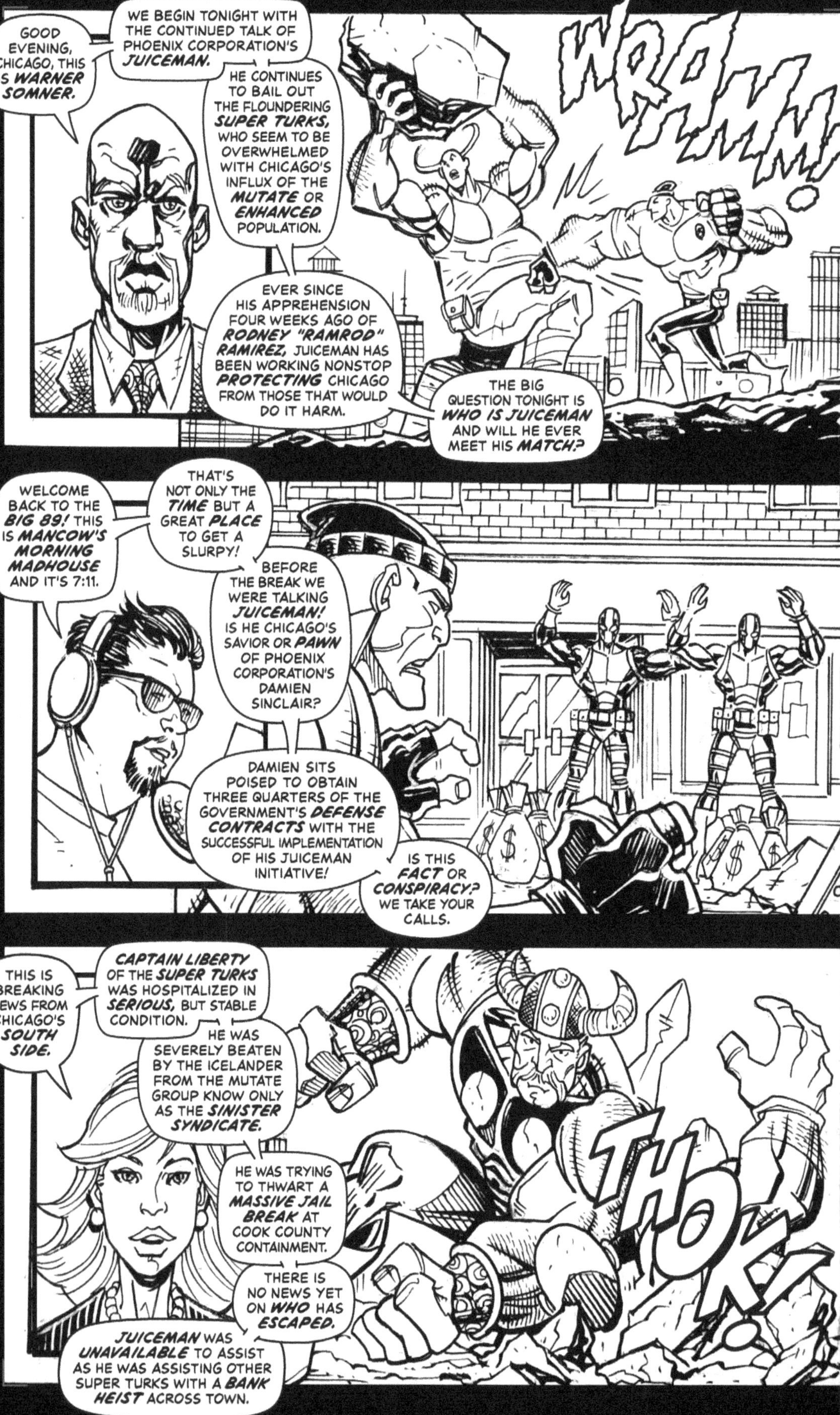

GOOD EVENING, CHICAGO, THIS IS WARNER SOMNER.
WE BEGIN TONIGHT WITH THE CONTINUED TALK OF PHOENIX CORPORATION'S JUICEMAN.
HE CONTINUES TO BAIL OUT THE FLOUNDERING SUPER TURKS, WHO SEEM TO BE OVERWHELMED WITH CHICAGO'S INFLUX OF THE MUTATE OR ENHANCED POPULATION.
EVER SINCE HIS APPREHENSION FOUR WEEKS AGO OF RODNEY "RAMROD" RAMIREZ, JUICEMAN HAS BEEN WORKING NONSTOP PROTECTING CHICAGO FROM THOSE THAT WOULD DO IT HARM.
THE BIG QUESTION TONIGHT IS WHO IS JUICEMAN AND WILL HE EVER MEET HIS MATCH?
WRAMM!
WELCOME BACK TO THE BIG 89! THIS IS MANCOW'S MORNING MADHOUSE AND IT'S 7:11.
THAT'S NOT ONLY THE TIME BUT A GREAT PLACE TO GET A SLURPY!
BEFORE THE BREAK WE WERE TALKING JUICEMAN! IS HE CHICAGO'S SAVIOR OR PAWN OF PHOENIX CORPORATION'S DAMIEN SINCLAIR?
DAMIEN SITS POISED TO OBTAIN THREE QUARTERS OF THE GOVERNMENT'S DEFENSE CONTRACTS WITH THE SUCCESSFUL IMPLEMENTATION OF HIS JUICEMAN INITIATIVE!
IS THIS FACT OR CONSPIRACY? WE TAKE YOUR CALLS.
THIS IS BREAKING NEWS FROM CHICAGO'S SOUTH SIDE.
CAPTAIN LIBERTY OF THE SUPER TURKS WAS HOSPITALIZED IN SERIOUS, BUT STABLE CONDITION.
HE WAS SEVERELY BEATEN BY THE ICELANDER FROM THE MUTATE GROUP KNOW ONLY AS THE SINISTER SYNDICATE.
HE WAS TRYING TO THWART A MASSIVE JAIL BREAK AT COOK COUNTY CONTAINMENT.
THERE IS NO NEWS YET ON WHO HAS ESCAPED.
JUICEMAN WAS UNAVAILABLE TO ASSIST AS HE WAS ASSISTING OTHER SUPER TURKS WITH A BANK HEIST ACROSS TOWN.
THOK!

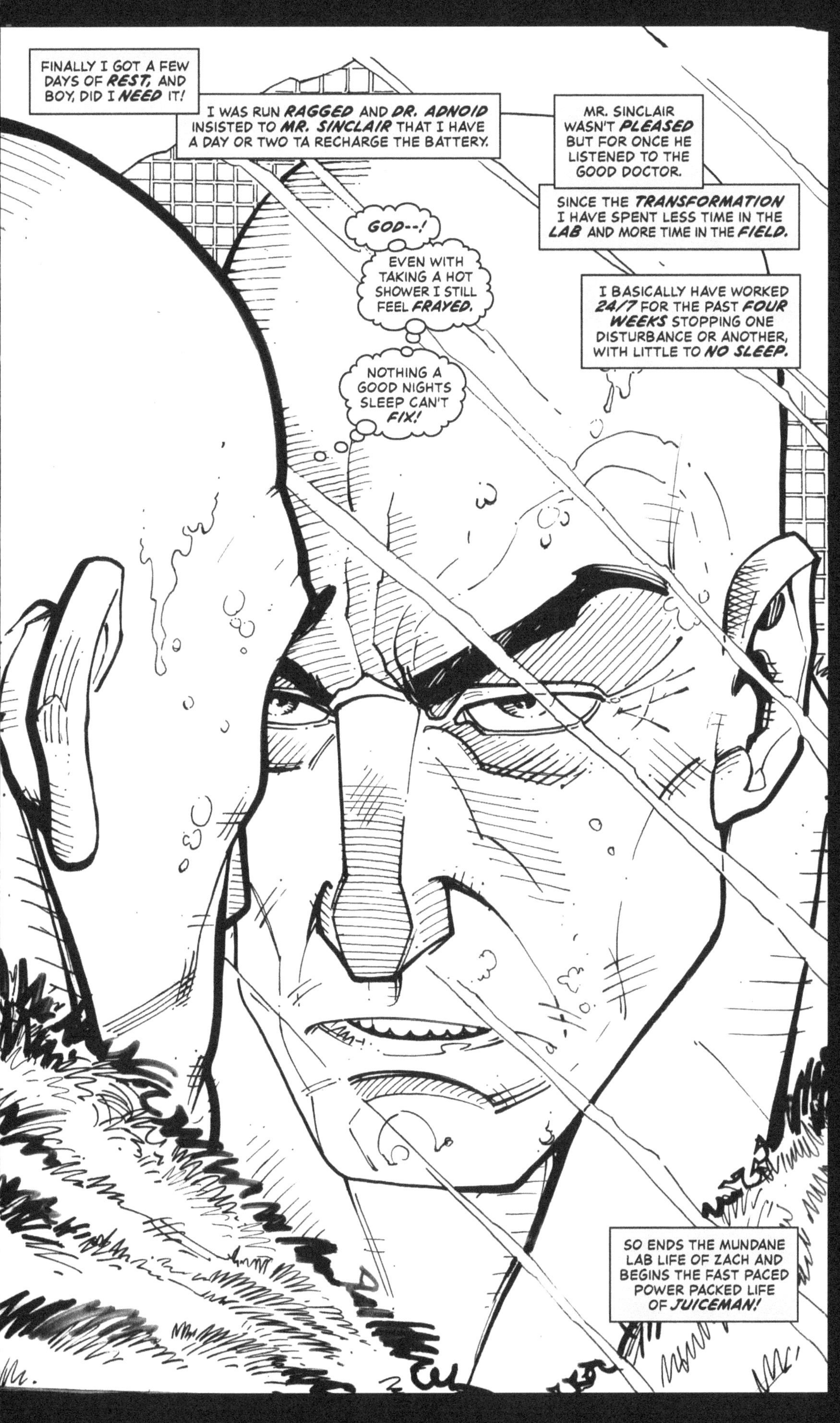
FINALLY I GOT A FEW DAYS OF REST, AND BOY, DID I NEED IT!
I WAS RUN RAGGED AND DR. ADNOID INSISTED TO MR. SINCLAIR THAT I HAVE A DAY OR TWO TA RECHARGE THE BATTERY.
MR. SINCLAIR WASN'T PLEASED BUT FOR ONCE HE LISTENED TO THE GOOD DOCTOR.
SINCE THE TRANSFORMATION I HAVE SPENT LESS TIME IN THE LAB AND MORE TIME IN THE FIELD.
GOD--!
EVEN WITH TAKING A HOT SHOWER I STILL FEEL FRAYED.
I BASICALLY HAVE WORKED 24/7 FOR THE PAST FOUR WEEKS STOPPING ONE DISTURBANCE OR ANOTHER, WITH LITTLE TO NO SLEEP.
NOTHING A GOOD NIGHTS SLEEP CAN'T FIX!
SO ENDS THE MUNDANE LAB LIFE OF ZACH AND BEGINS THE FAST PACED POWER PACKED LIFE OF JUICEMAN!

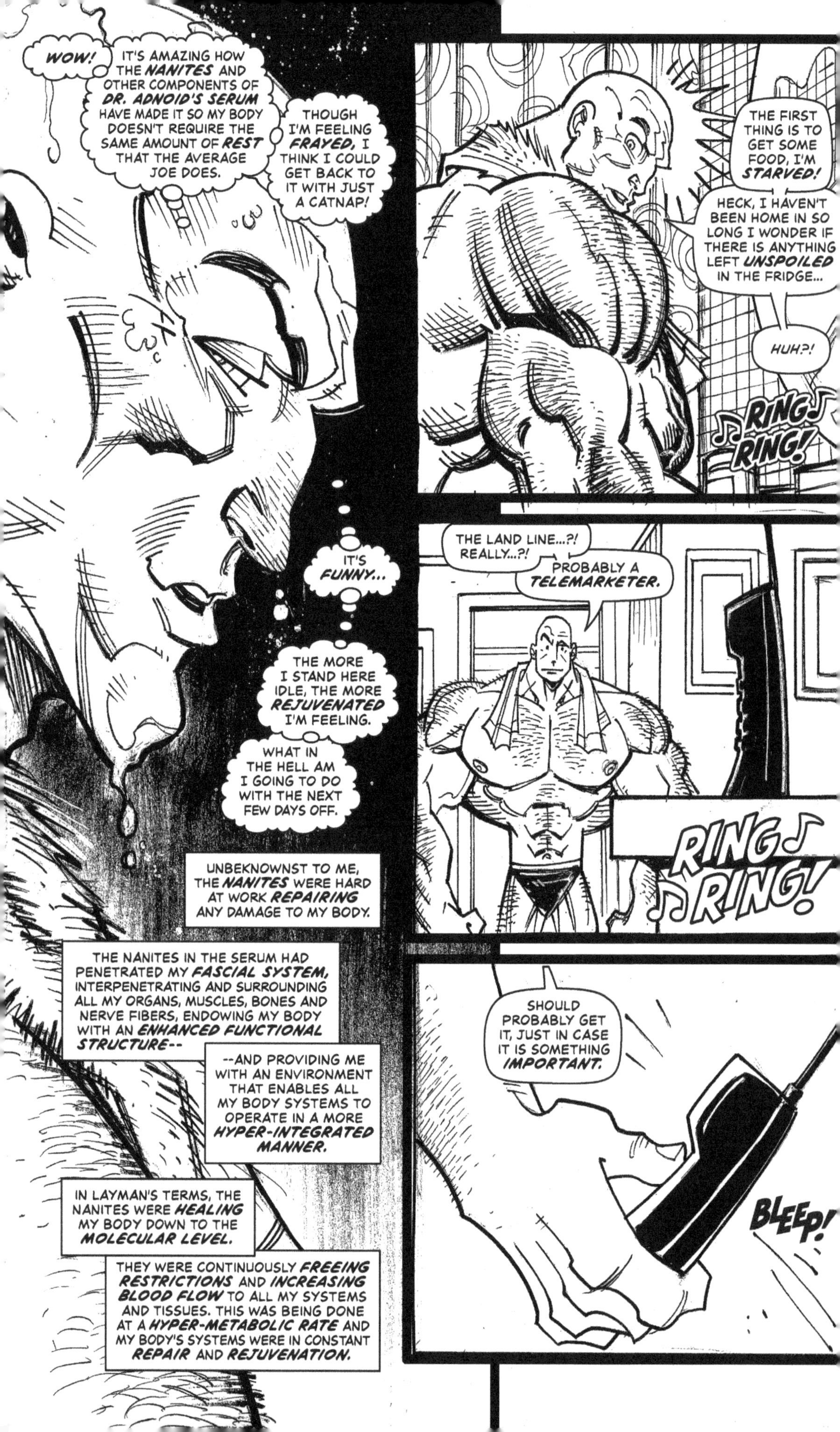
WOW!
IT'S AMAZING HOW THE NANITES AND OTHER COMPONENTS OF DR. ADNOID'S SERUM HAVE MADE IT SO MY BODY DOESN'T REQUIRE THE SAME AMOUNT OF REST THAT THE AVERAGE JOE DOES.
THOUGH I'M FEELING FRAYED, I THINK I COULD GET BACK TO IT WITH JUST A CATNAP!
IT'S FUNNY...
THE MORE I STAND HERE IDLE, THE MORE REJUVENATED I'M FEELING.
WHAT IN THE HELL AM I GOING TO DO WITH THE NEXT FEW DAYS OFF.
UNBEKNOWNST TO ME, THE NANITES WERE HARD AT WORK REPAIRING ANY DAMAGE TO MY BODY.
THE NANITES IN THE SERUM HAD PENETRATED MY FASCIAL SYSTEM, INTERPENETRATING AND SURROUNDING ALL MY ORGANS, MUSCLES, BONES AND NERVE FIBERS, ENDOWING MY BODY WITH AN ENHANCED FUNCTIONAL STRUCTURE--
--AND PROVIDING ME WITH AN ENVIRONMENT THAT ENABLES ALL MY BODY SYSTEMS TO OPERATE IN A MORE HYPER-INTEGRATED MANNER.
IN LAYMAN'S TERMS, THE NANITES WERE HEALING MY BODY DOWN TO THE MOLECULAR LEVEL.
THEY WERE CONTINUOUSLY FREEING RESTRICTIONS AND INCREASING BLOOD FLOW TO ALL MY SYSTEMS AND TISSUES. THIS WAS BEING DONE AT A HYPER-METABOLIC RATE AND MY BODY'S SYSTEMS WERE IN CONSTANT REPAIR AND REJUVENATION.
THE FIRST THING IS TO GET SOME FOOD, I'M STARVED!
HECK, I HAVEN'T BEEN HOME IN SO LONG I WONDER IF THERE IS ANYTHING LEFT UNSPOILED IN THE FRIDGE...
HUH?!
RING♪ ♪RING!
THE LAND LINE...?! REALLY...?!
PROBABLY A TELEMARKETER.
RING♪ ♪RING!
SHOULD PROBABLY GET IT, JUST IN CASE IT IS SOMETHING IMPORTANT.
BLEEP!

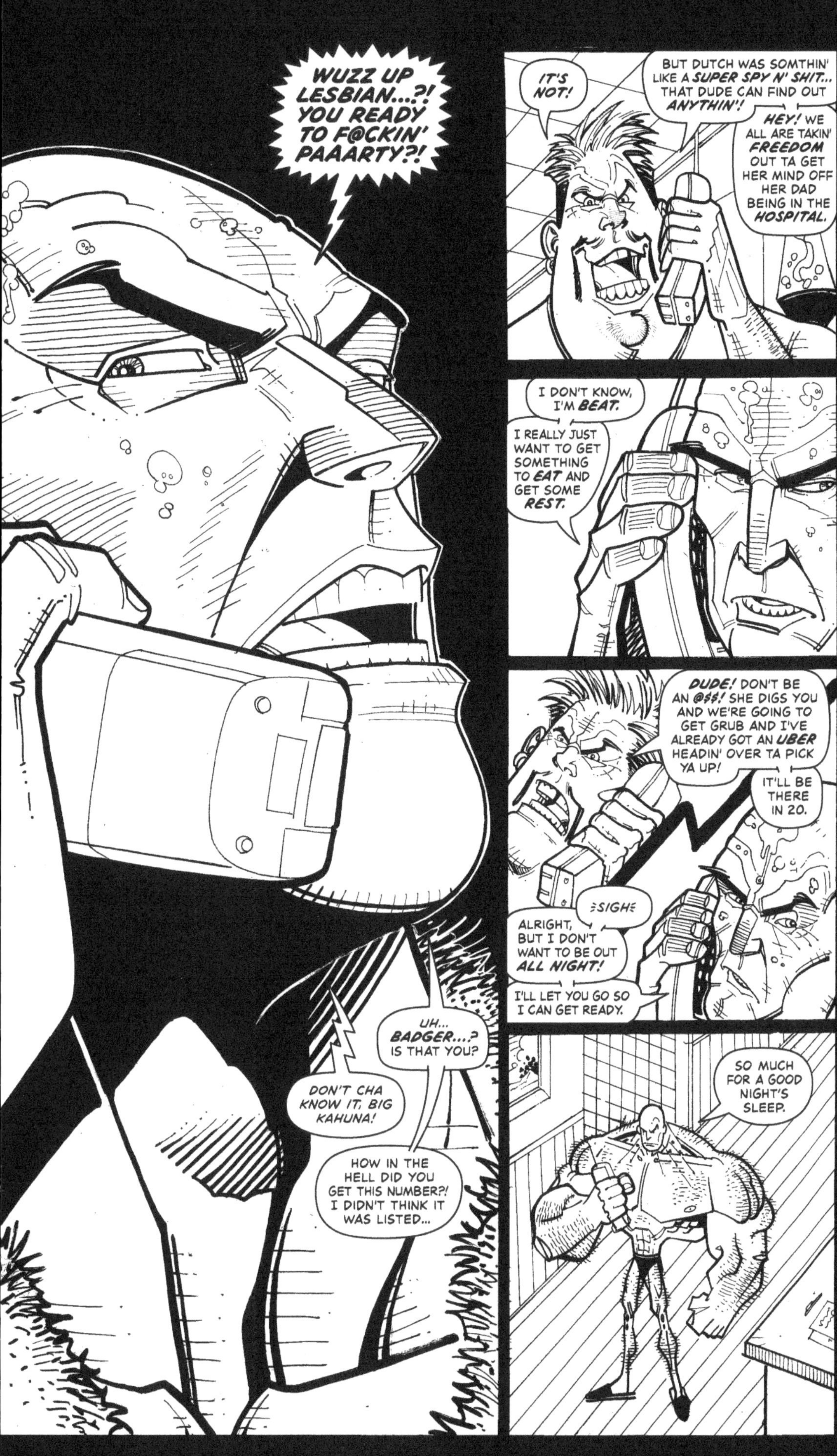
WUZZ UP LESBIAN...?! YOU READY TO F@CKIN' PAAARTY?!
UH... BADGER...? IS THAT YOU?
DON'T CHA KNOW IT, BIG KAHUNA!
HOW IN THE HELL DID YOU GET THIS NUMBER?! I DIDN'T THINK IT WAS LISTED...
IT'S NOT!
BUT DUTCH WAS SOMTHIN' LIKE A SUPER SPY N' SHIT... THAT DUDE CAN FIND OUT ANYTHIN'!
HEY! WE ALL ARE TAKIN' FREEDOM OUT TA GET HER MIND OFF HER DAD BEING IN THE HOSPITAL.
I DON'T KNOW, I'M BEAT.
I REALLY JUST WANT TO GET SOMETHING TO EAT AND GET SOME REST.
DUDE! DON'T BE AN @$$! SHE DIGS YOU AND WE'RE GOING TO GET GRUB AND I'VE ALREADY GOT AN UBER HEADIN' OVER TA PICK YA UP!
IT'LL BE THERE IN 20.
SIGH
ALRIGHT, BUT I DON'T WANT TO BE OUT ALL NIGHT!
I'LL LET YOU GO SO I CAN GET READY.
SO MUCH FOR A GOOD NIGHT'S SLEEP.

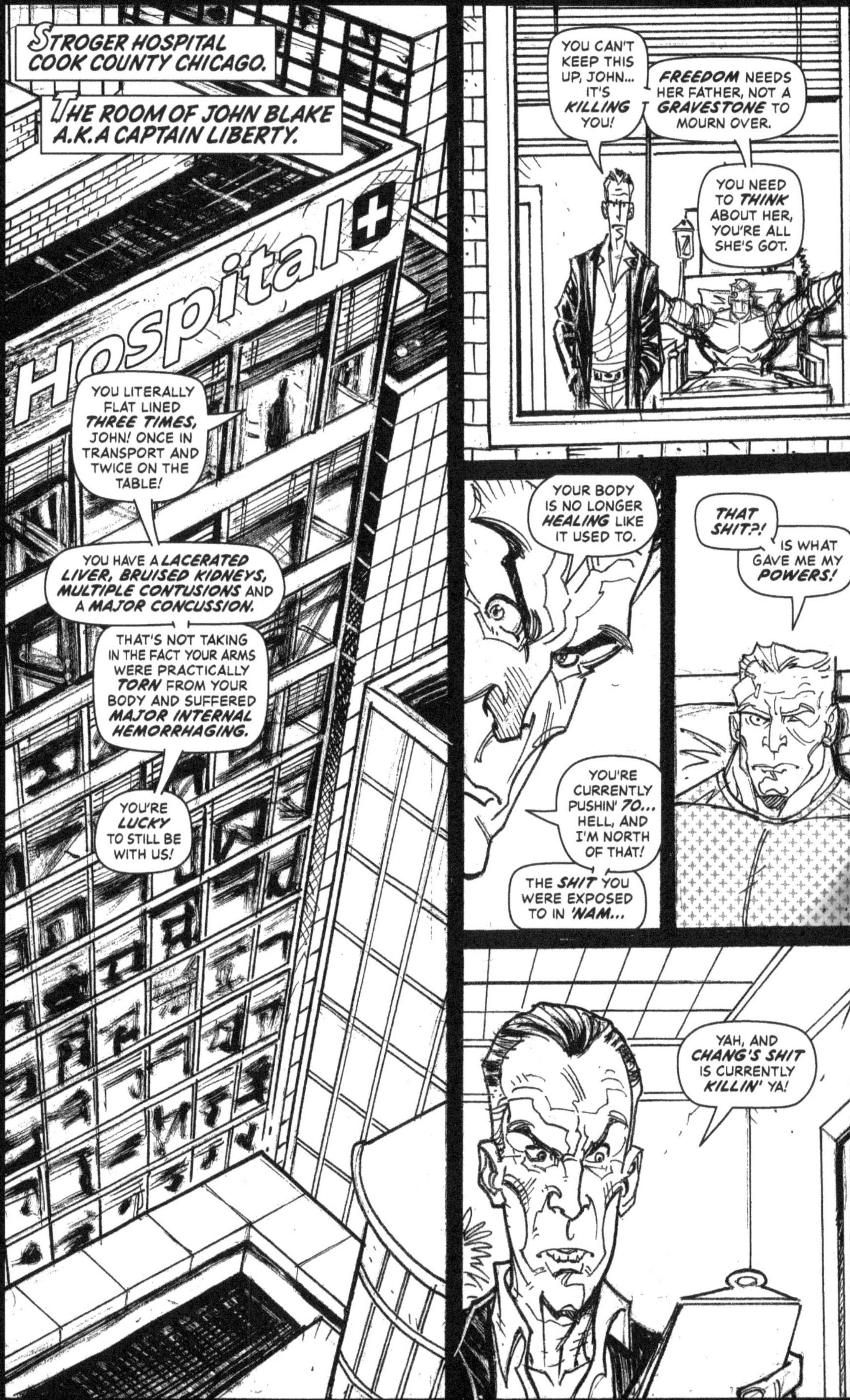
STROGER HOSPITAL COOK COUNTY CHICAGO.
THE ROOM OF JOHN BLAKE A.K.A CAPTAIN LIBERTY.
Hospital
YOU LITERALLY FLAT LINED THREE TIMES, JOHN! ONCE IN TRANSPORT AND TWICE ON THE TABLE!
YOU HAVE A LACERATED LIVER, BRUISED KIDNEYS, MULTIPLE CONTUSIONS AND A MAJOR CONCUSSION.
THAT'S NOT TAKING IN THE FACT YOUR ARMS WERE PRACTICALLY TORN FROM YOUR BODY AND SUFFERED MAJOR INTERNAL HEMORRHAGING.
YOU'RE LUCKY TO STILL BE WITH US!
YOU CAN'T KEEP THIS UP, JOHN... IT'S KILLING YOU!
FREEDOM NEEDS HER FATHER, NOT A GRAVESTONE TO MOURN OVER.
YOU NEED TO THINK ABOUT HER, YOU'RE ALL SHE'S GOT.
YOUR BODY IS NO LONGER HEALING LIKE IT USED TO.
YOU'RE CURRENTLY PUSHIN' 70... HELL, AND I'M NORTH OF THAT!
THE SHIT YOU WERE EXPOSED TO IN 'NAM...
THAT SHIT?!
IS WHAT GAVE ME MY POWERS!
YAH, AND CHANG'S SHIT IS CURRENTLY KILLIN' YA!

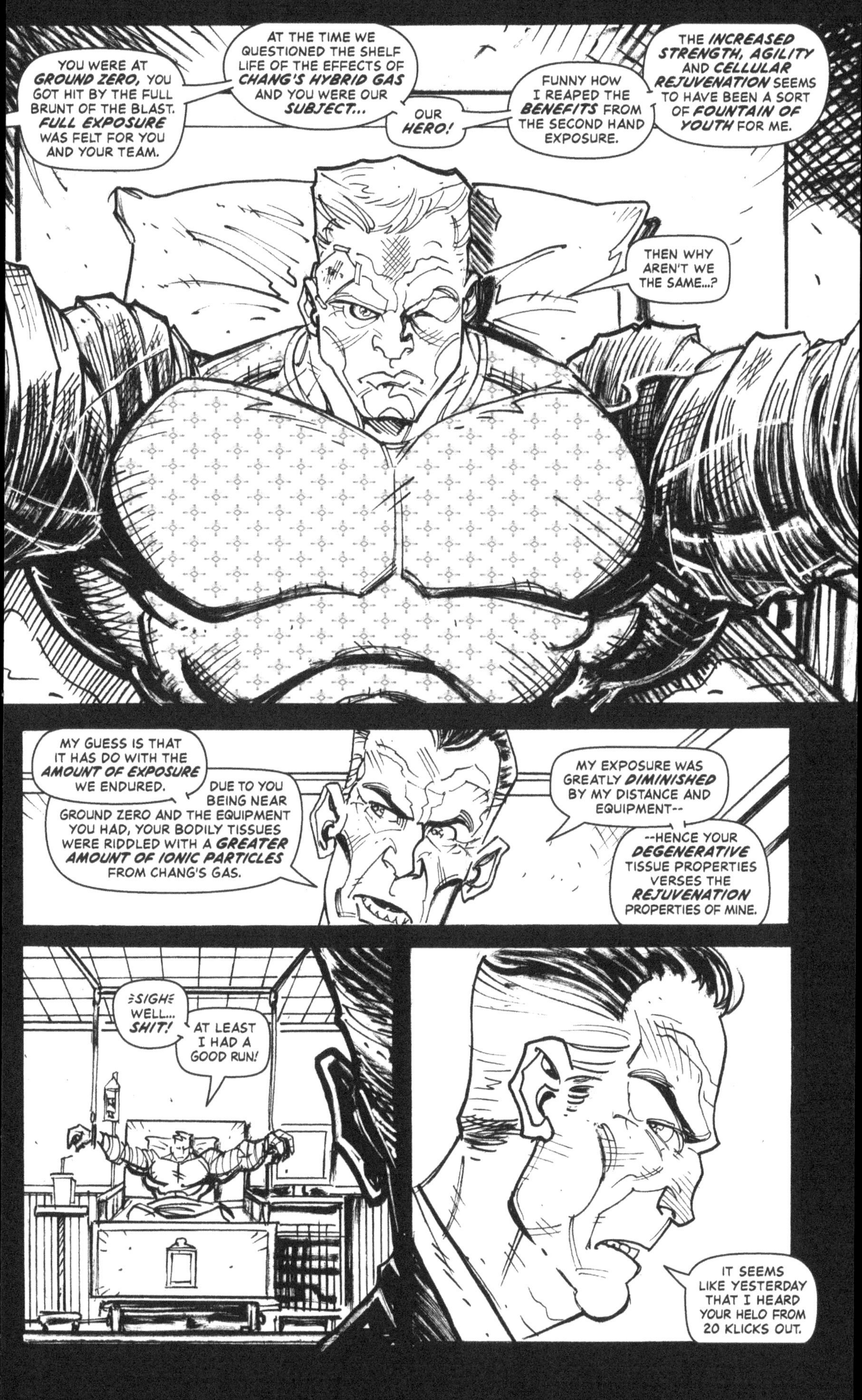

YOU WERE AT GROUND ZERO, YOU GOT HIT BY THE FULL BRUNT OF THE BLAST. FULL EXPOSURE WAS FELT FOR YOU AND YOUR TEAM.
AT THE TIME WE QUESTIONED THE SHELF LIFE OF THE EFFECTS OF CHANG'S HYBRID GAS AND YOU WERE OUR SUBJECT...
OUR HERO!
FUNNY HOW I REAPED THE BENEFITS FROM THE SECOND HAND EXPOSURE.
THE INCREASED STRENGTH, AGILITY AND CELLULAR REJUVENATION SEEMS TO HAVE BEEN A SORT OF FOUNTAIN OF YOUTH FOR ME.
THEN WHY AREN'T WE THE SAME...?
MY GUESS IS THAT IT HAS DO WITH THE AMOUNT OF EXPOSURE WE ENDURED.
DUE TO YOU BEING NEAR GROUND ZERO AND THE EQUIPMENT YOU HAD, YOUR BODILY TISSUES WERE RIDDLED WITH A GREATER AMOUNT OF IONIC PARTICLES FROM CHANG'S GAS.
MY EXPOSURE WAS GREATLY DIMINISHED BY MY DISTANCE AND EQUIPMENT--
--HENCE YOUR DEGENERATIVE TISSUE PROPERTIES VERSES THE REJUVENATION PROPERTIES OF MINE.
SIGH WELL... SHIT!
AT LEAST I HAD A GOOD RUN!
IT SEEMS LIKE YESTERDAY THAT I HEARD YOUR HELO FROM 20 KLICKS OUT.

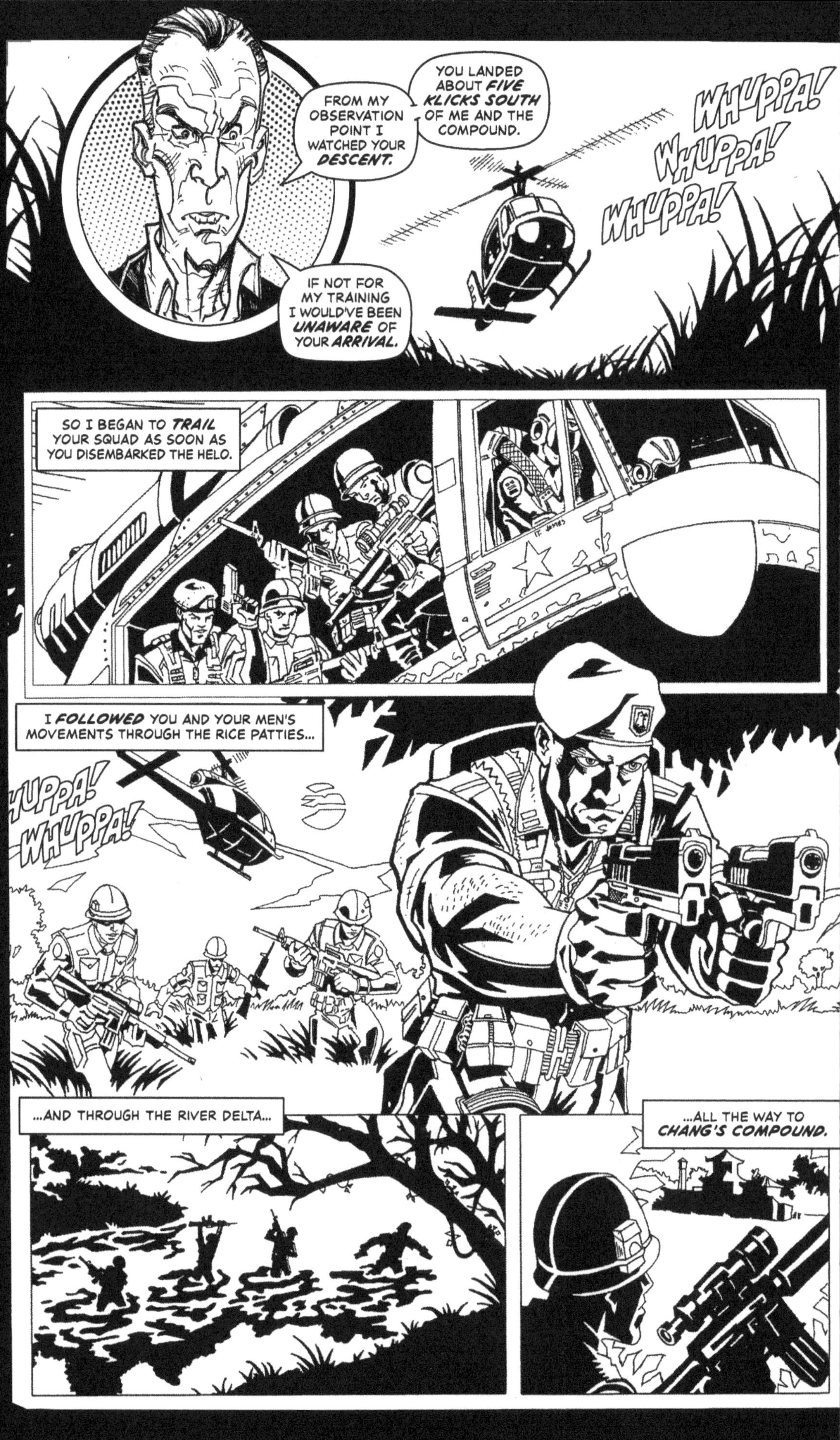
FROM MY OBSERVATION POINT I WATCHED YOUR DESCENT.
YOU LANDED ABOUT FIVE KLICKS SOUTH OF ME AND THE COMPOUND.
WHUPPA! WHUPPA! WHUPPA!
IF NOT FOR MY TRAINING I WOULD'VE BEEN UNAWARE OF YOUR ARRIVAL.
SO I BEGAN TO TRAIL YOUR SQUAD AS SOON AS YOU DISEMBARKED THE HELO.
I FOLLOWED YOU AND YOUR MEN'S MOVEMENTS THROUGH THE RICE PATTIES...
HUPPA! WHUPPA!
...AND THROUGH THE RIVER DELTA...
...ALL THE WAY TO CHANG'S COMPOUND.

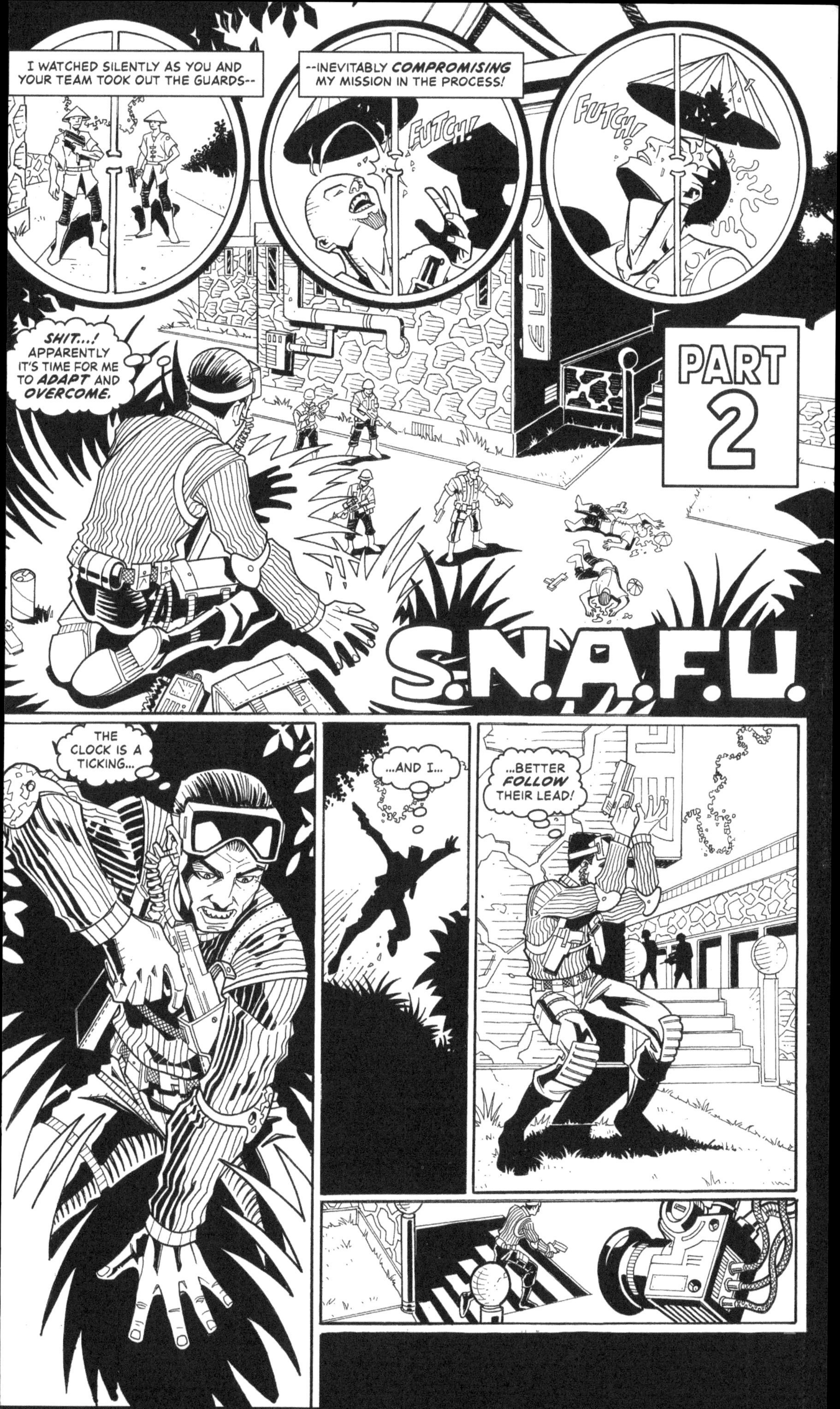
I WATCHED SILENTLY AS YOU AND YOUR TEAM TOOK OUT THE GUARDS--
--INEVITABLY COMPROMISING MY MISSION IN THE PROCESS!
FUTCH!
FUTCH!
SHIT...! APPARENTLY IT'S TIME FOR ME TO ADAPT AND OVERCOME.
PART 2
S.N.A.F.U.
THE CLOCK IS A TICKING...
...AND I...
...BETTER FOLLOW THEIR LEAD!

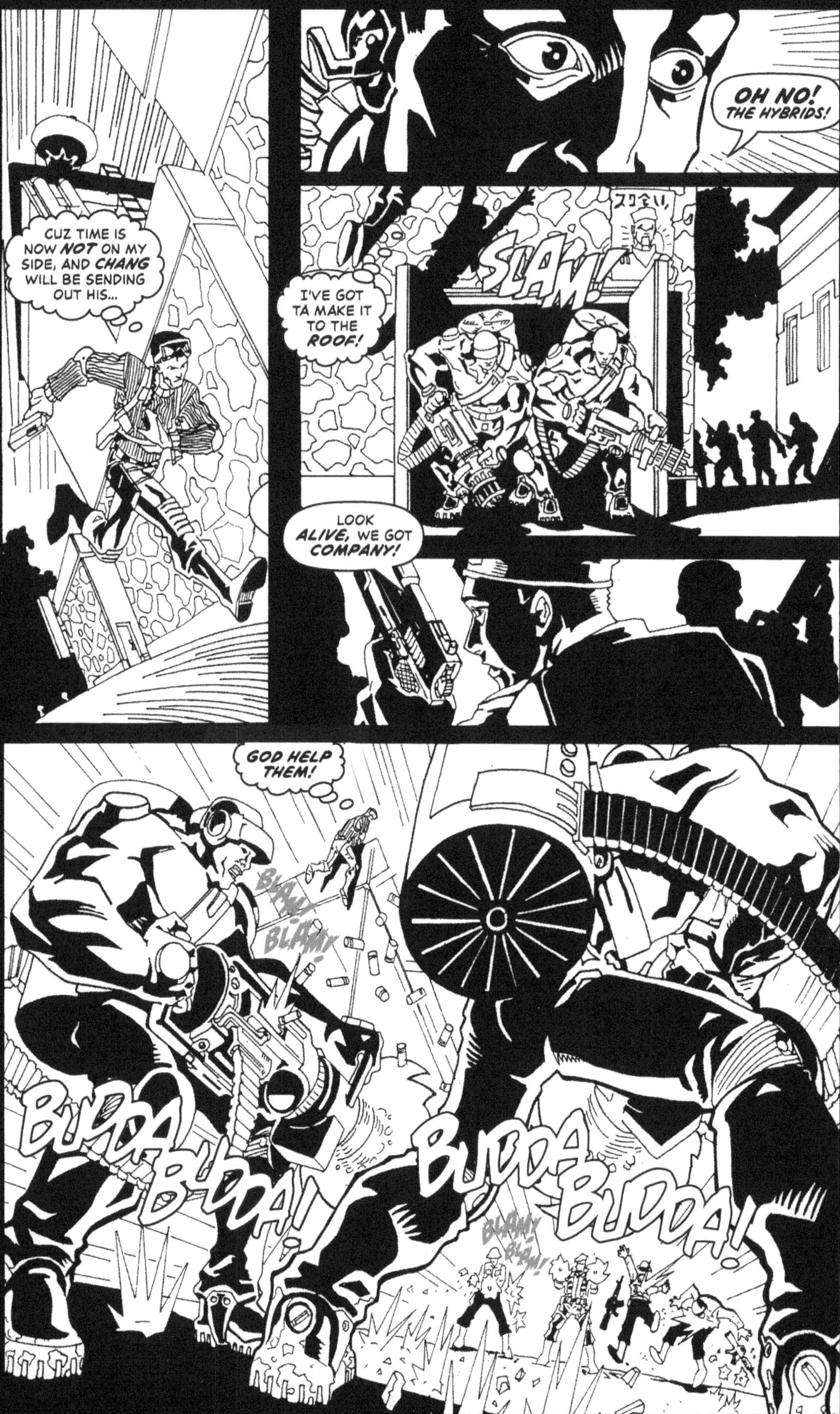

CUZ TIME IS NOW NOT ON MY SIDE, AND CHANG WILL BE SENDING OUT HIS...
OH NO! THE HYBRIDS!
I'VE GOT TA MAKE IT TO THE ROOF!
SLAM!
LOOK ALIVE, WE GOT COMPANY!
GOD HELP THEM!
BLAM! BLAM!
BUDDA BUDDA!
BUDDA BUDDA!
BLAM! BLAM!

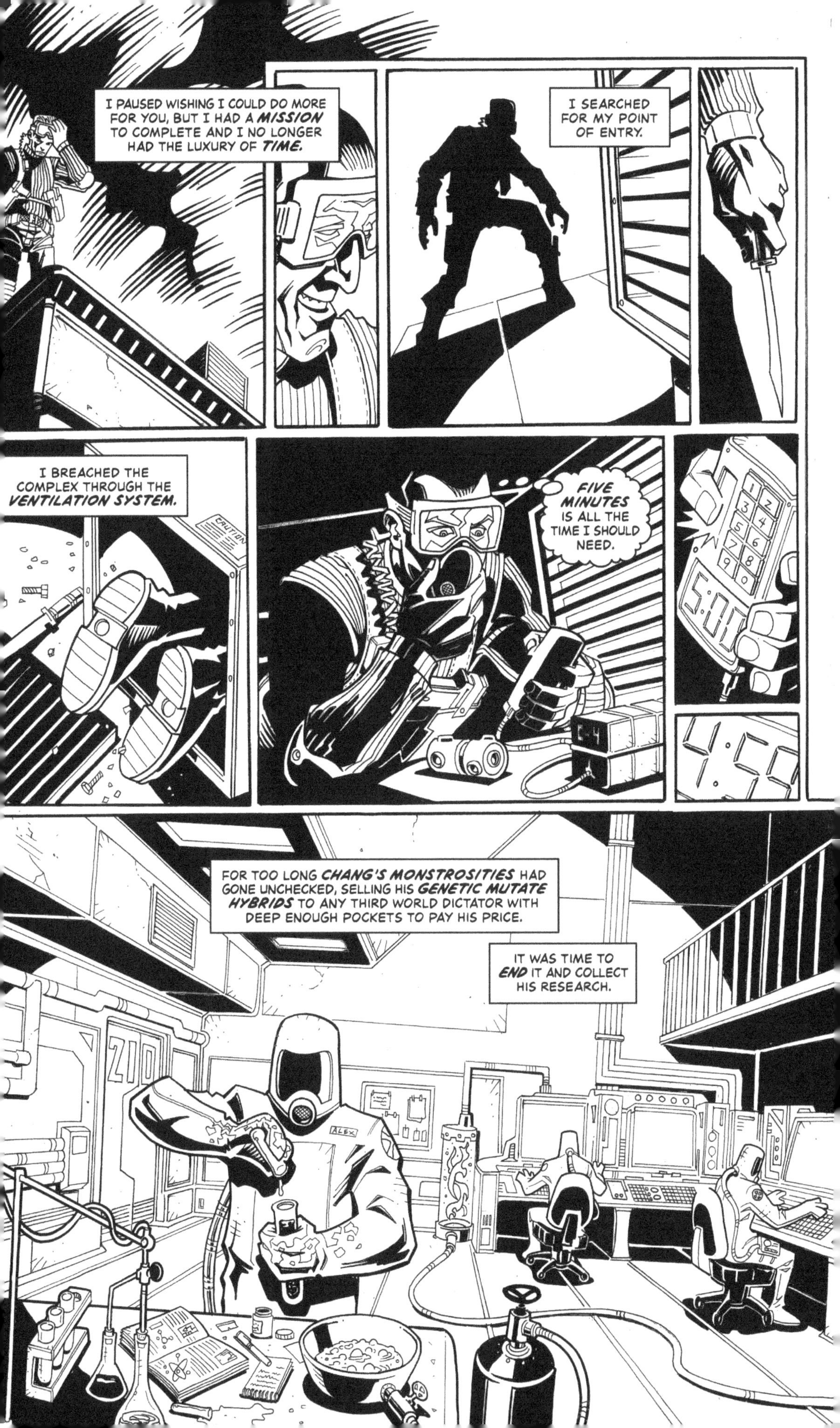

I PAUSED WISHING I COULD DO MORE FOR YOU, BUT I HAD A *MISSION* TO COMPLETE AND I NO LONGER HAD THE LUXURY OF *TIME.*
I SEARCHED FOR MY POINT OF ENTRY.
I BREACHED THE COMPLEX THROUGH THE *VENTILATION SYSTEM.*
CAUTION
FIVE MINUTES IS ALL THE TIME I SHOULD NEED.
C-4
FOR TOO LONG *CHANG'S MONSTROSITIES* HAD GONE UNCHECKED, SELLING HIS *GENETIC MUTATE HYBRIDS* TO ANY THIRD WORLD DICTATOR WITH DEEP ENOUGH POCKETS TO PAY HIS PRICE.
IT WAS TIME TO *END* IT AND COLLECT HIS RESEARCH.
210
ALEX

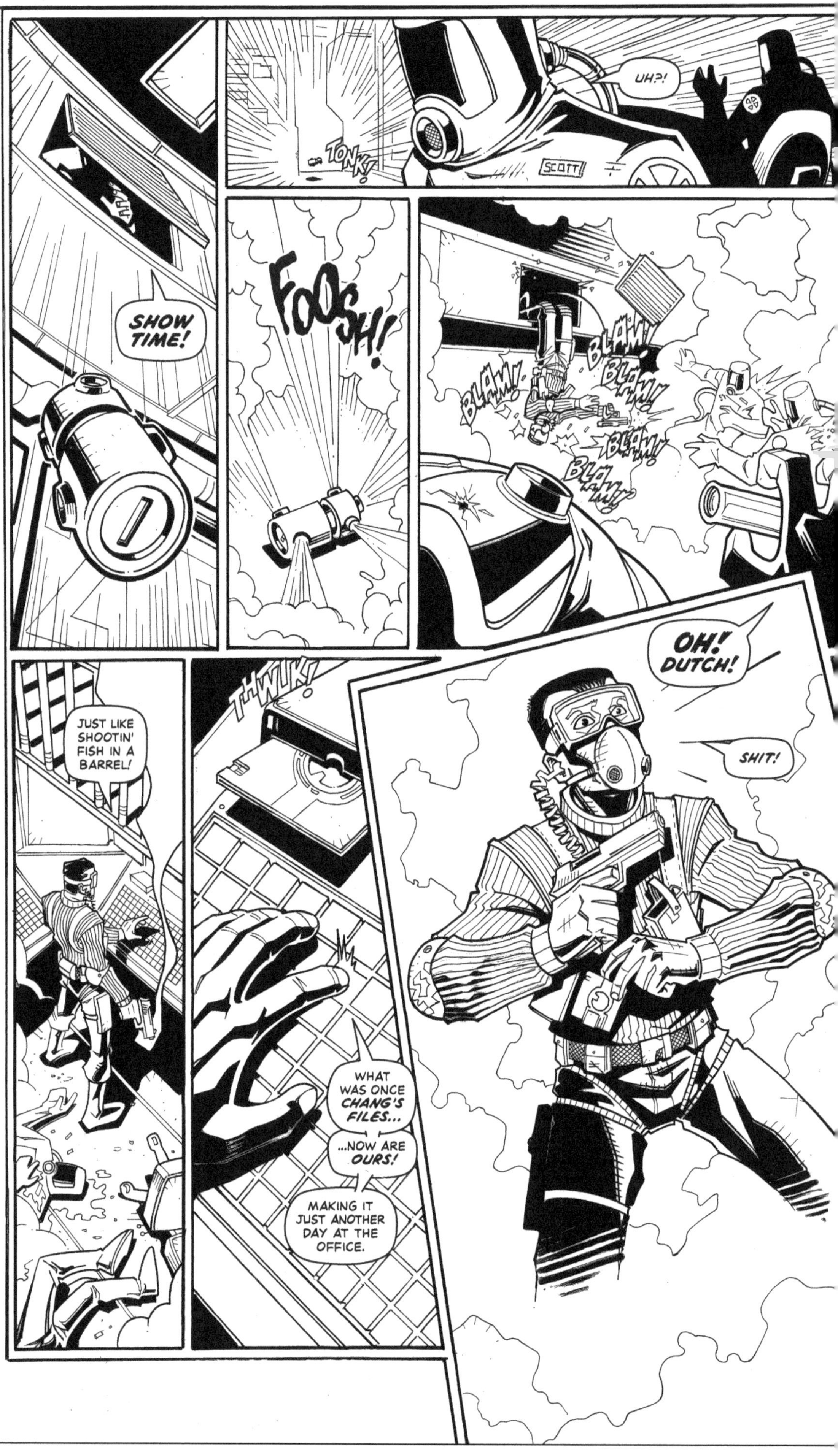

SHOW TIME!
TONK!
UH?!
SCOTT
FOOSH!
BLAM!
BLAM!
BLAM!
BLAM!
BLAM!
JUST LIKE SHOOTIN' FISH IN A BARREL!
THWUK!
WHAT WAS ONCE CHANG'S FILES...
...NOW ARE OURS!
MAKING IT JUST ANOTHER DAY AT THE OFFICE.
OH! DUTCH!
SHIT!

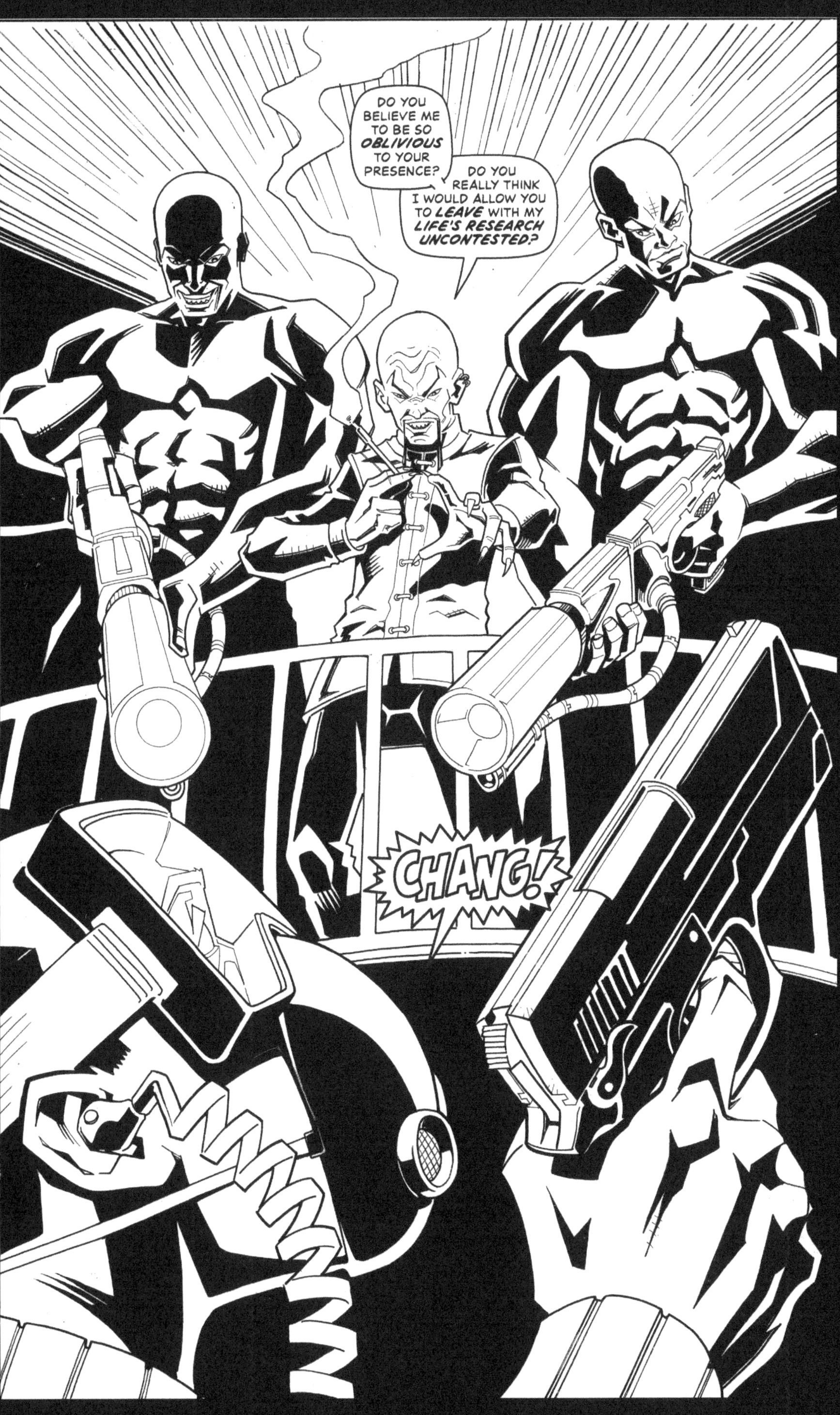
DO YOU BELIEVE ME TO BE SO OBLIVIOUS TO YOUR PRESENCE?
DO YOU REALLY THINK I WOULD ALLOW YOU TO LEAVE WITH MY LIFE'S RESEARCH UNCONTESTED?
CHANG!

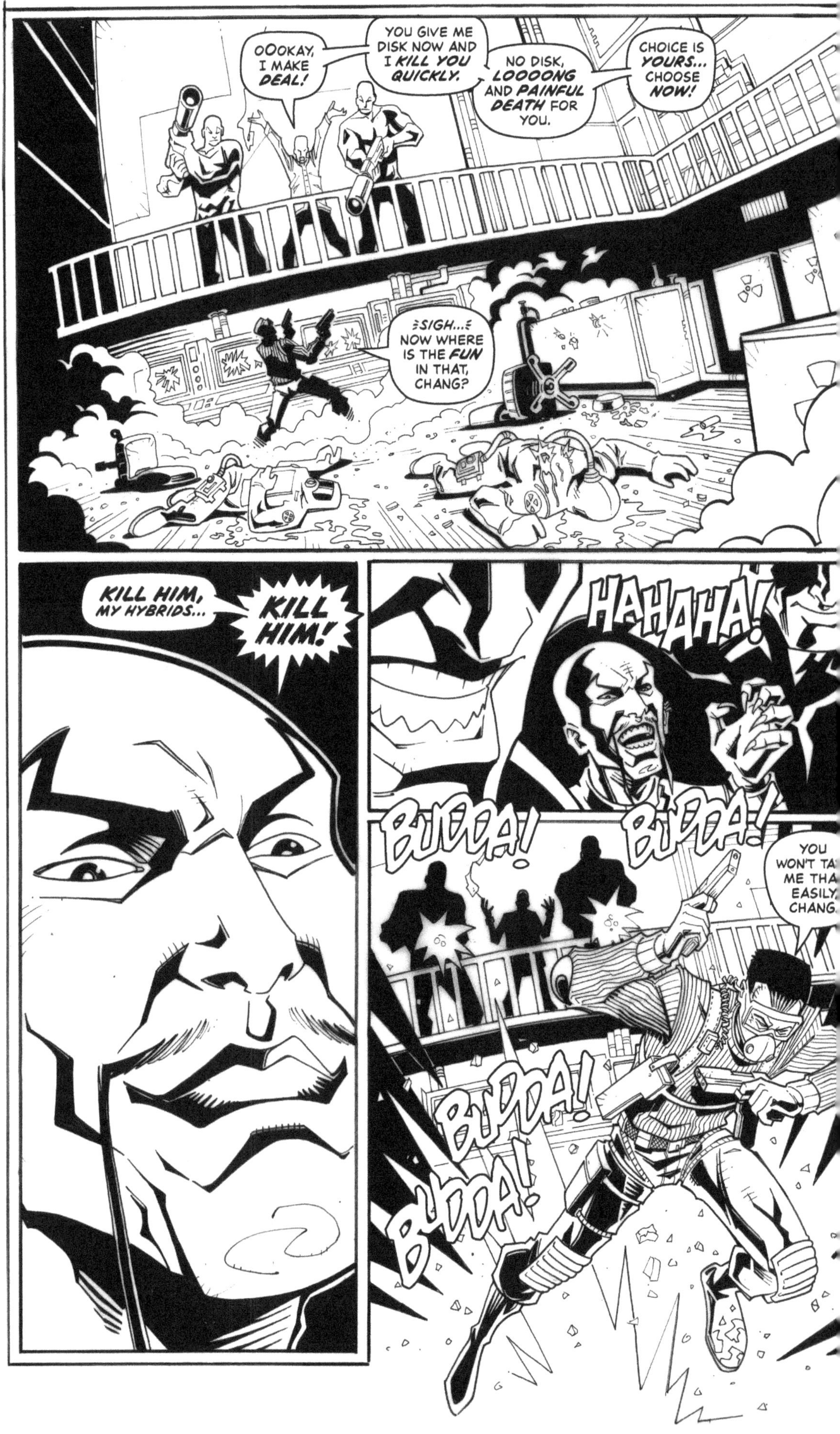
OOOKAY, I MAKE DEAL!
YOU GIVE ME DISK NOW AND I KILL YOU QUICKLY.
NO DISK, LOOOONG AND PAINFUL DEATH FOR YOU.
CHOICE IS YOURS... CHOOSE NOW!
SIGH... NOW WHERE IS THE FUN IN THAT, CHANG?
KILL HIM, MY HYBRIDS...
KILL HIM!
HAHAHA!
BUDDA!
BUDDA!
YOU WON'T TA ME THA EASILY, CHANG.
BUDDA!
BUDDA!

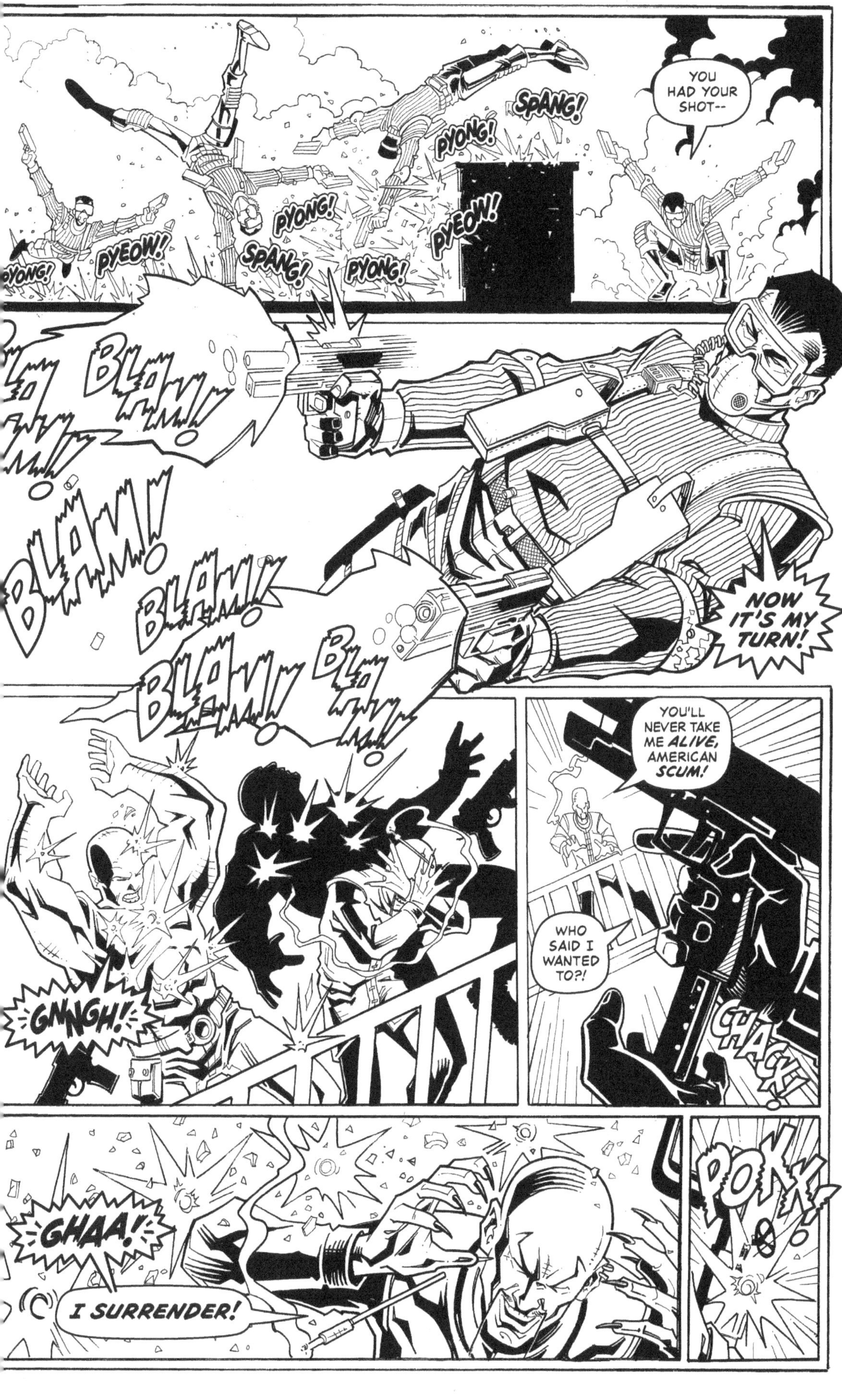
PYONG!
PYEOW!
PYONG!
SPANG!
PYONG!
PYONG!
PYEOW!
SPANG!
YOU HAD YOUR SHOT--
BLAM! BLAM!
BLAM!
BLAM!
BLAM! BLAM!
NOW IT'S MY TURN!
GNNGH!
YOU'LL NEVER TAKE ME ALIVE, AMERICAN SCUM!
WHO SAID I WANTED TO?!
CHACK!
GHAA!
I SURRENDER!
POK!

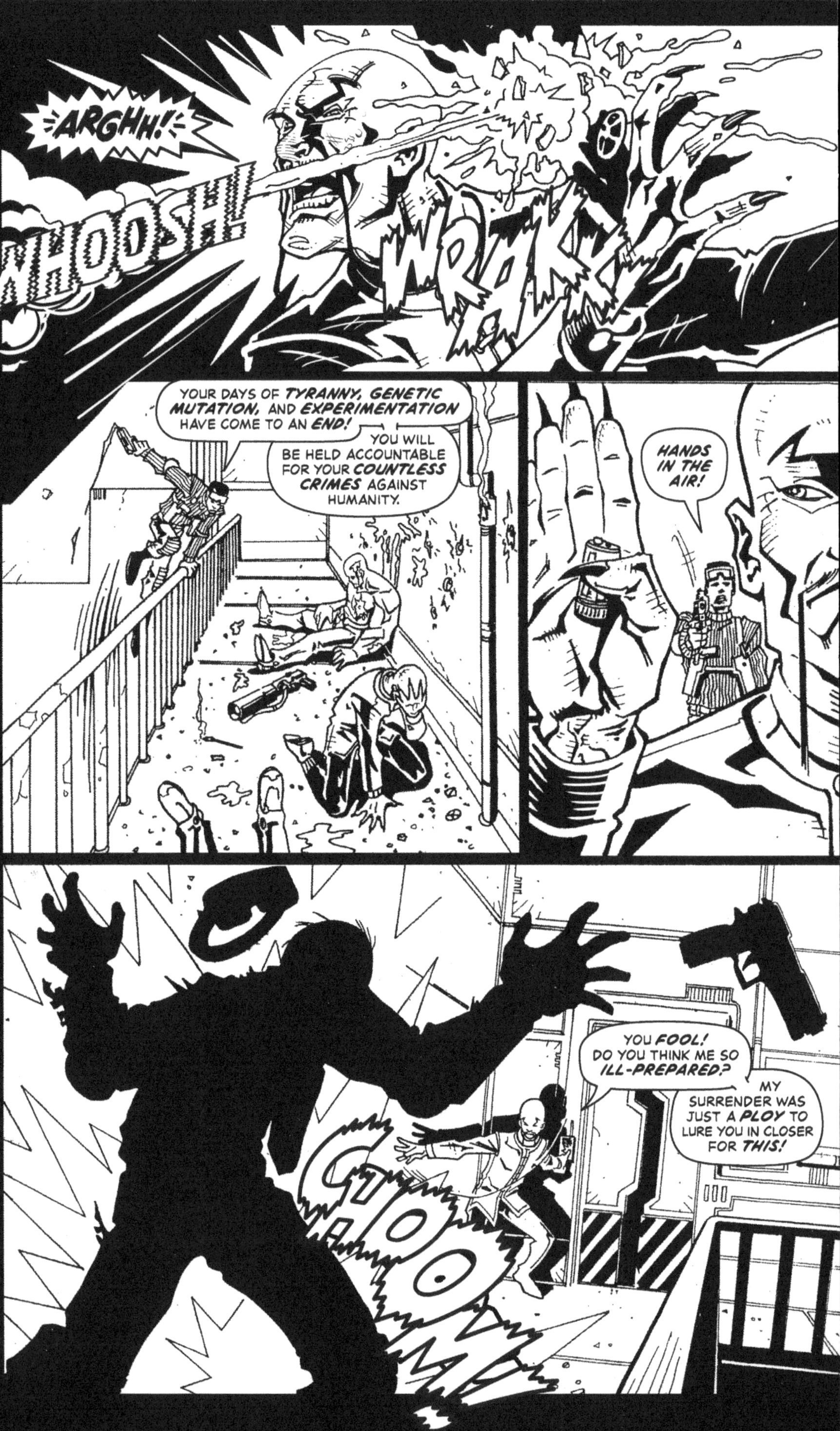
ARGHH!
WHOOSH!
WRAK!
YOUR DAYS OF TYRANNY, GENETIC MUTATION, AND EXPERIMENTATION HAVE COME TO AN END!
YOU WILL BE HELD ACCOUNTABLE FOR YOUR COUNTLESS CRIMES AGAINST HUMANITY.
HANDS IN THE AIR!
YOU FOOL! DO YOU THINK ME SO ILL-PREPARED?
MY SURRENDER WAS JUST A PLOY TO LURE YOU IN CLOSER FOR THIS!

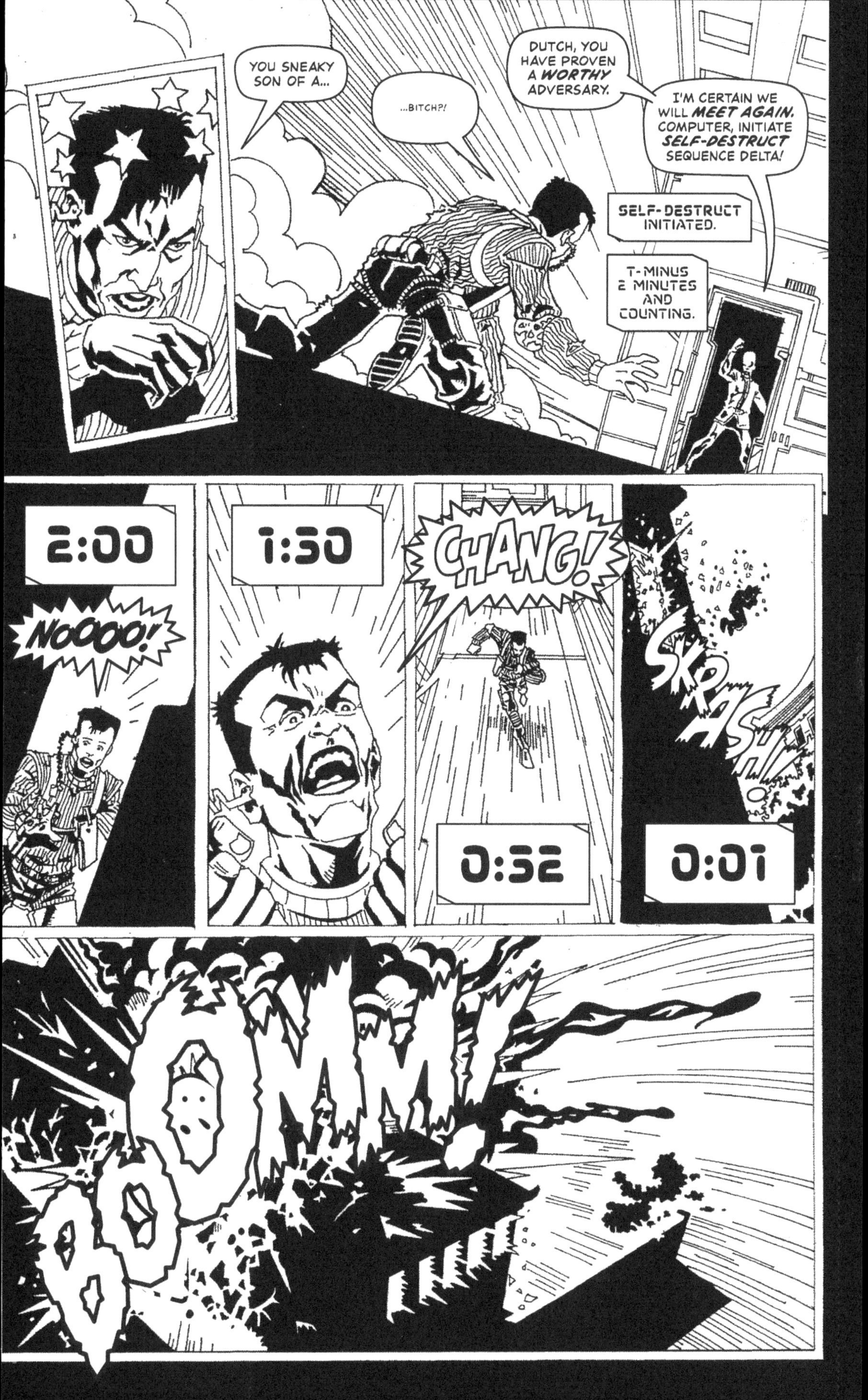
YOU SNEAKY SON OF A...
...BITCH?!
DUTCH, YOU HAVE PROVEN A WORTHY ADVERSARY.
I'M CERTAIN WE WILL MEET AGAIN. COMPUTER, INITIATE SELF-DESTRUCT SEQUENCE DELTA!
SELF-DESTRUCT INITIATED.
T-MINUS 2 MINUTES AND COUNTING.
2:00
NOOOO!
1:50
CHANG!
0:52
SKRASH!
0:01
BOOM!

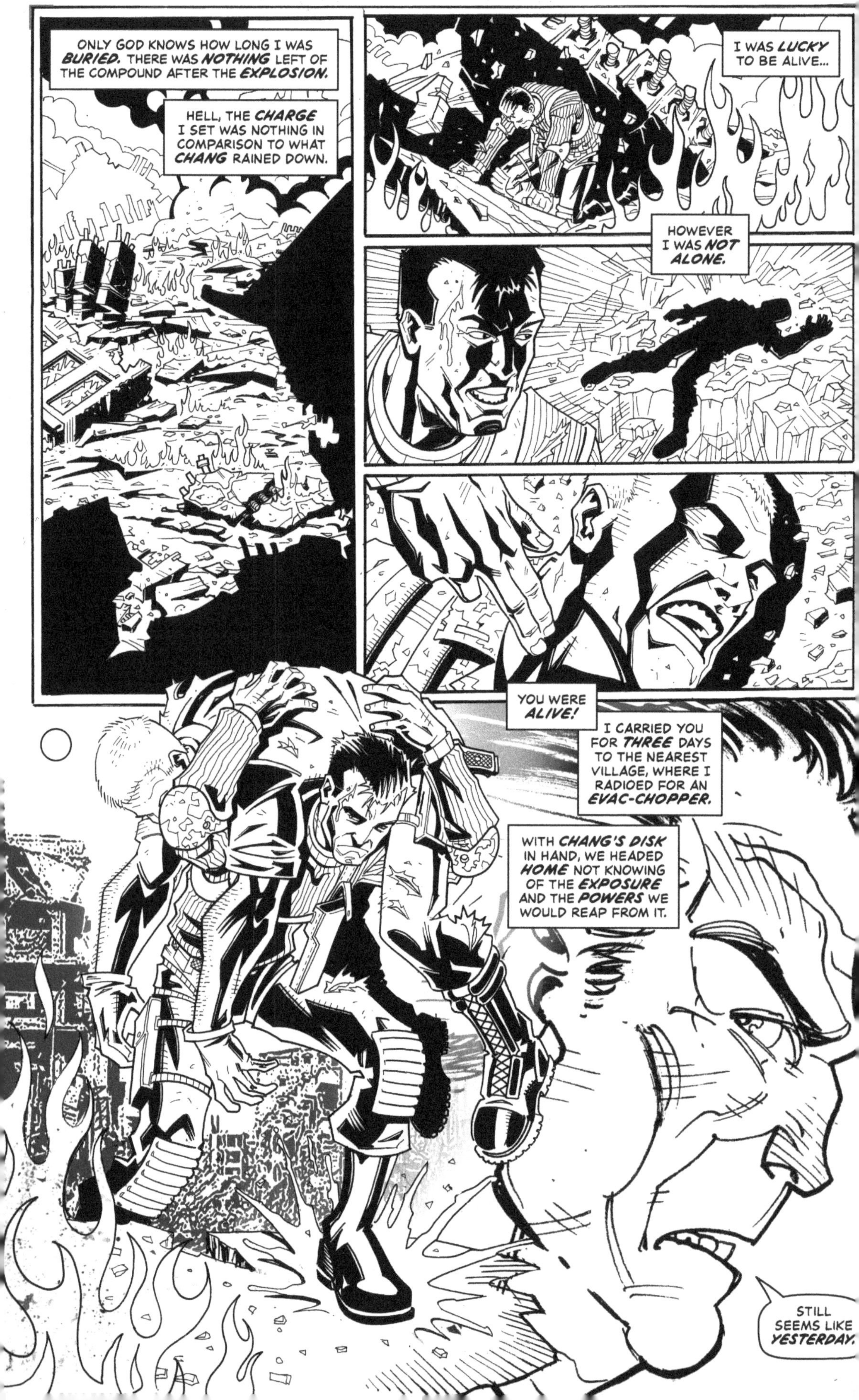
ONLY GOD KNOWS HOW LONG I WAS BURIED. THERE WAS NOTHING LEFT OF THE COMPOUND AFTER THE EXPLOSION.
HELL, THE CHARGE I SET WAS NOTHING IN COMPARISON TO WHAT CHANG RAINED DOWN.
I WAS LUCKY TO BE ALIVE...
HOWEVER I WAS NOT ALONE.
YOU WERE ALIVE!
I CARRIED YOU FOR THREE DAYS TO THE NEAREST VILLAGE, WHERE I RADIOED FOR AN EVAC-CHOPPER.
WITH CHANG'S DISK IN HAND, WE HEADED HOME NOT KNOWING OF THE EXPOSURE AND THE POWERS WE WOULD REAP FROM IT.
STILL SEEMS LIKE YESTERDAY.

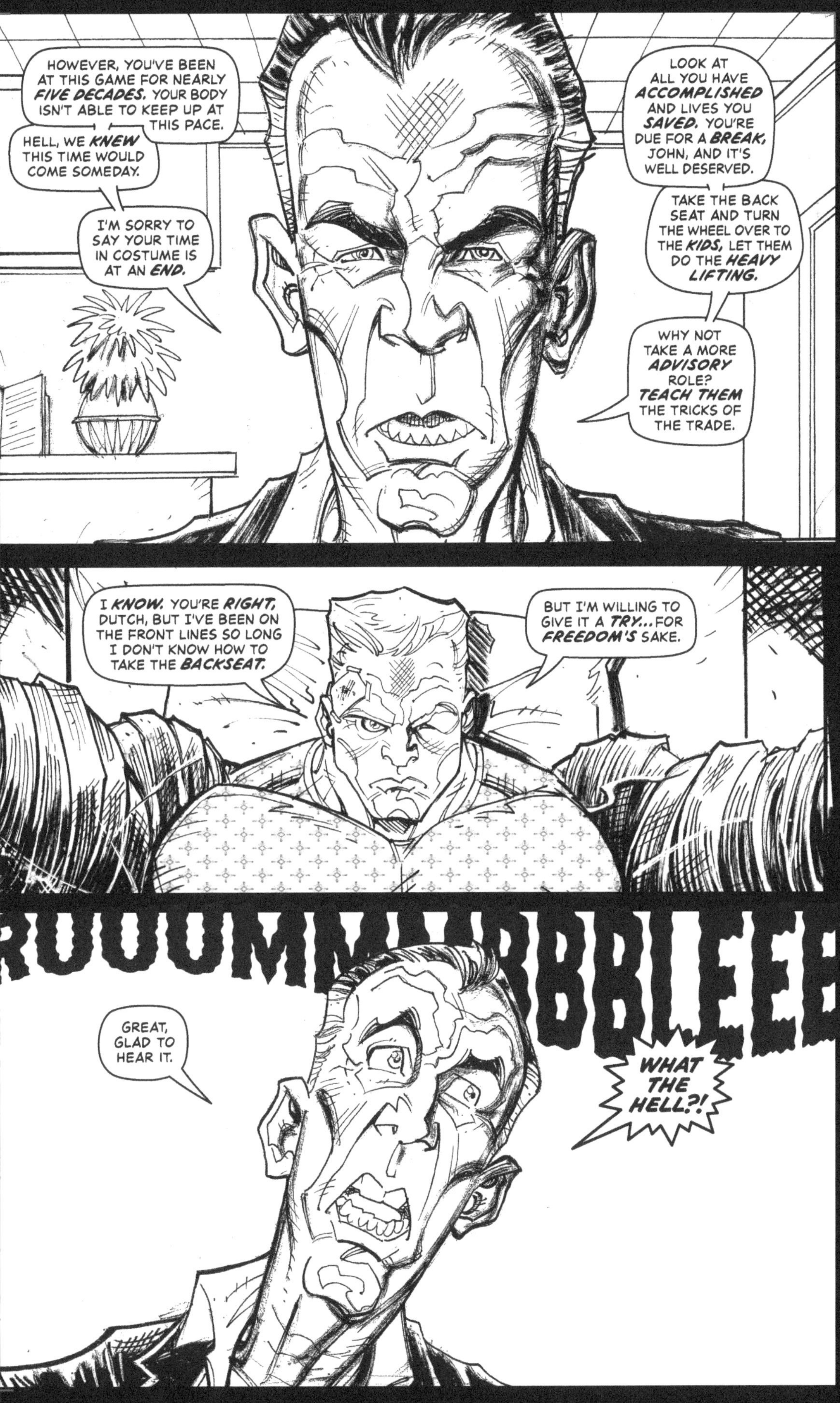
HOWEVER, YOU'VE BEEN AT THIS GAME FOR NEARLY FIVE DECADES. YOUR BODY ISN'T ABLE TO KEEP UP AT THIS PACE.
HELL, WE KNEW THIS TIME WOULD COME SOMEDAY.
I'M SORRY TO SAY YOUR TIME IN COSTUME IS AT AN END.
LOOK AT ALL YOU HAVE ACCOMPLISHED AND LIVES YOU SAVED. YOU'RE DUE FOR A BREAK, JOHN, AND IT'S WELL DESERVED.
TAKE THE BACK SEAT AND TURN THE WHEEL OVER TO THE KIDS, LET THEM DO THE HEAVY LIFTING.
WHY NOT TAKE A MORE ADVISORY ROLE? TEACH THEM THE TRICKS OF THE TRADE.
I KNOW. YOU'RE RIGHT, DUTCH, BUT I'VE BEEN ON THE FRONT LINES SO LONG I DON'T KNOW HOW TO TAKE THE BACKSEAT.
BUT I'M WILLING TO GIVE IT A TRY... FOR FREEDOM'S SAKE.
GREAT, GLAD TO HEAR IT.
WHAT THE HELL?!

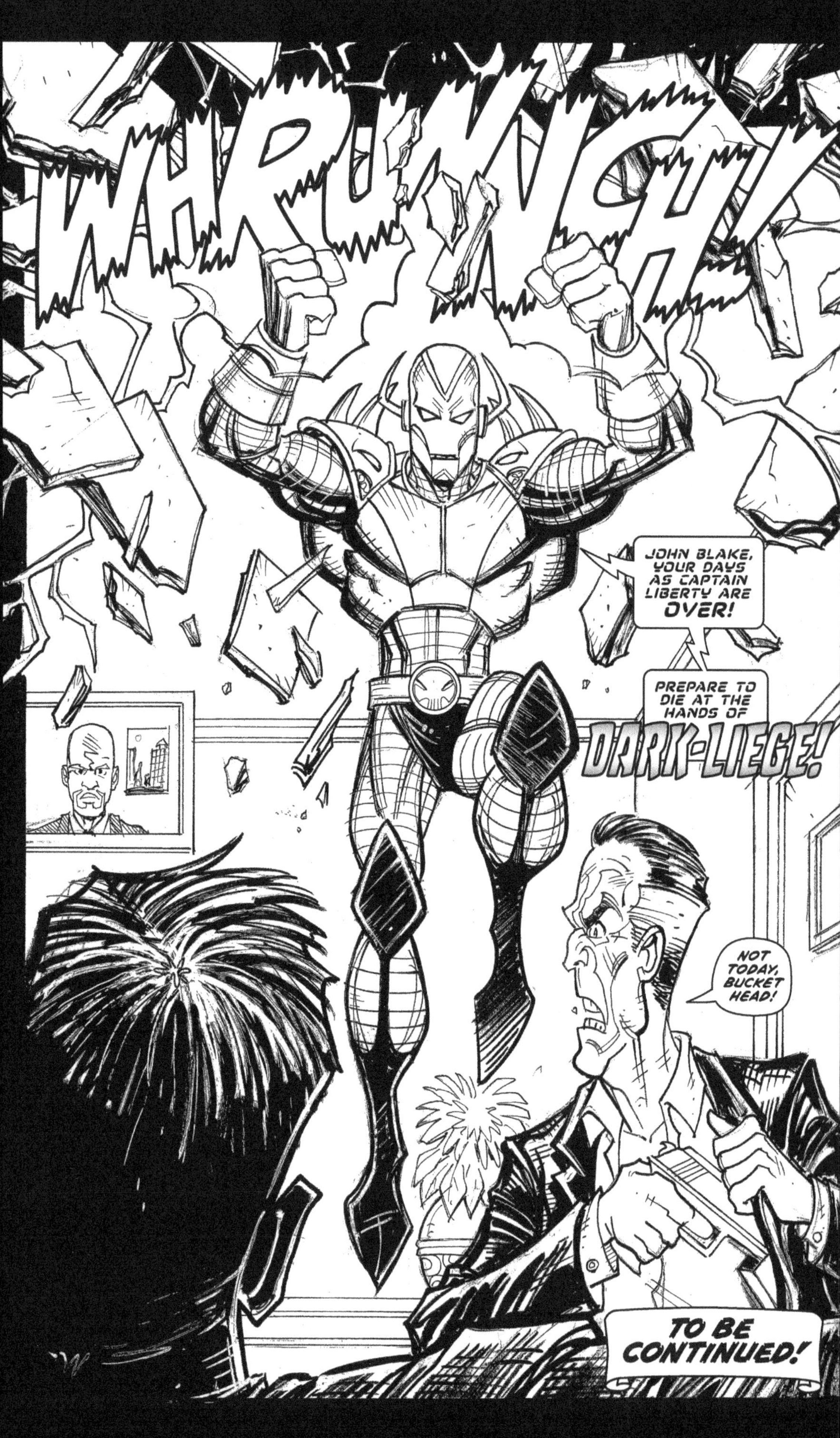

WHRUNCH!
JOHN BLAKE, YOUR DAYS AS CAPTAIN LIBERTY ARE OVER!
PREPARE TO DIE AT THE HANDS OF
DARK-LIEGE!
NOT TODAY, BUCKET HEAD!
TO BE CONTINUED!

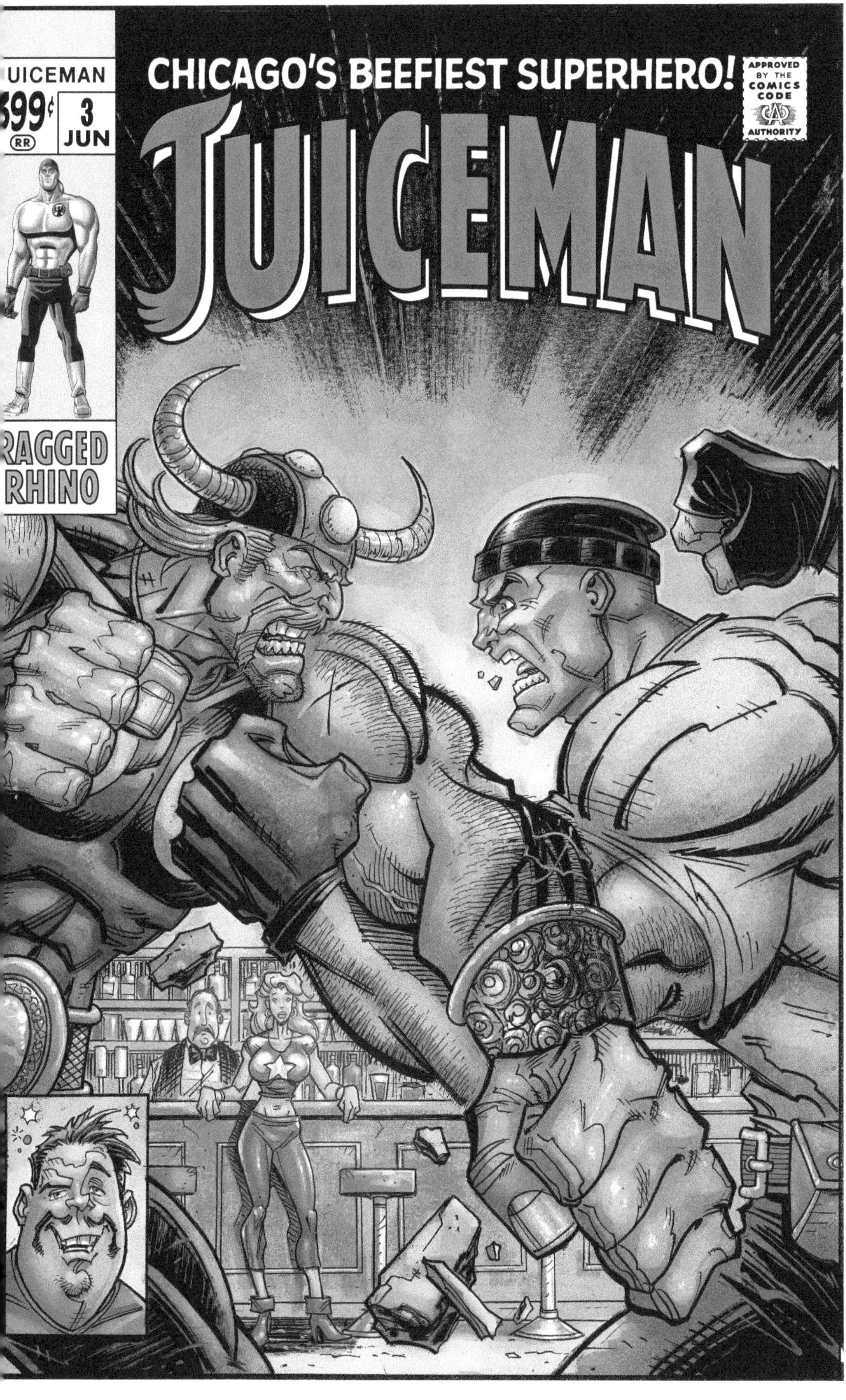

UICEMAN
$99¢
RR
3
JUN
CHICAGO'S BEEFIEST SUPERHERO!
APPROVED BY THE COMICS CODE AUTHORITY
JUICEMAN
RAGGED RHINO

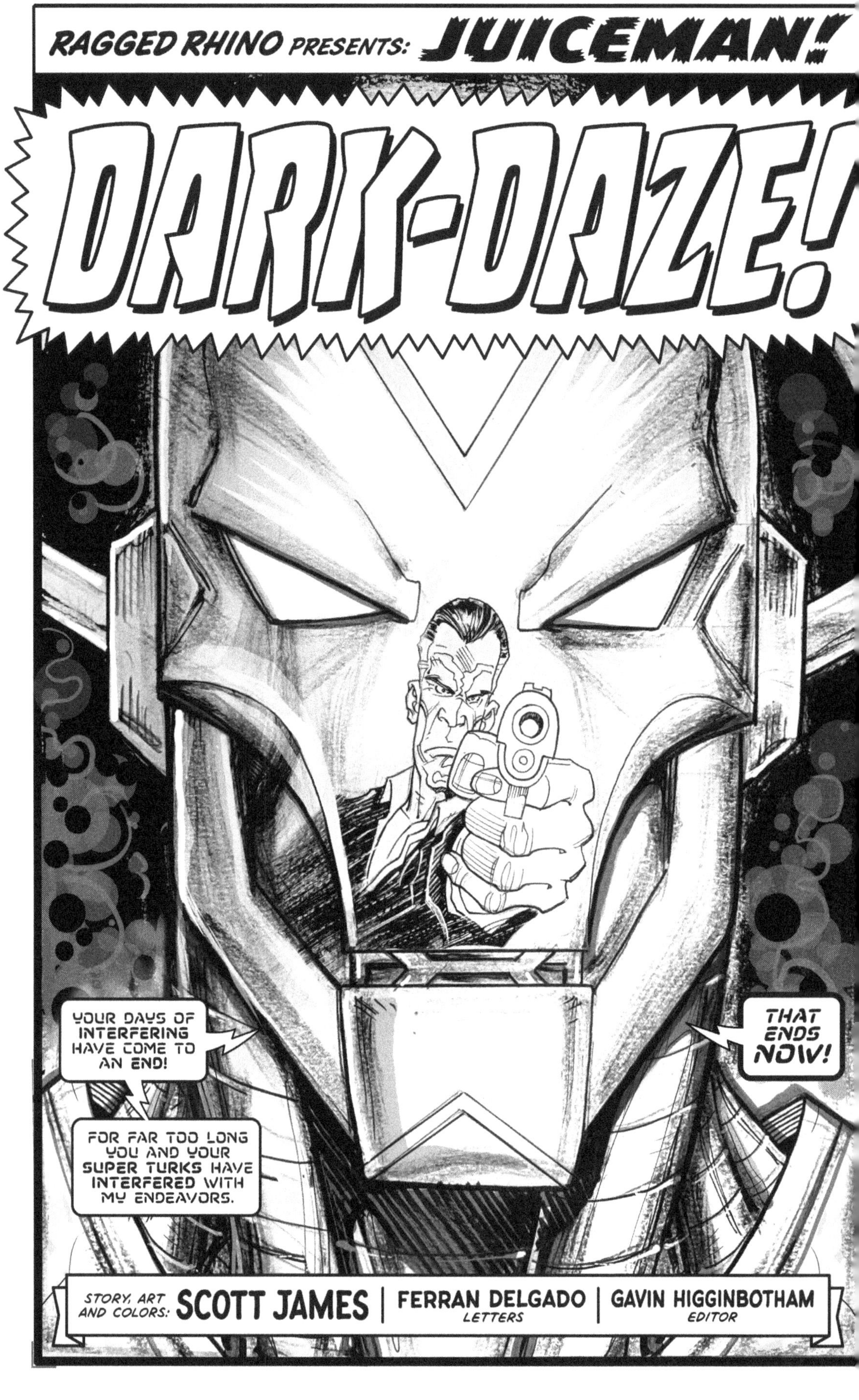

RAGGED RHINO PRESENTS: JUICEMAN!
DARK-DAZE!
YOUR DAYS OF INTERFERING HAVE COME TO AN END!
FOR FAR TOO LONG YOU AND YOUR SUPER TURKS HAVE INTERFERED WITH MY ENDEAVORS.
THAT ENDS NOW!
STORY, ART AND COLORS: SCOTT JAMES | FERRAN DELGADO LETTERS | GAVIN HIGGINBOTHAM EDITOR

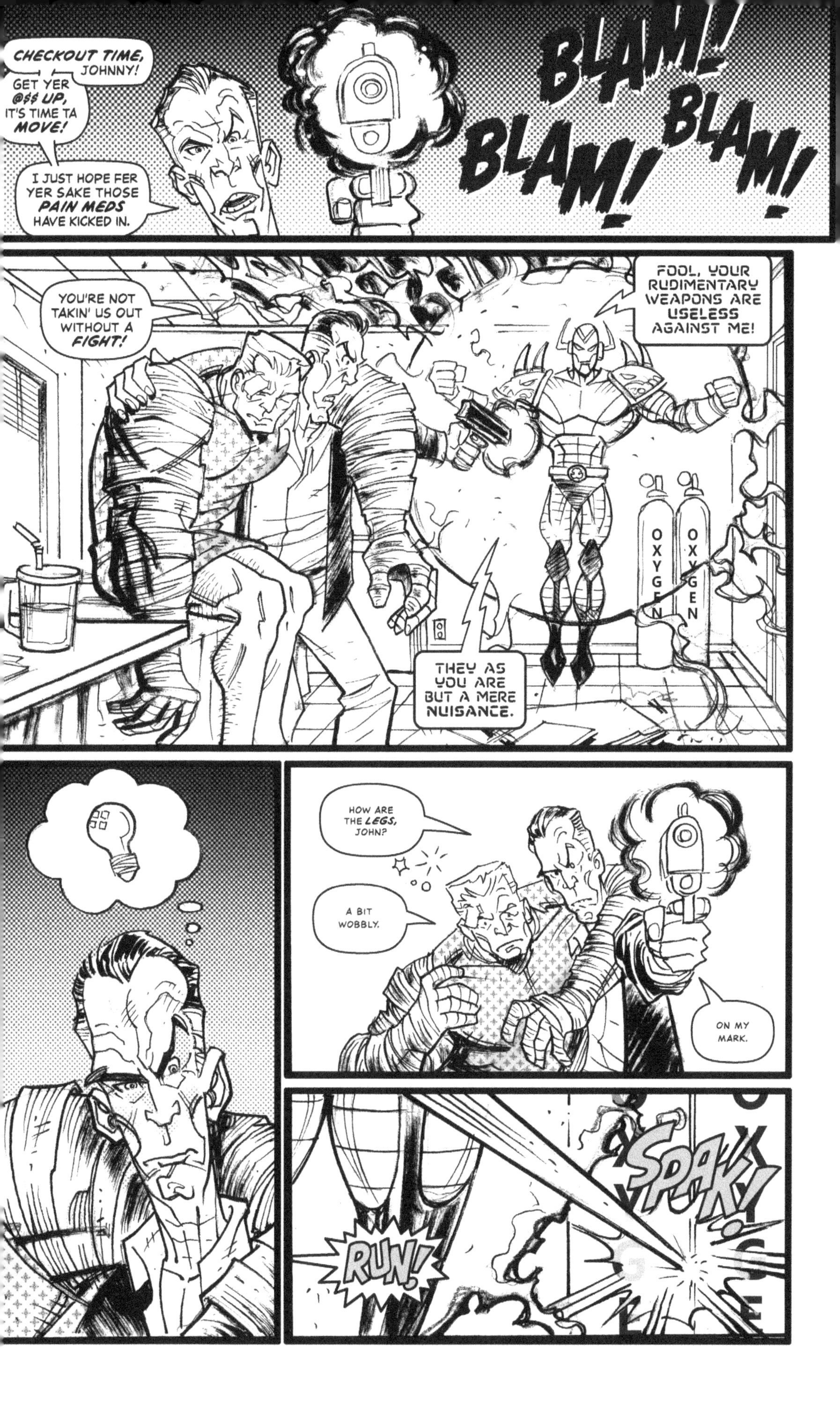
CHECKOUT TIME, JOHNNY!
GET YER @$$ UP, IT'S TIME TA MOVE!
I JUST HOPE FER YER SAKE THOSE PAIN MEDS HAVE KICKED IN.
BLAM! BLAM! BLAM! BLAM!
YOU'RE NOT TAKIN' US OUT WITHOUT A FIGHT!
FOOL, YOUR RUDIMENTARY WEAPONS ARE USELESS AGAINST ME!
THEY AS YOU ARE BUT A MERE NUISANCE.
OXYGEN
OXYGEN
HOW ARE THE LEGS, JOHN?
A BIT WOBBLY.
ON MY MARK.
SPAK!
RUN!

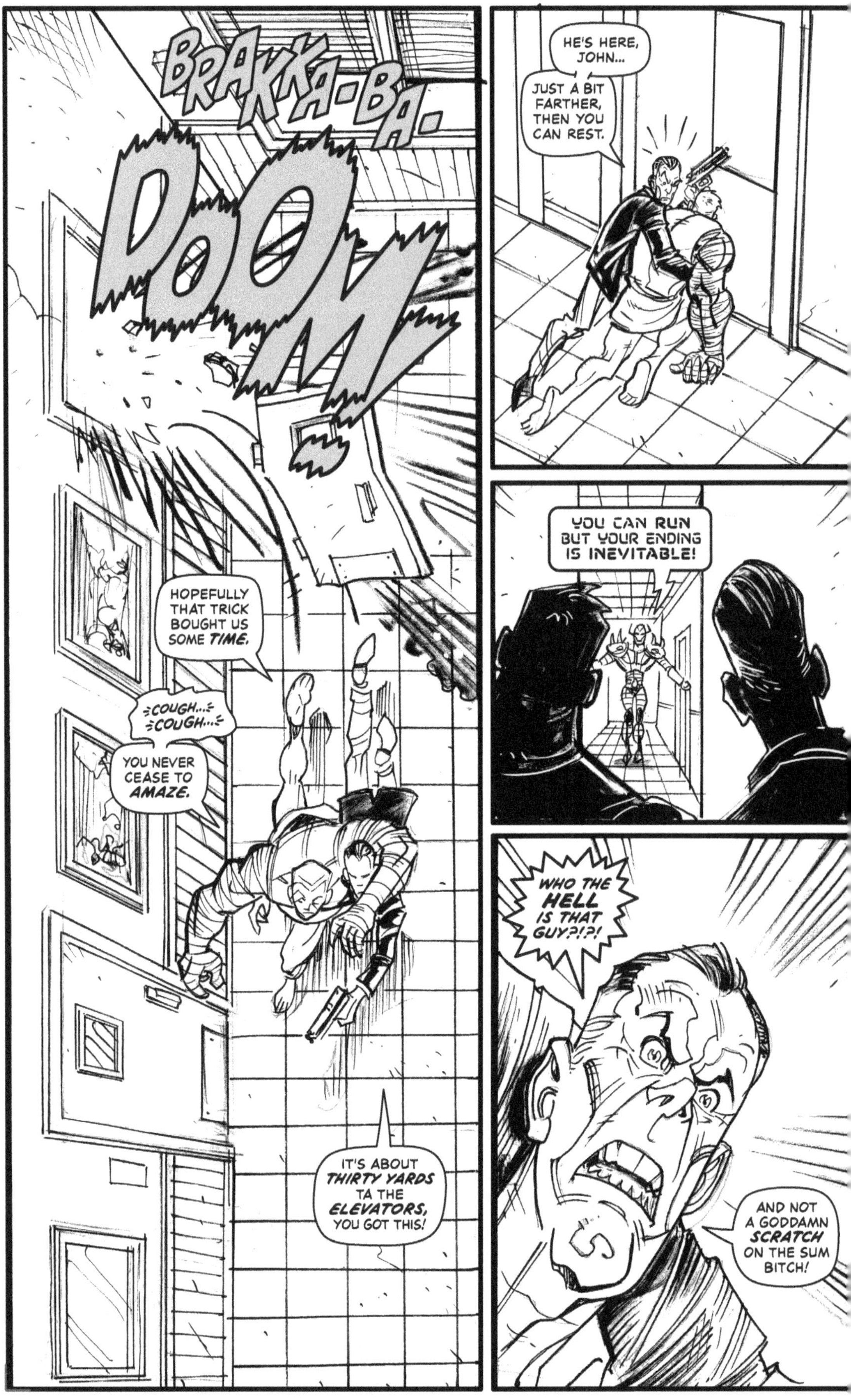
BRAKKA-BA-DOOM!
HE'S HERE, JOHN...
JUST A BIT FARTHER, THEN YOU CAN REST.
HOPEFULLY THAT TRICK BOUGHT US SOME TIME.
COUGH... COUGH...
YOU NEVER CEASE TO AMAZE.
IT'S ABOUT THIRTY YARDS TA THE ELEVATORS, YOU GOT THIS!
YOU CAN RUN BUT YOUR ENDING IS INEVITABLE!
WHO THE HELL IS THAT GUY?!?!
AND NOT A GODDAMN SCRATCH ON THE SUM BITCH!

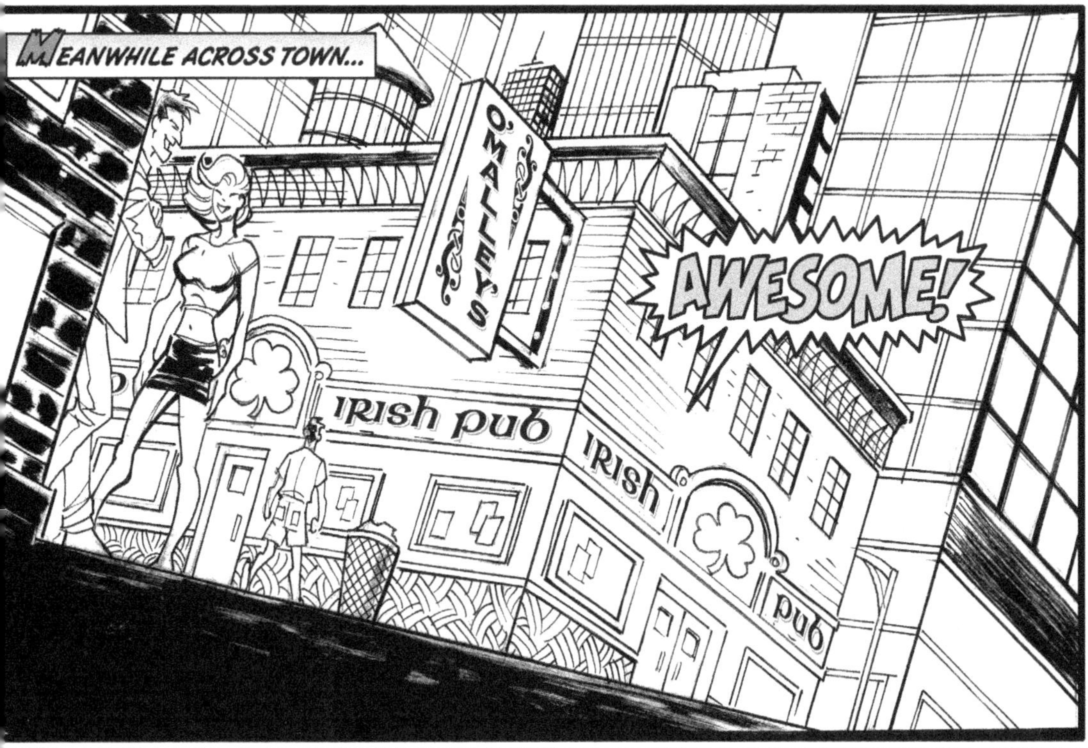
MEANWHILE ACROSS TOWN...
O'MALLEY'S
IRISH PUB
IRISH
PUB
AWESOME!

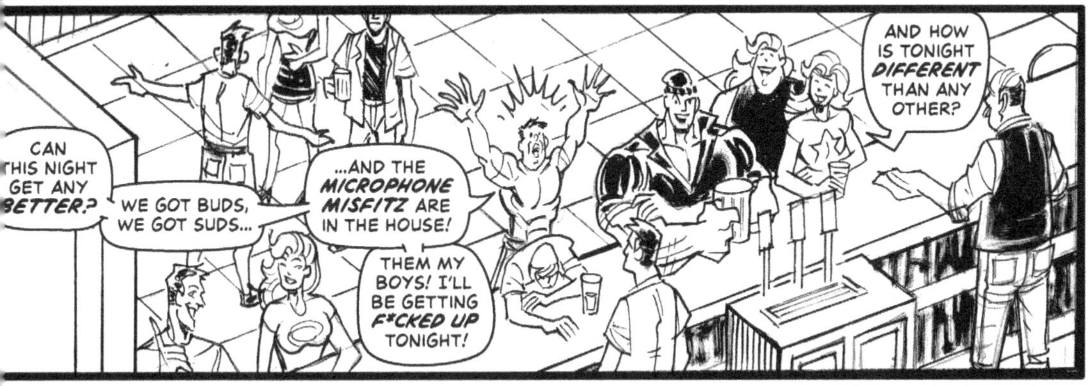
CAN THIS NIGHT GET ANY BETTER?
WE GOT BUDS, WE GOT SUDS...
...AND THE MICROPHONE MISFITZ ARE IN THE HOUSE!
THEM MY BOYS! I'LL BE GETTING F*CKED UP TONIGHT!
AND HOW IS TONIGHT DIFFERENT THAN ANY OTHER?

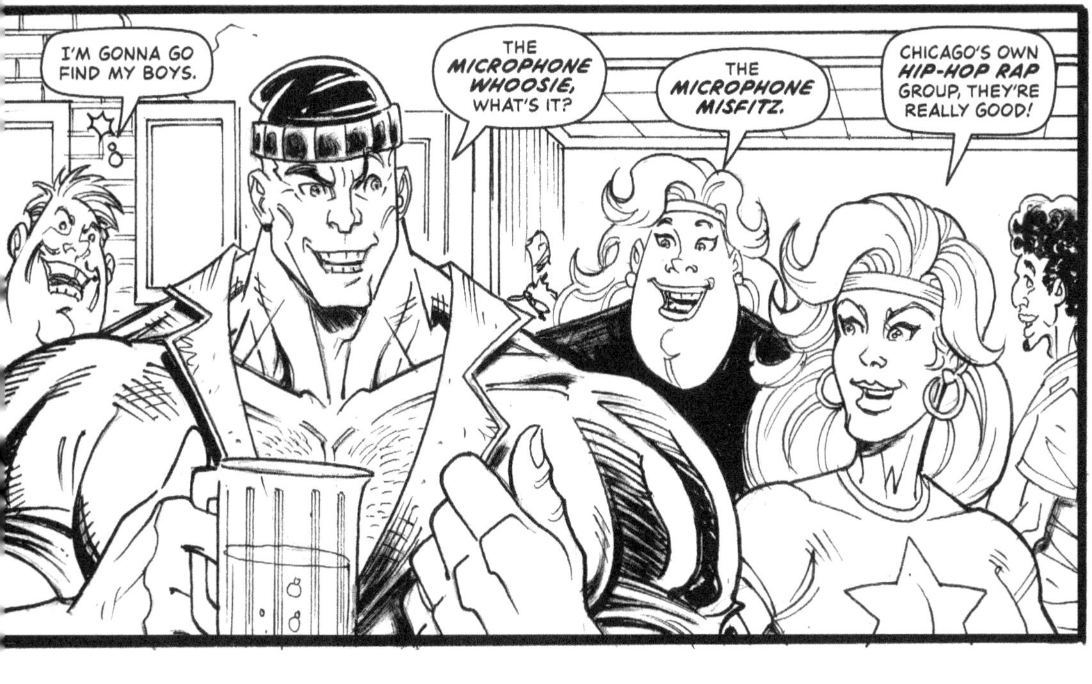
I'M GONNA GO FIND MY BOYS.
THE MICROPHONE WHOOSIE, WHAT'S IT?
THE MICROPHONE MISFITZ.
CHICAGO'S OWN HIP-HOP RAP GROUP, THEY'RE REALLY GOOD!

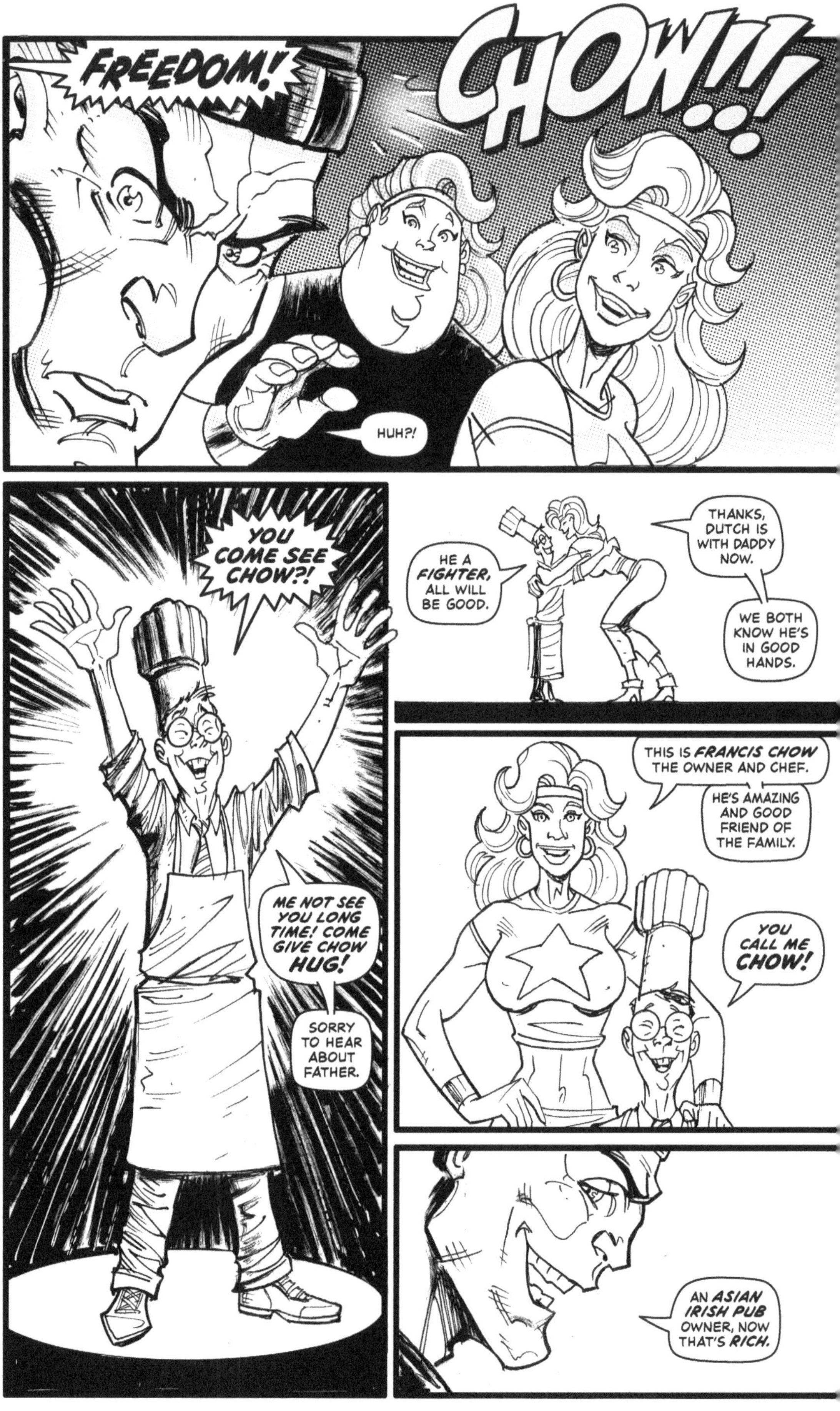
FREEDOM!
CHOW!!!
HUH?!
YOU COME SEE CHOW?!
ME NOT SEE YOU LONG TIME! COME GIVE CHOW HUG!
SORRY TO HEAR ABOUT FATHER.
HE A FIGHTER, ALL WILL BE GOOD.
THANKS, DUTCH IS WITH DADDY NOW.
WE BOTH KNOW HE'S IN GOOD HANDS.
THIS IS FRANCIS CHOW THE OWNER AND CHEF.
HE'S AMAZING AND GOOD FRIEND OF THE FAMILY.
YOU CALL ME CHOW!
AN ASIAN IRISH PUB OWNER, NOW THAT'S RICH.

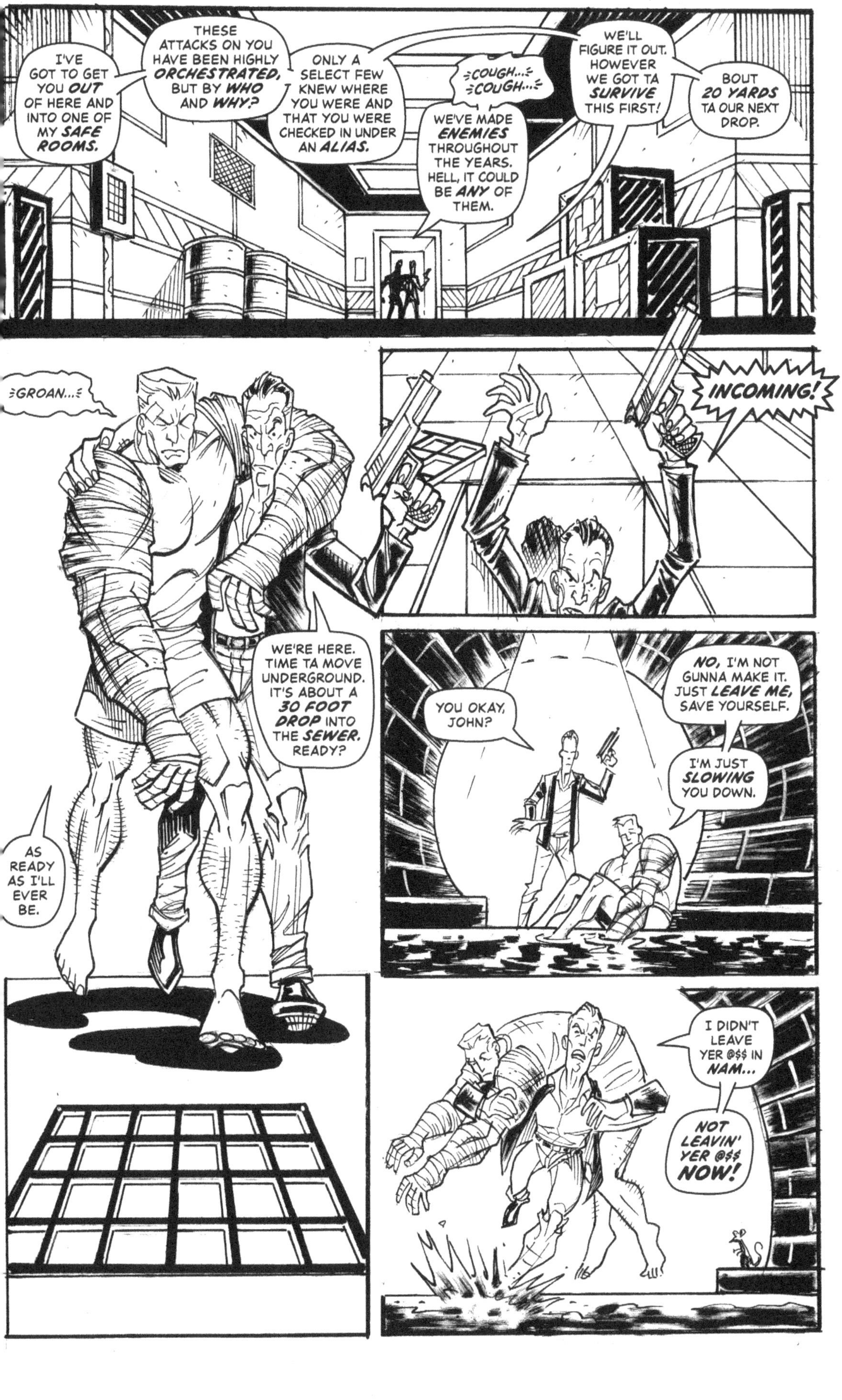
I'VE GOT TO GET YOU OUT OF HERE AND INTO ONE OF MY SAFE ROOMS.
THESE ATTACKS ON YOU HAVE BEEN HIGHLY ORCHESTRATED, BUT BY WHO AND WHY?
ONLY A SELECT FEW KNEW WHERE YOU WERE AND THAT YOU WERE CHECKED IN UNDER AN ALIAS.
COUGH... COUGH...
WE'VE MADE ENEMIES THROUGHOUT THE YEARS. HELL, IT COULD BE ANY OF THEM.
WE'LL FIGURE IT OUT. HOWEVER WE GOT TA SURVIVE THIS FIRST!
BOUT 20 YARDS TA OUR NEXT DROP.
GROAN...
INCOMING!
WE'RE HERE. TIME TA MOVE UNDERGROUND. IT'S ABOUT A 30 FOOT DROP INTO THE SEWER. READY?
AS READY AS I'LL EVER BE.
YOU OKAY, JOHN?
NO, I'M NOT GUNNA MAKE IT. JUST LEAVE ME, SAVE YOURSELF.
I'M JUST SLOWING YOU DOWN.
I DIDN'T LEAVE YER @$$ IN NAM...
NOT LEAVIN' YER @$$ NOW!

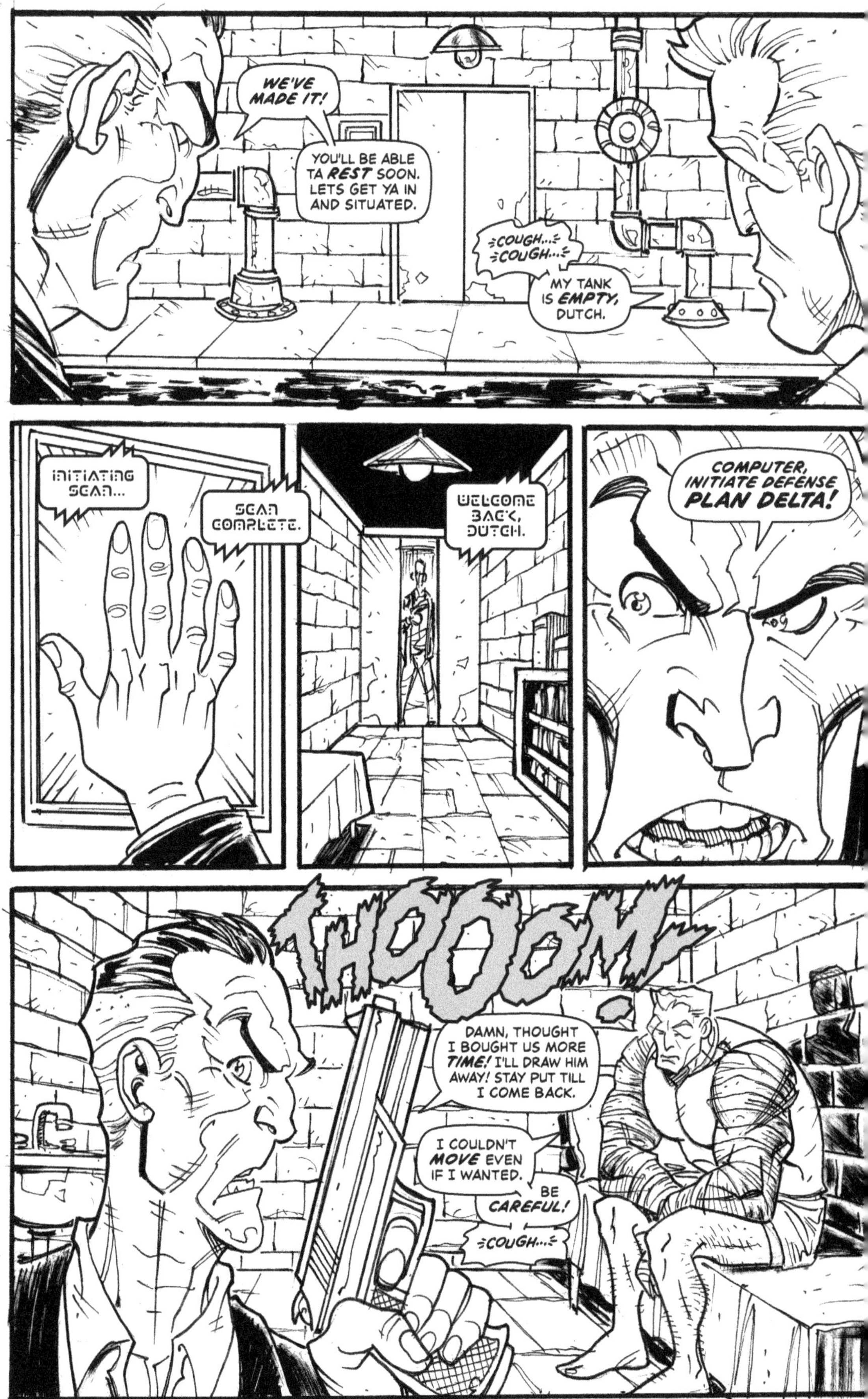
WE'VE MADE IT!
YOU'LL BE ABLE TA REST SOON. LETS GET YA IN AND SITUATED.
COUGH... COUGH...
MY TANK IS EMPTY, DUTCH.
INITIATING SCAN...
SCAN COMPLETE.
WELCOME BACK, DUTCH.
COMPUTER, INITIATE DEFENSE PLAN DELTA!
THOOOM!
DAMN, THOUGHT I BOUGHT US MORE TIME! I'LL DRAW HIM AWAY! STAY PUT TILL I COME BACK.
I COULDN'T MOVE EVEN IF I WANTED.
BE CAREFUL!
COUGH...

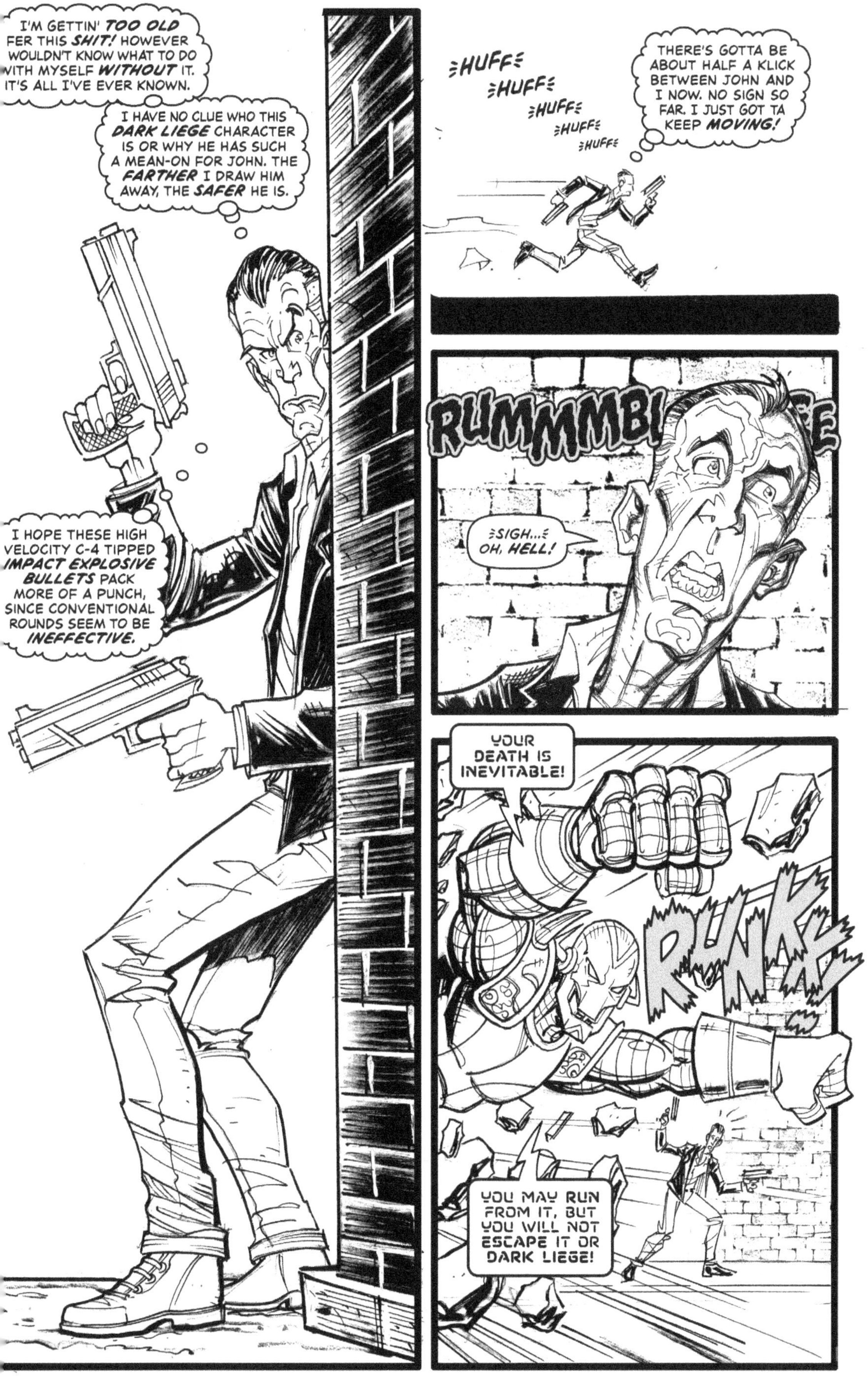
I'M GETTIN' TOO OLD FER THIS SHIT! HOWEVER WOULDN'T KNOW WHAT TO DO WITH MYSELF WITHOUT IT. IT'S ALL I'VE EVER KNOWN.
I HAVE NO CLUE WHO THIS DARK LIEGE CHARACTER IS OR WHY HE HAS SUCH A MEAN-ON FOR JOHN. THE FARTHER I DRAW HIM AWAY, THE SAFER HE IS.
I HOPE THESE HIGH VELOCITY C-4 TIPPED IMPACT EXPLOSIVE BULLETS PACK MORE OF A PUNCH, SINCE CONVENTIONAL ROUNDS SEEM TO BE INEFFECTIVE.
HUFF HUFF HUFF HUFF HUFF
THERE'S GOTTA BE ABOUT HALF A KLICK BETWEEN JOHN AND I NOW. NO SIGN SO FAR. I JUST GOT TA KEEP MOVING!
RUMMMBLE
SIGH... OH, HELL!
YOUR DEATH IS INEVITABLE!
RUNK
YOU MAY RUN FROM IT, BUT YOU WILL NOT ESCAPE IT OR DARK LIEGE!

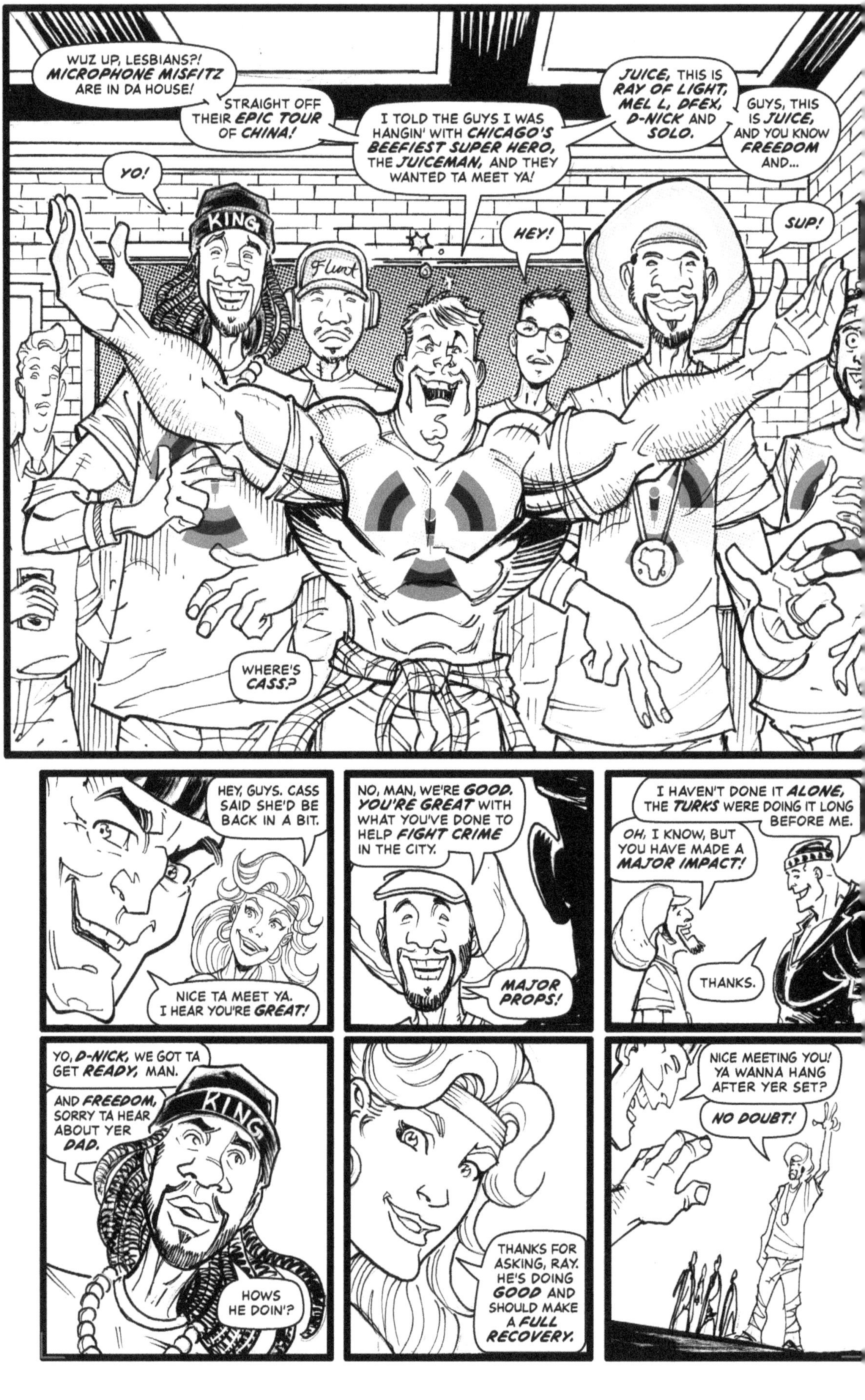
WUZ UP, LESBIANS?! MICROPHONE MISFITZ ARE IN DA HOUSE!
STRAIGHT OFF THEIR EPIC TOUR OF CHINA!
I TOLD THE GUYS I WAS HANGIN' WITH CHICAGO'S BEEFIEST SUPER HERO, THE JUICEMAN, AND THEY WANTED TA MEET YA!
JUICE, THIS IS RAY OF LIGHT, MEL L, DFEX, D-NICK AND SOLO.
GUYS, THIS IS JUICE, AND YOU KNOW FREEDOM AND...
YO!
HEY!
SUP!
WHERE'S CASS?
HEY, GUYS. CASS SAID SHE'D BE BACK IN A BIT.
NICE TA MEET YA. I HEAR YOU'RE GREAT!
NO, MAN, WE'RE GOOD. YOU'RE GREAT WITH WHAT YOU'VE DONE TO HELP FIGHT CRIME IN THE CITY.
MAJOR PROPS!
I HAVEN'T DONE IT ALONE, THE TURKS WERE DOING IT LONG BEFORE ME.
OH, I KNOW, BUT YOU HAVE MADE A MAJOR IMPACT!
THANKS.
YO, D-NICK, WE GOT TA GET READY, MAN.
AND FREEDOM, SORRY TA HEAR ABOUT YER DAD.
HOWS HE DOIN'?
THANKS FOR ASKING, RAY. HE'S DOING GOOD AND SHOULD MAKE A FULL RECOVERY.
NICE MEETING YOU! YA WANNA HANG AFTER YER SET?
NO DOUBT!

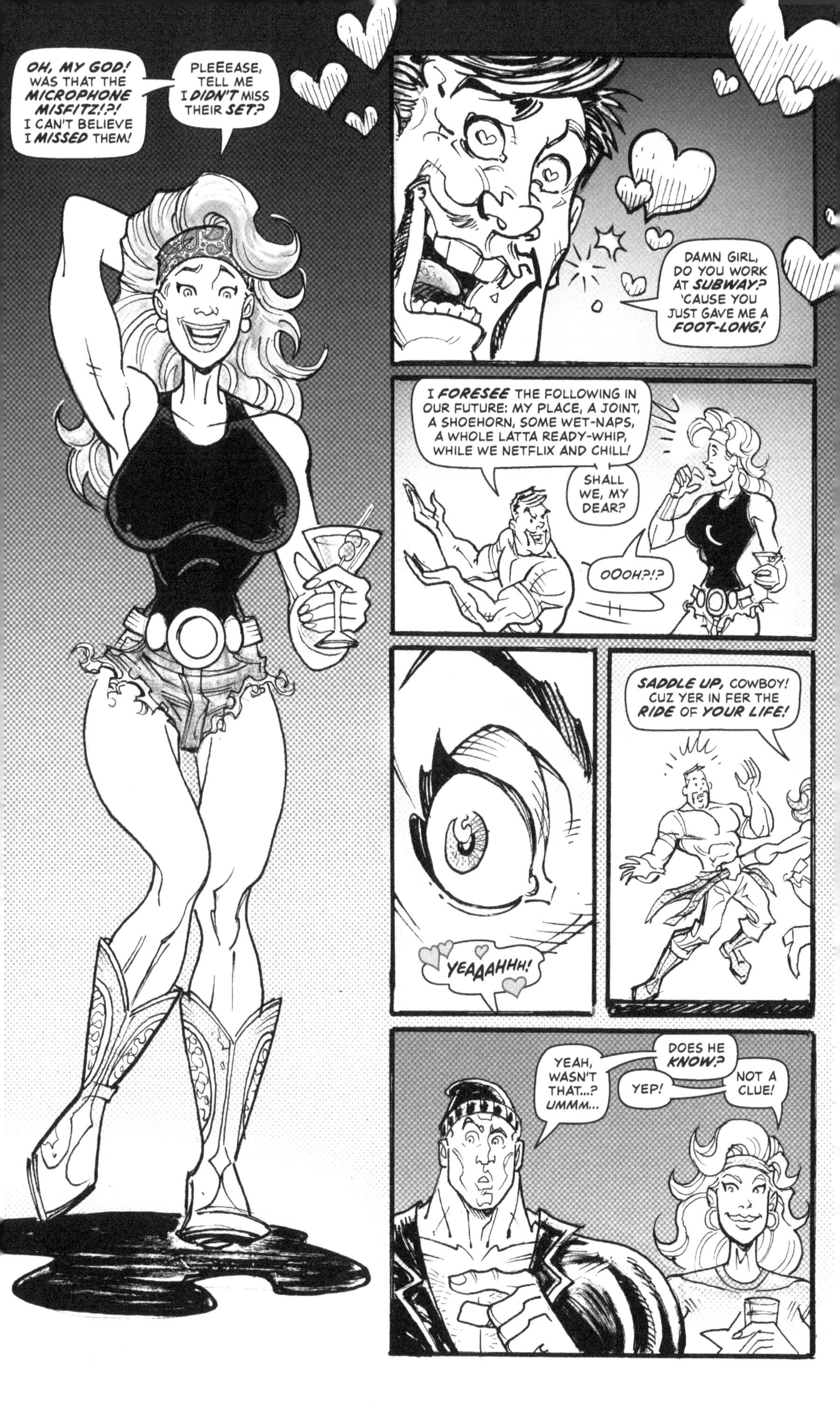
OH, MY GOD! WAS THAT THE MICROPHONE MISFITZ!?! I CAN'T BELIEVE I MISSED THEM!
PLEEEASE, TELL ME I DIDN'T MISS THEIR SET?
DAMN GIRL, DO YOU WORK AT SUBWAY? 'CAUSE YOU JUST GAVE ME A FOOT-LONG!
I FORESEE THE FOLLOWING IN OUR FUTURE: MY PLACE, A JOINT, A SHOEHORN, SOME WET-NAPS, A WHOLE LATTA READY-WHIP, WHILE WE NETFLIX AND CHILL!
SHALL WE, MY DEAR?
OOOH?!?
YEAAAHHH!
SADDLE UP, COWBOY! CUZ YER IN FER THE RIDE OF YOUR LIFE!
DOES HE KNOW?
YEAH, WASN'T THAT...? UMMM...
YEP!
NOT A CLUE!

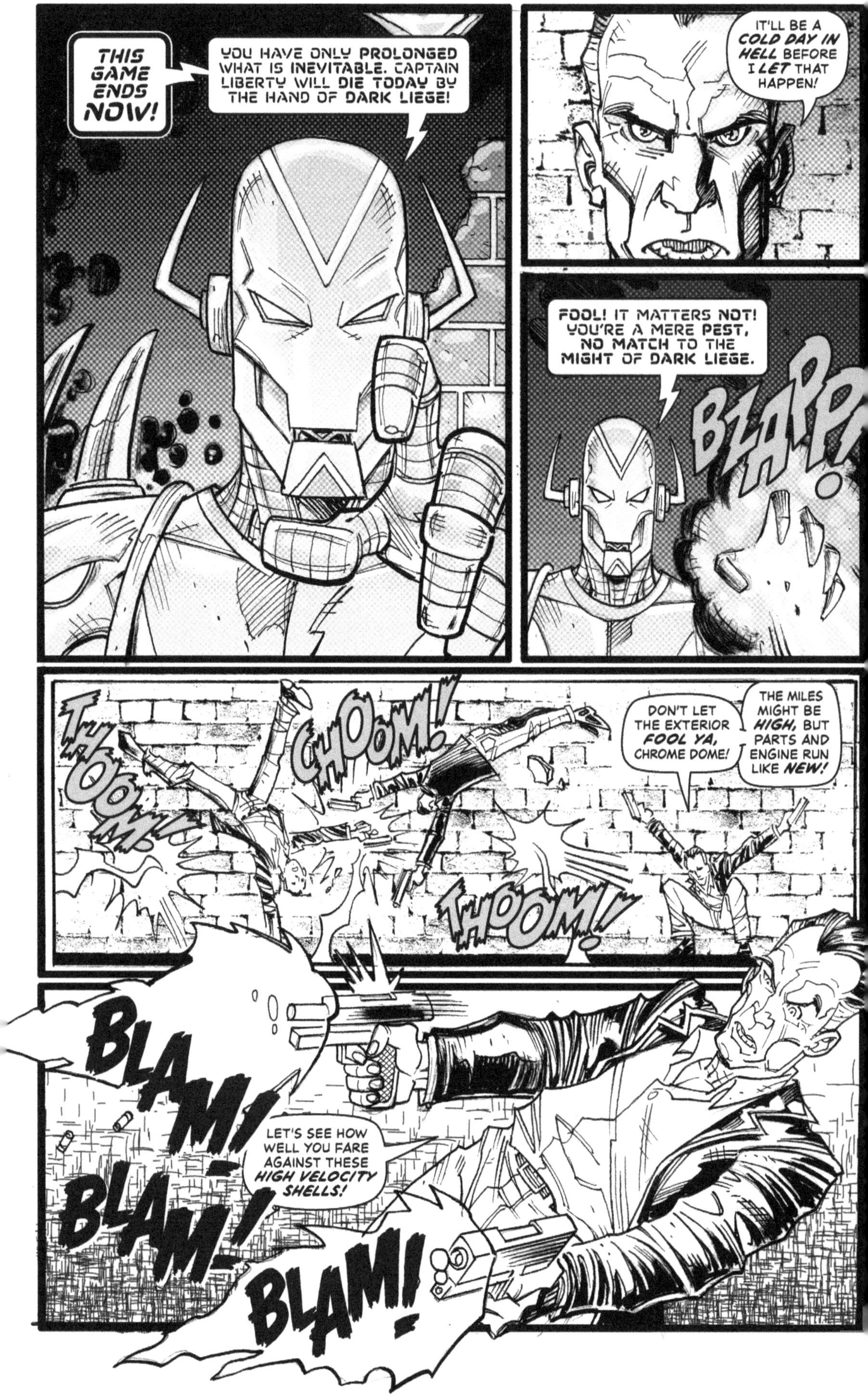
THIS GAME ENDS NOW!
YOU HAVE ONLY PROLONGED WHAT IS INEVITABLE. CAPTAIN LIBERTY WILL DIE TODAY BY THE HAND OF DARK LIEGE!
IT'LL BE A COLD DAY IN HELL BEFORE I LET THAT HAPPEN!
FOOL! IT MATTERS NOT! YOU'RE A MERE PEST, NO MATCH TO THE MIGHT OF DARK LIEGE.
BZAPP!
THOOM!
CHOOM!
THOOM!
DON'T LET THE EXTERIOR FOOL YA, CHROME DOME!
THE MILES MIGHT BE HIGH, BUT PARTS AND ENGINE RUN LIKE NEW!
BLAM!
BLAM!
BLAM!
LET'S SEE HOW WELL YOU FARE AGAINST THESE HIGH VELOCITY SHELLS!

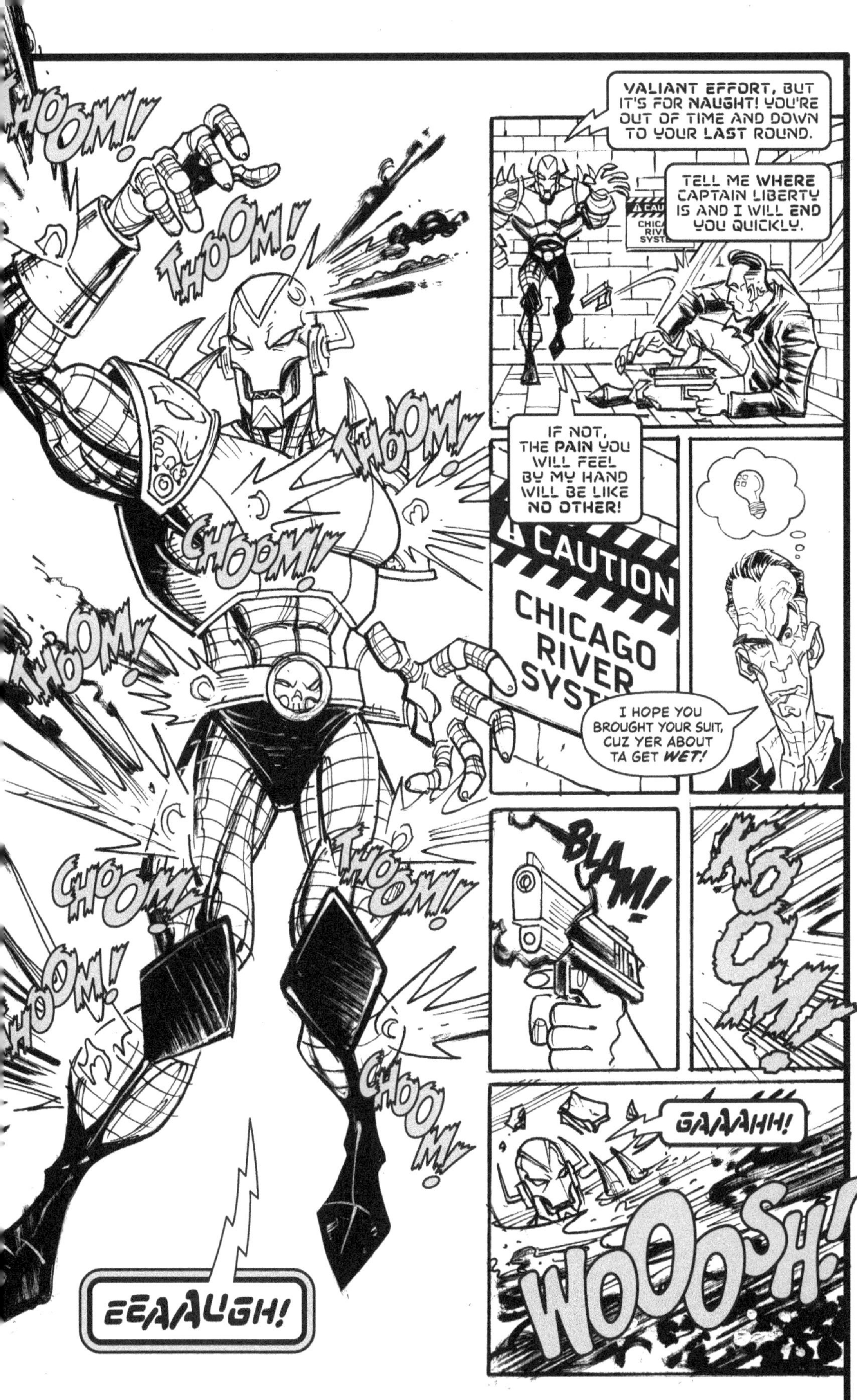
THOOM!
THOOM!
THOOM!
CHOOM!
THOOM!
CHOOM!
THOOM!
HOOM!
CHOOM!
EEAAAUGH!
VALIANT EFFORT, BUT IT'S FOR NAUGHT! YOU'RE OUT OF TIME AND DOWN TO YOUR LAST ROUND.
TELL ME WHERE CAPTAIN LIBERTY IS AND I WILL END YOU QUICKLY.
IF NOT, THE PAIN YOU WILL FEEL BY MY HAND WILL BE LIKE NO OTHER!
CAUTION
CHICAGO RIVER SYST
I HOPE YOU BROUGHT YOUR SUIT, CUZ YER ABOUT TA GET WET!
BLAM!
KOOM!
GAAAHH!
WOOOSH!

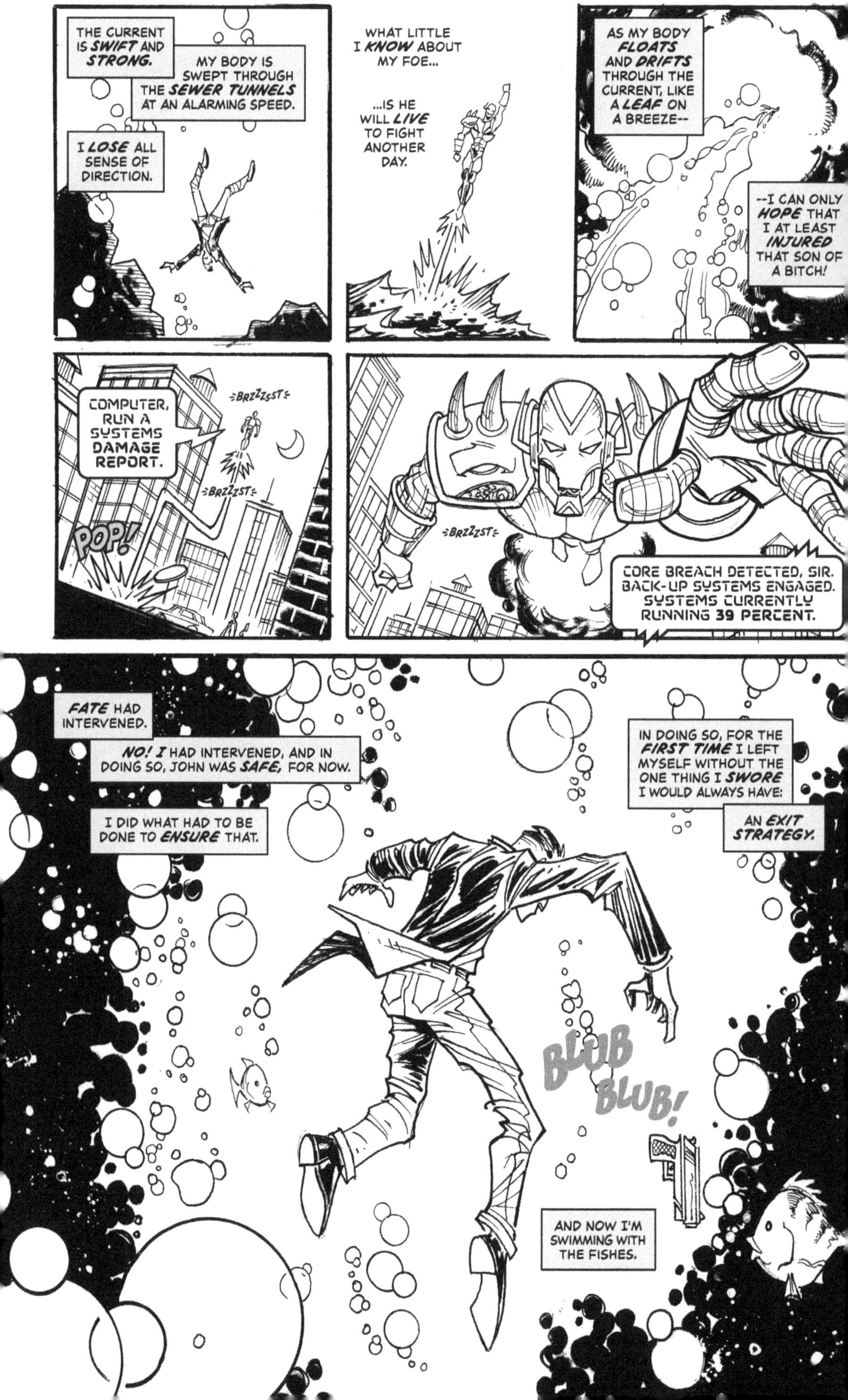
THE CURRENT IS SWIFT AND STRONG.
MY BODY IS SWEPT THROUGH THE SEWER TUNNELS AT AN ALARMING SPEED.
I LOSE ALL SENSE OF DIRECTION.
WHAT LITTLE I KNOW ABOUT MY FOE...
...IS HE WILL LIVE TO FIGHT ANOTHER DAY.
AS MY BODY FLOATS AND DRIFTS THROUGH THE CURRENT, LIKE A LEAF ON A BREEZE--
--I CAN ONLY HOPE THAT I AT LEAST INJURED THAT SON OF A BITCH!
COMPUTER, RUN A SYSTEMS DAMAGE REPORT.
BRZZZSST
BRZZZST
POP!
BRZZZST
CORE BREACH DETECTED, SIR. BACK-UP SYSTEMS ENGAGED. SYSTEMS CURRENTLY RUNNING 39 PERCENT.
FATE HAD INTERVENED.
NO! I HAD INTERVENED, AND IN DOING SO, JOHN WAS SAFE, FOR NOW.
I DID WHAT HAD TO BE DONE TO ENSURE THAT.
IN DOING SO, FOR THE FIRST TIME I LEFT MYSELF WITHOUT THE ONE THING I SWORE I WOULD ALWAYS HAVE:
AN EXIT STRATEGY.
BLUB BLUB!
AND NOW I'M SWIMMING WITH THE FISHES.

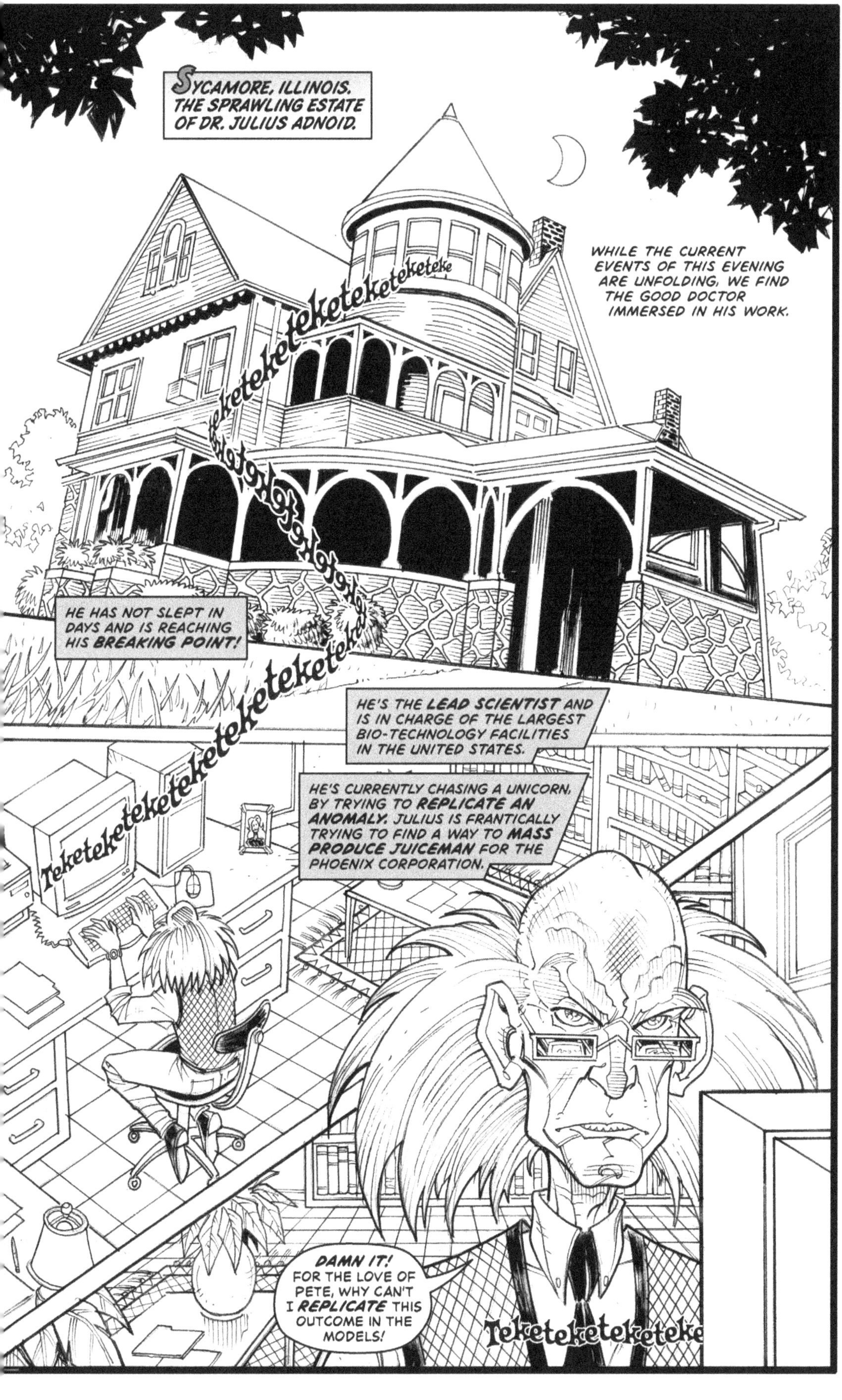
SYCAMORE, ILLINOIS. THE SPRAWLING ESTATE OF DR. JULIUS ADNOID.
WHILE THE CURRENT EVENTS OF THIS EVENING ARE UNFOLDING, WE FIND THE GOOD DOCTOR IMMERSED IN HIS WORK.
teketeketeketeketeke
HE HAS NOT SLEPT IN DAYS AND IS REACHING HIS BREAKING POINT!
HE'S THE LEAD SCIENTIST AND IS IN CHARGE OF THE LARGEST BIO-TECHNOLOGY FACILITIES IN THE UNITED STATES.
HE'S CURRENTLY CHASING A UNICORN, BY TRYING TO REPLICATE AN ANOMALY. JULIUS IS FRANTICALLY TRYING TO FIND A WAY TO MASS PRODUCE JUICEMAN FOR THE PHOENIX CORPORATION.
Teketeketeketeke
DAMN IT! FOR THE LOVE OF PETE, WHY CAN'T I REPLICATE THIS OUTCOME IN THE MODELS!
Teketeketeketeke

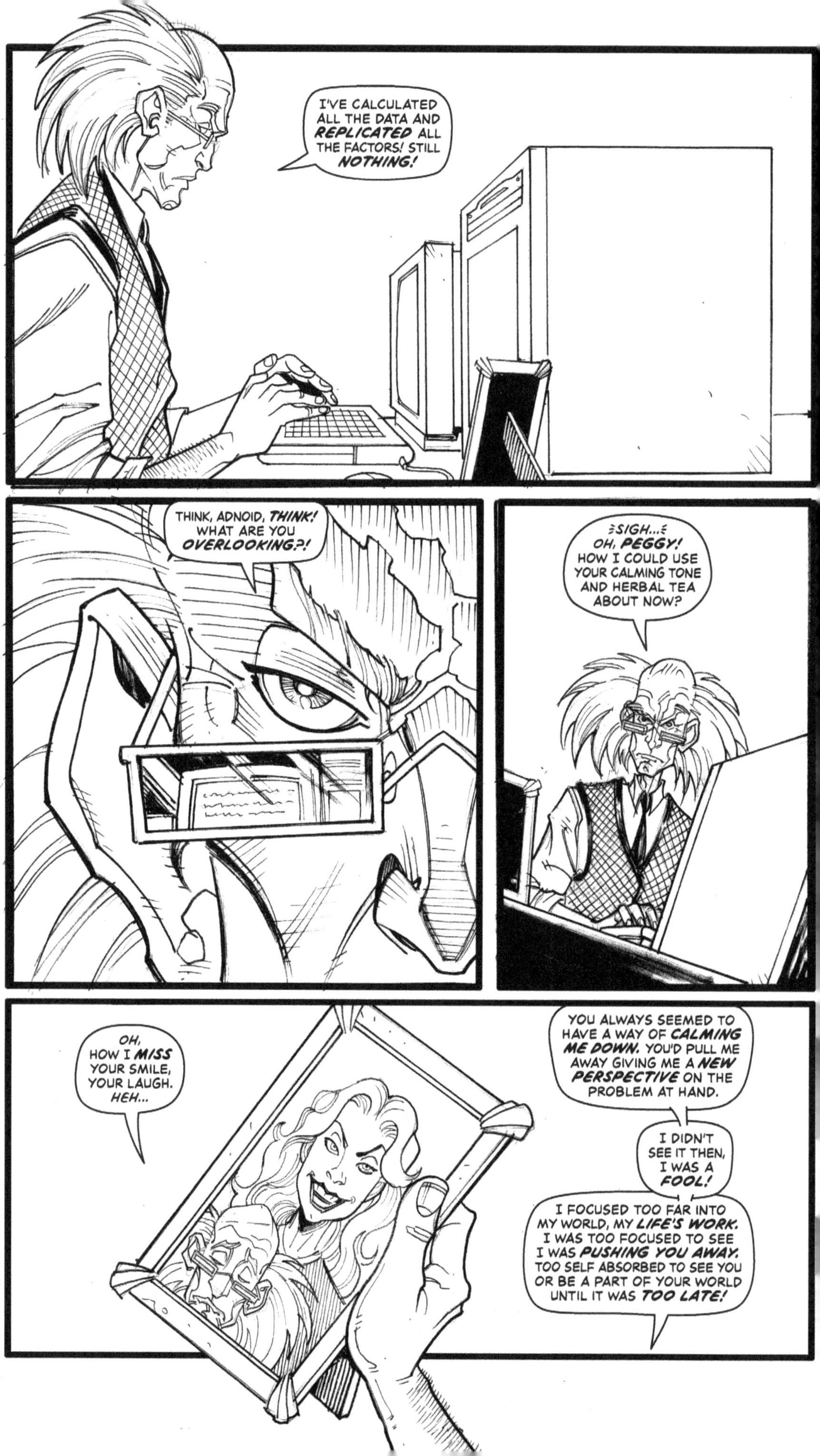
I'VE CALCULATED ALL THE DATA AND REPLICATED ALL THE FACTORS! STILL NOTHING!
THINK, ADNOID, THINK! WHAT ARE YOU OVERLOOKING?!
SIGH... OH, PEGGY! HOW I COULD USE YOUR CALMING TONE AND HERBAL TEA ABOUT NOW?
OH, HOW I MISS YOUR SMILE, YOUR LAUGH. HEH...
YOU ALWAYS SEEMED TO HAVE A WAY OF CALMING ME DOWN. YOU'D PULL ME AWAY GIVING ME A NEW PERSPECTIVE ON THE PROBLEM AT HAND.
I DIDN'T SEE IT THEN, I WAS A FOOL!
I FOCUSED TOO FAR INTO MY WORLD, MY LIFE'S WORK. I WAS TOO FOCUSED TO SEE I WAS PUSHING YOU AWAY. TOO SELF ABSORBED TO SEE YOU OR BE A PART OF YOUR WORLD UNTIL IT WAS TOO LATE!

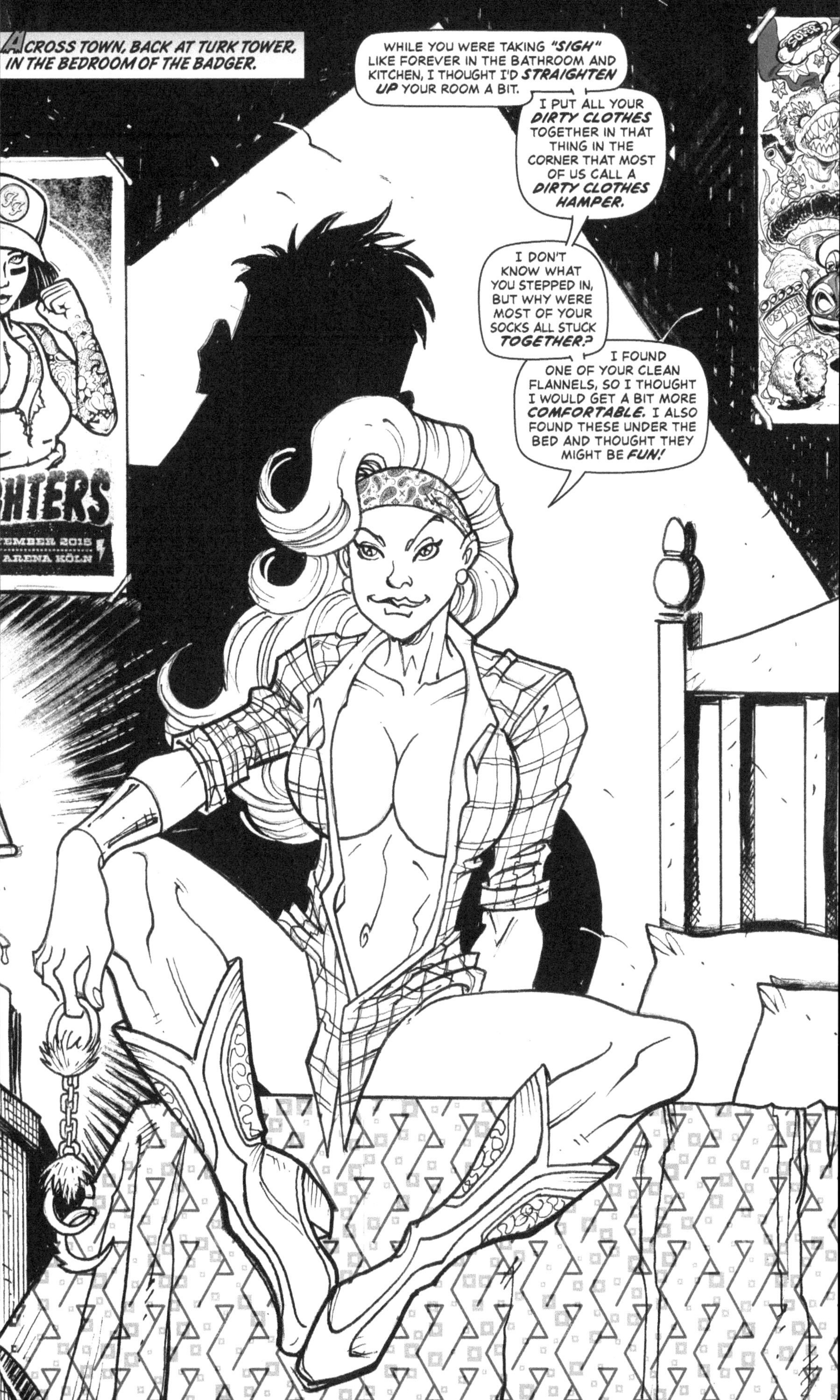
ACROSS TOWN, BACK AT TURK TOWER, IN THE BEDROOM OF THE BADGER.
WHILE YOU WERE TAKING "SIGH" LIKE FOREVER IN THE BATHROOM AND KITCHEN, I THOUGHT I'D STRAIGHTEN UP YOUR ROOM A BIT.
I PUT ALL YOUR DIRTY CLOTHES TOGETHER IN THAT THING IN THE CORNER THAT MOST OF US CALL A DIRTY CLOTHES HAMPER.
I DON'T KNOW WHAT YOU STEPPED IN, BUT WHY WERE MOST OF YOUR SOCKS ALL STUCK TOGETHER?
I FOUND ONE OF YOUR CLEAN FLANNELS, SO I THOUGHT I WOULD GET A BIT MORE COMFORTABLE. I ALSO FOUND THESE UNDER THE BED AND THOUGHT THEY MIGHT BE FUN!
GHTERS
TEMBER 2015
ARENA KÖLN

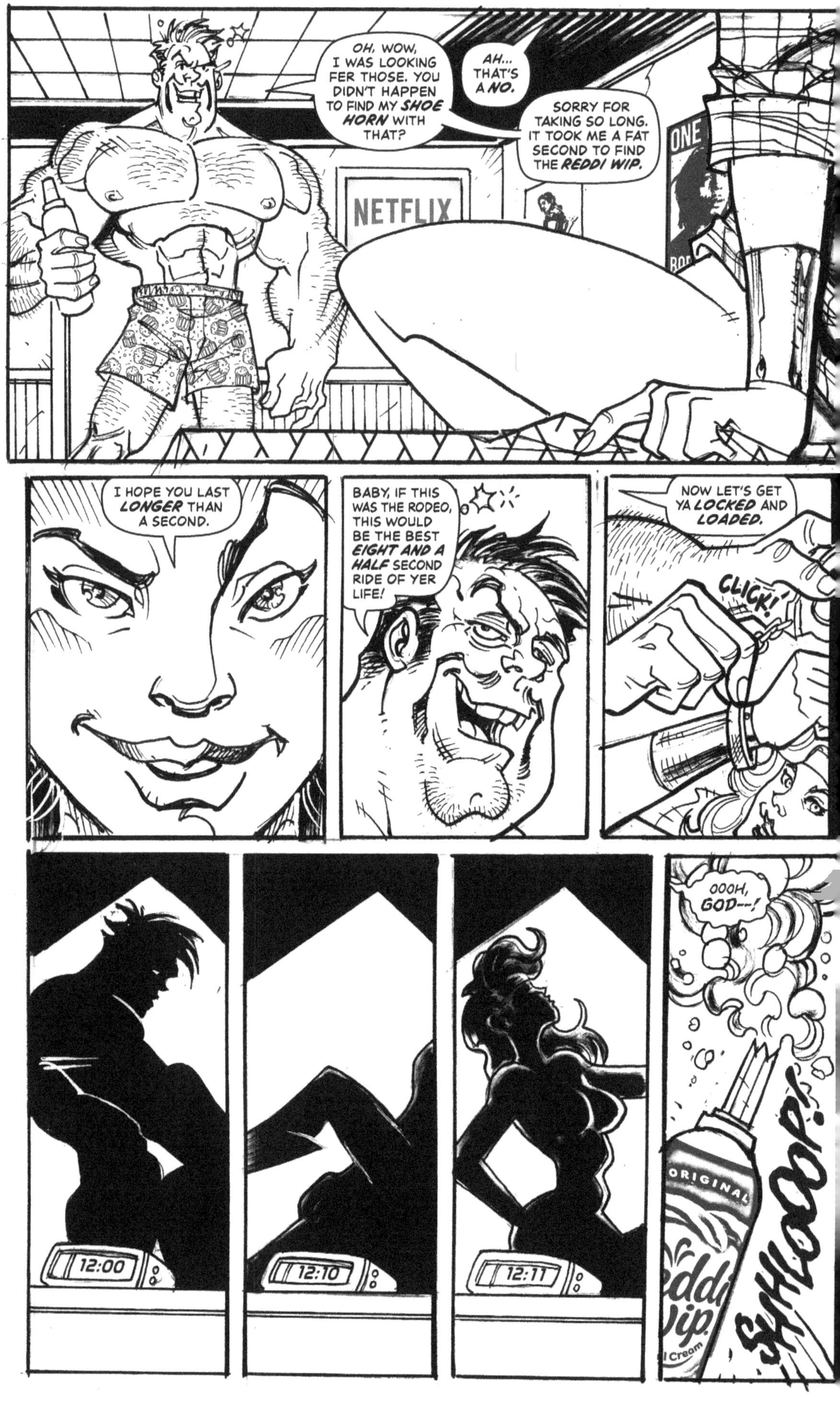
OH, WOW, I WAS LOOKING FER THOSE. YOU DIDN'T HAPPEN TO FIND MY SHOE HORN WITH THAT?
AH... THAT'S A NO.
SORRY FOR TAKING SO LONG. IT TOOK ME A FAT SECOND TO FIND THE REDDI WIP.
NETFLIX
ONE
I HOPE YOU LAST LONGER THAN A SECOND.
BABY, IF THIS WAS THE RODEO, THIS WOULD BE THE BEST EIGHT AND A HALF SECOND RIDE OF YER LIFE!
NOW LET'S GET YA LOCKED AND LOADED.
CLICK!
12:00
12:10
12:11
OOOH, GOD--!
ORIGINAL
SHLOOOP!

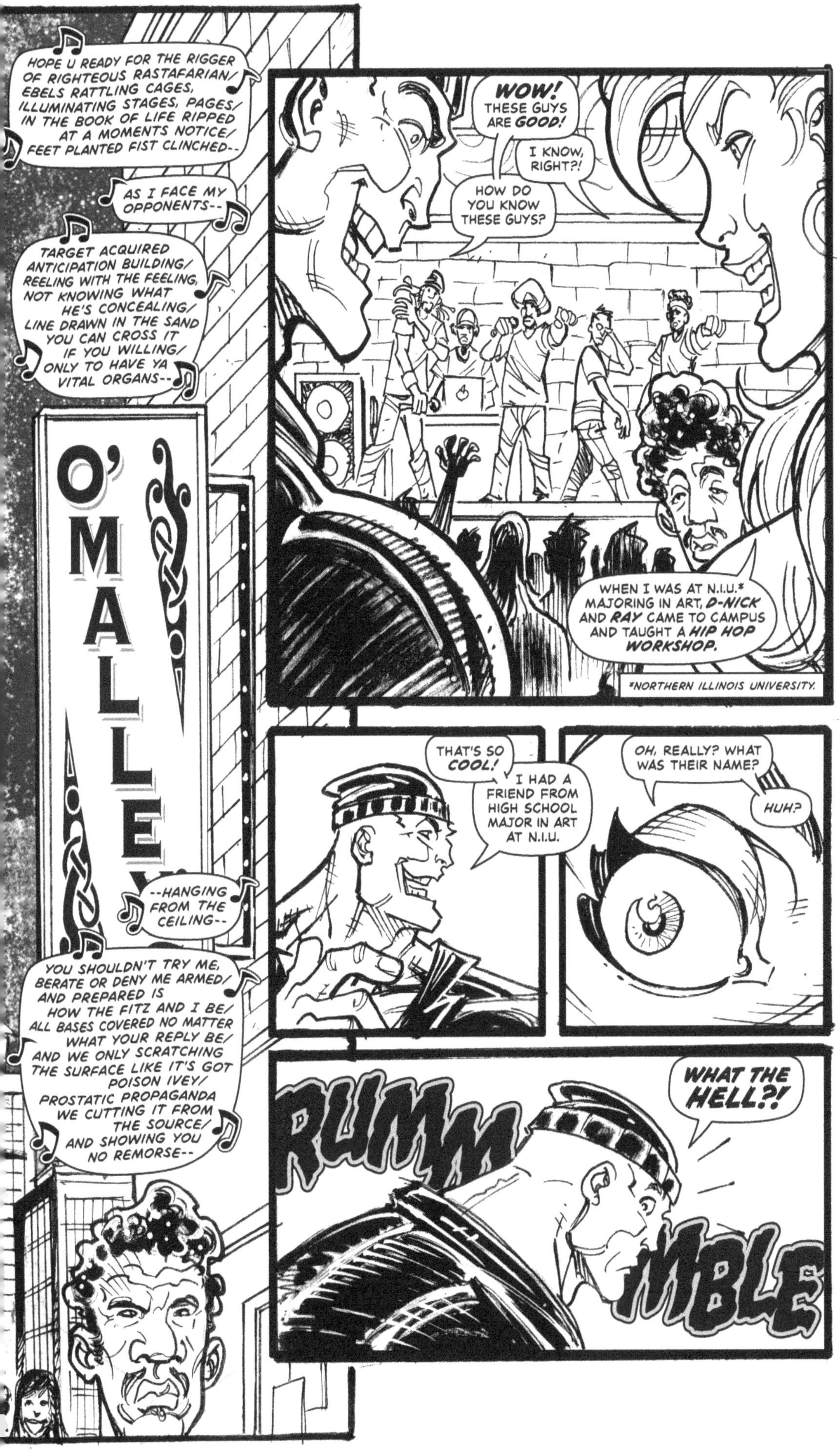

HOPE U READY FOR THE RIGGER OF RIGHTEOUS RASTAFARIAN/ EBELS RATTLING CAGES, ILLUMINATING STAGES, PAGES/ IN THE BOOK OF LIFE RIPPED AT A MOMENTS NOTICE/ FEET PLANTED FIST CLINCHED--
AS I FACE MY OPPONENTS--
TARGET ACQUIRED ANTICIPATION BUILDING/ REELING WITH THE FEELING, NOT KNOWING WHAT HE'S CONCEALING/ LINE DRAWN IN THE SAND YOU CAN CROSS IT IF YOU WILLING/ ONLY TO HAVE YA VITAL ORGANS--
O'MALLEY
WOW! THESE GUYS ARE GOOD!
I KNOW, RIGHT?!
HOW DO YOU KNOW THESE GUYS?
WHEN I WAS AT N.I.U.* MAJORING IN ART, D-NICK AND RAY CAME TO CAMPUS AND TAUGHT A HIP HOP WORKSHOP.
*NORTHERN ILLINOIS UNIVERSITY.
THAT'S SO COOL!
I HAD A FRIEND FROM HIGH SCHOOL MAJOR IN ART AT N.I.U.
OH, REALLY? WHAT WAS THEIR NAME?
HUH?
--HANGING FROM THE CEILING--
YOU SHOULDN'T TRY ME, BERATE OR DENY ME ARMED/ AND PREPARED IS HOW THE FITZ AND I BE/ ALL BASES COVERED NO MATTER WHAT YOUR REPLY BE/ AND WE ONLY SCRATCHING THE SURFACE LIKE IT'S GOT POISON IVEY/ PROSTATIC PROPAGANDA WE CUTTING IT FROM THE SOURCE/ AND SHOWING YOU NO REMORSE--
RUMM
WHAT THE HELL?!
MBLE

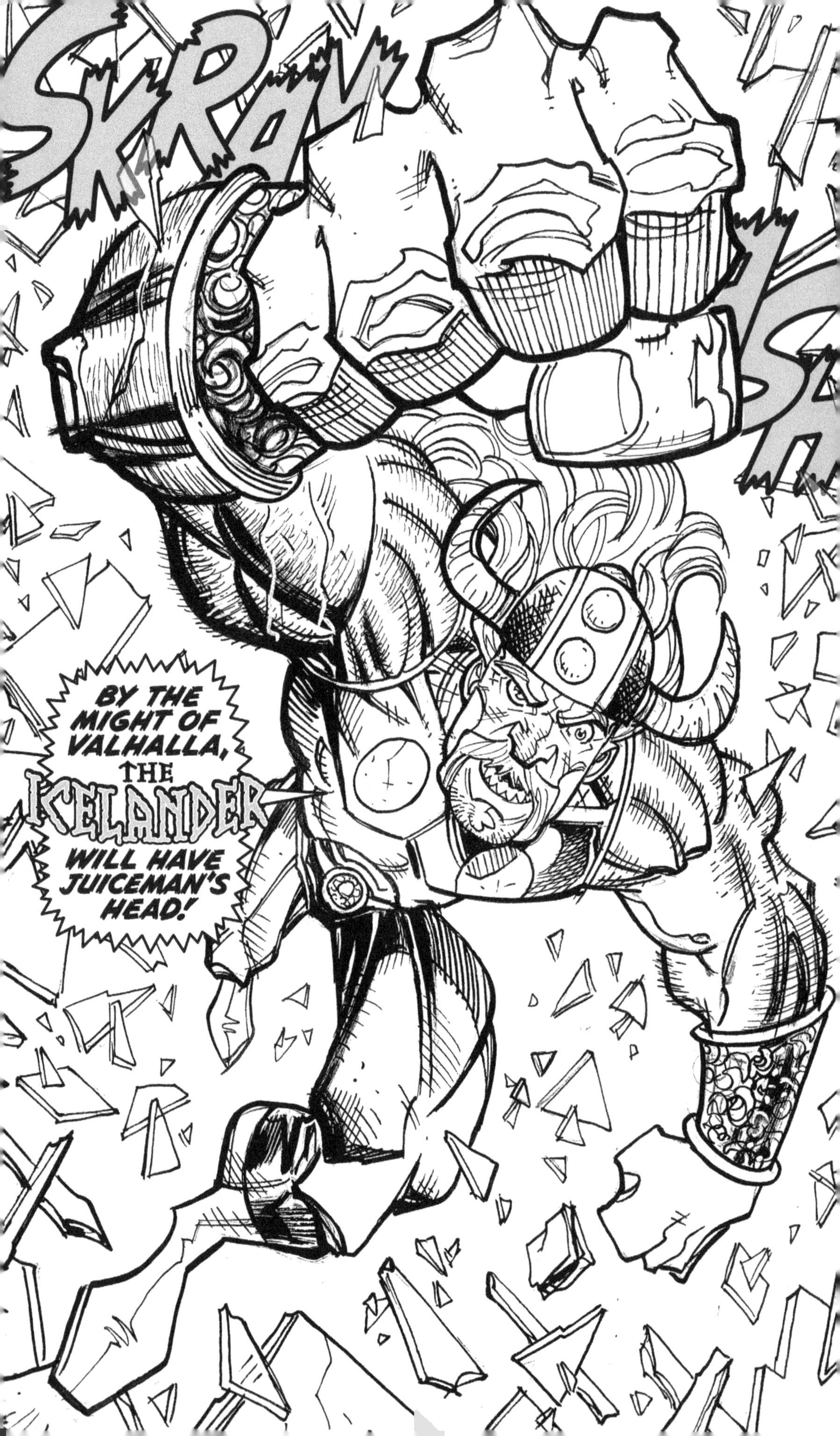

BY THE MIGHT OF VALHALLA, THE ICELANDER WILL HAVE JUICEMAN'S HEAD!

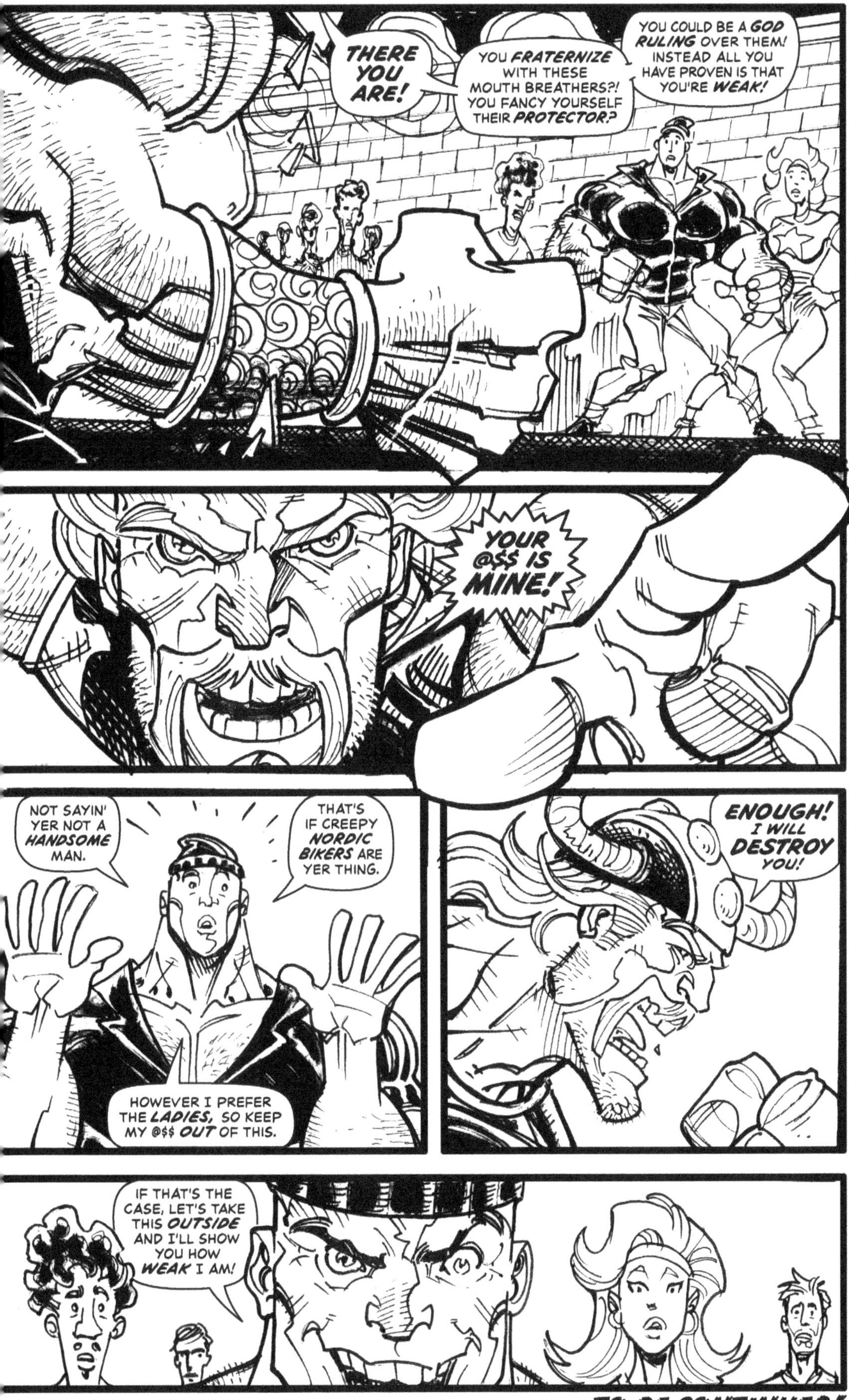
THERE YOU ARE!
YOU FRATERNIZE WITH THESE MOUTH BREATHERS?! YOU FANCY YOURSELF THEIR PROTECTOR?
YOU COULD BE A GOD RULING OVER THEM! INSTEAD ALL YOU HAVE PROVEN IS THAT YOU'RE WEAK!
YOUR @$$ IS MINE!
NOT SAYIN' YER NOT A HANDSOME MAN.
THAT'S IF CREEPY NORDIC BIKERS ARE YER THING.
HOWEVER I PREFER THE LADIES, SO KEEP MY @$$ OUT OF THIS.
ENOUGH! I WILL DESTROY YOU!
IF THAT'S THE CASE, LET'S TAKE THIS OUTSIDE AND I'LL SHOW YOU HOW WEAK I AM!

TO BE CONTINUED!

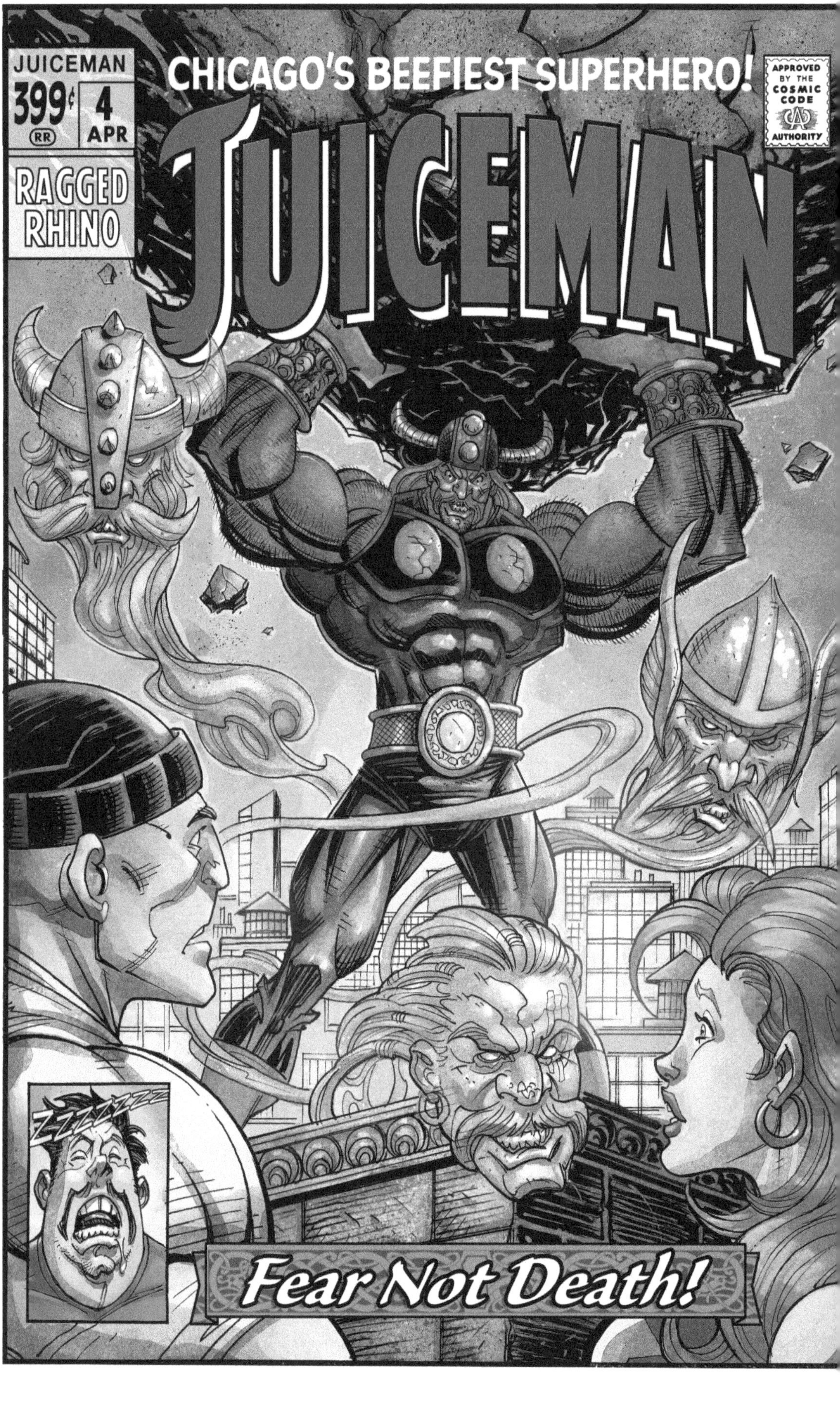
JUICEMAN
399¢
4
APR
RR
RAGGED RHINO
CHICAGO'S BEEFIEST SUPERHERO!
APPROVED BY THE COSMIC CODE AUTHORITY
JUICEMAN
ZZZZZZZ
Fear Not Death!

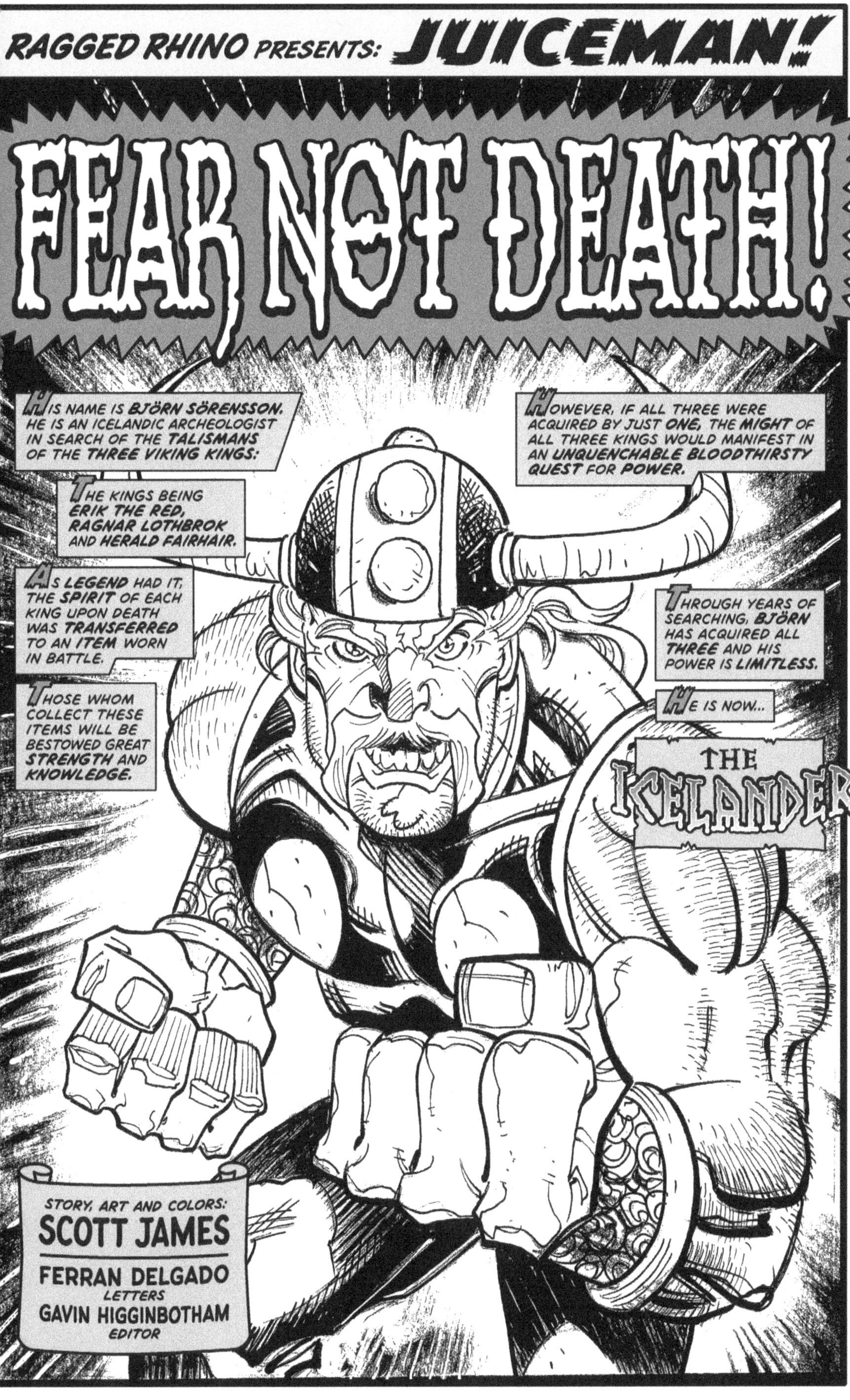

RAGGED RHINO PRESENTS: JUICEMAN!
FEAR NOT DEATH!
HIS NAME IS BJÖRN SÖRENSSON. HE IS AN ICELANDIC ARCHEOLOGIST IN SEARCH OF THE TALISMANS OF THE THREE VIKING KINGS:
THE KINGS BEING ERIK THE RED, RAGNAR LOTHBROK AND HERALD FAIRHAIR.
AS LEGEND HAD IT, THE SPIRIT OF EACH KING UPON DEATH WAS TRANSFERRED TO AN ITEM WORN IN BATTLE.
THOSE WHOM COLLECT THESE ITEMS WILL BE BESTOWED GREAT STRENGTH AND KNOWLEDGE.
HOWEVER, IF ALL THREE WERE ACQUIRED BY JUST ONE, THE MIGHT OF ALL THREE KINGS WOULD MANIFEST IN AN UNQUENCHABLE BLOODTHIRSTY QUEST FOR POWER.
THROUGH YEARS OF SEARCHING, BJÖRN HAS ACQUIRED ALL THREE AND HIS POWER IS LIMITLESS.
HE IS NOW...
THE ICELANDER
STORY, ART AND COLORS: SCOTT JAMES
FERRAN DELGADO LETTERS
GAVIN HIGGINBOTHAM EDITOR

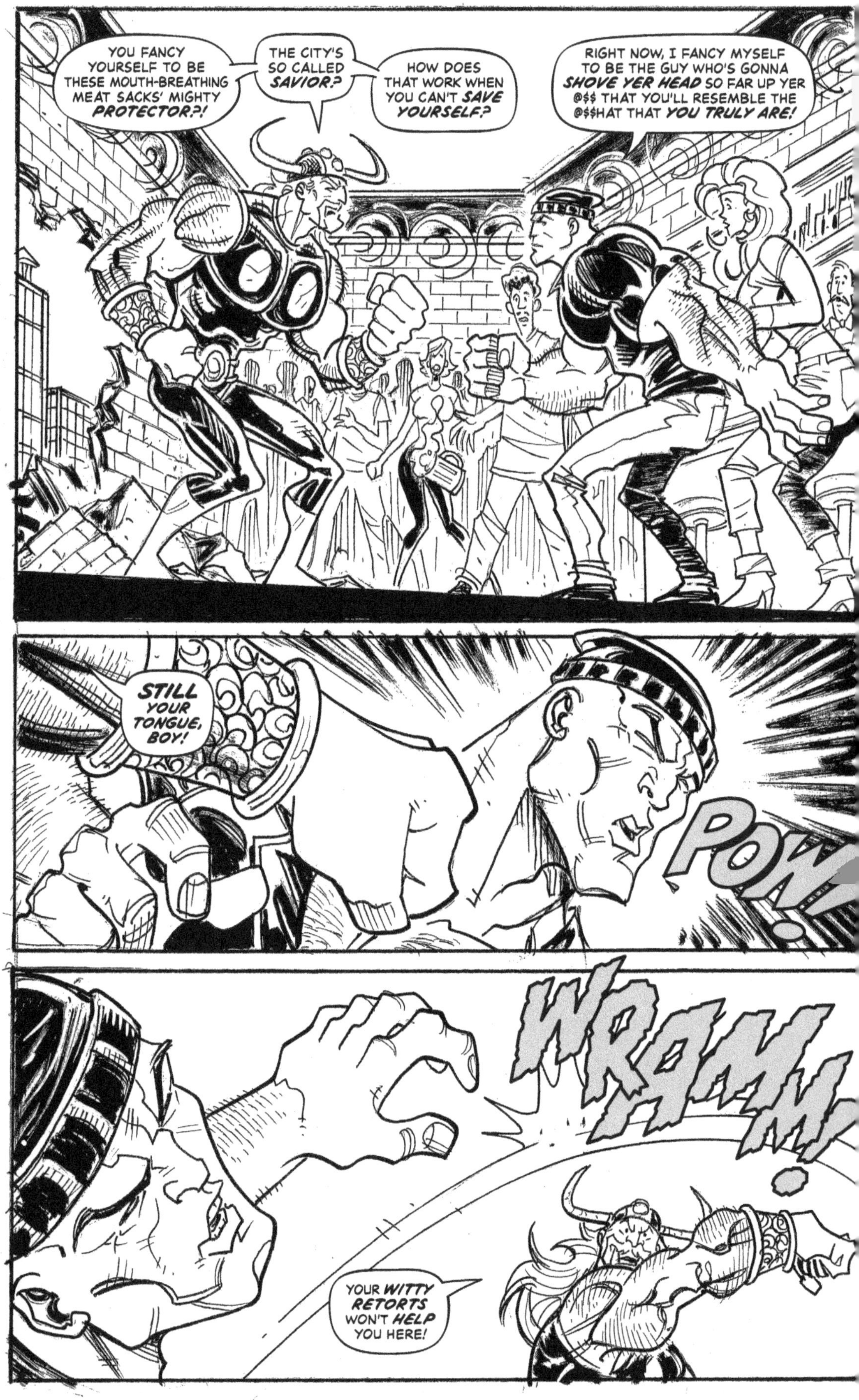
YOU FANCY YOURSELF TO BE THESE MOUTH-BREATHING MEAT SACKS' MIGHTY PROTECTOR?!
THE CITY'S SO CALLED SAVIOR?
HOW DOES THAT WORK WHEN YOU CAN'T SAVE YOURSELF?
RIGHT NOW, I FANCY MYSELF TO BE THE GUY WHO'S GONNA SHOVE YER HEAD SO FAR UP YER @$$ THAT YOU'LL RESEMBLE THE @$$HAT THAT YOU TRULY ARE!
STILL YOUR TONGUE, BOY!
POW!
WRAMM!
YOUR WITTY RETORTS WON'T HELP YOU HERE!

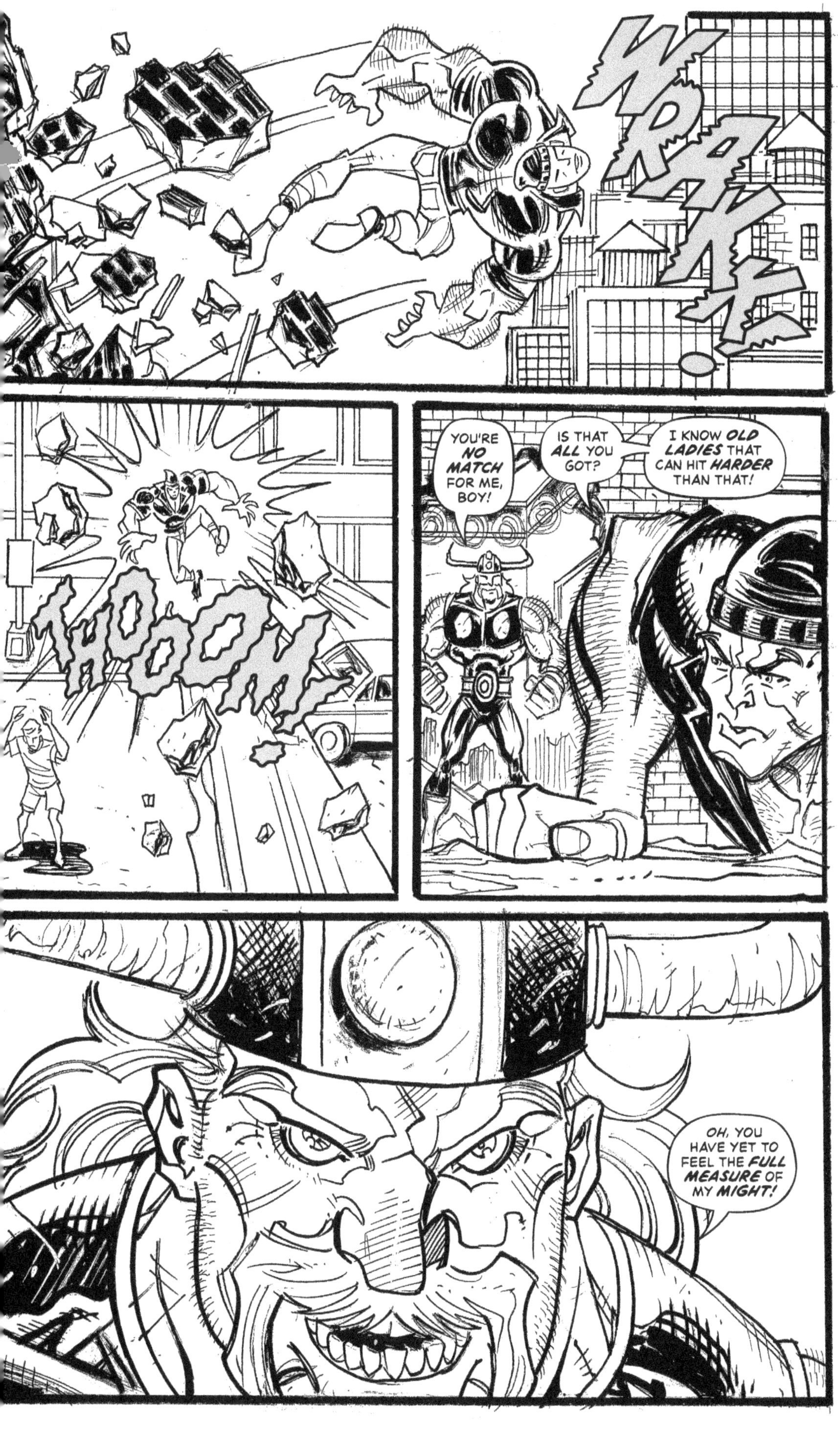
WRAKK!
THOOOM!
YOU'RE NO MATCH FOR ME, BOY!
IS THAT ALL YOU GOT?
I KNOW OLD LADIES THAT CAN HIT HARDER THAN THAT!
OH, YOU HAVE YET TO FEEL THE FULL MEASURE OF MY MIGHT!

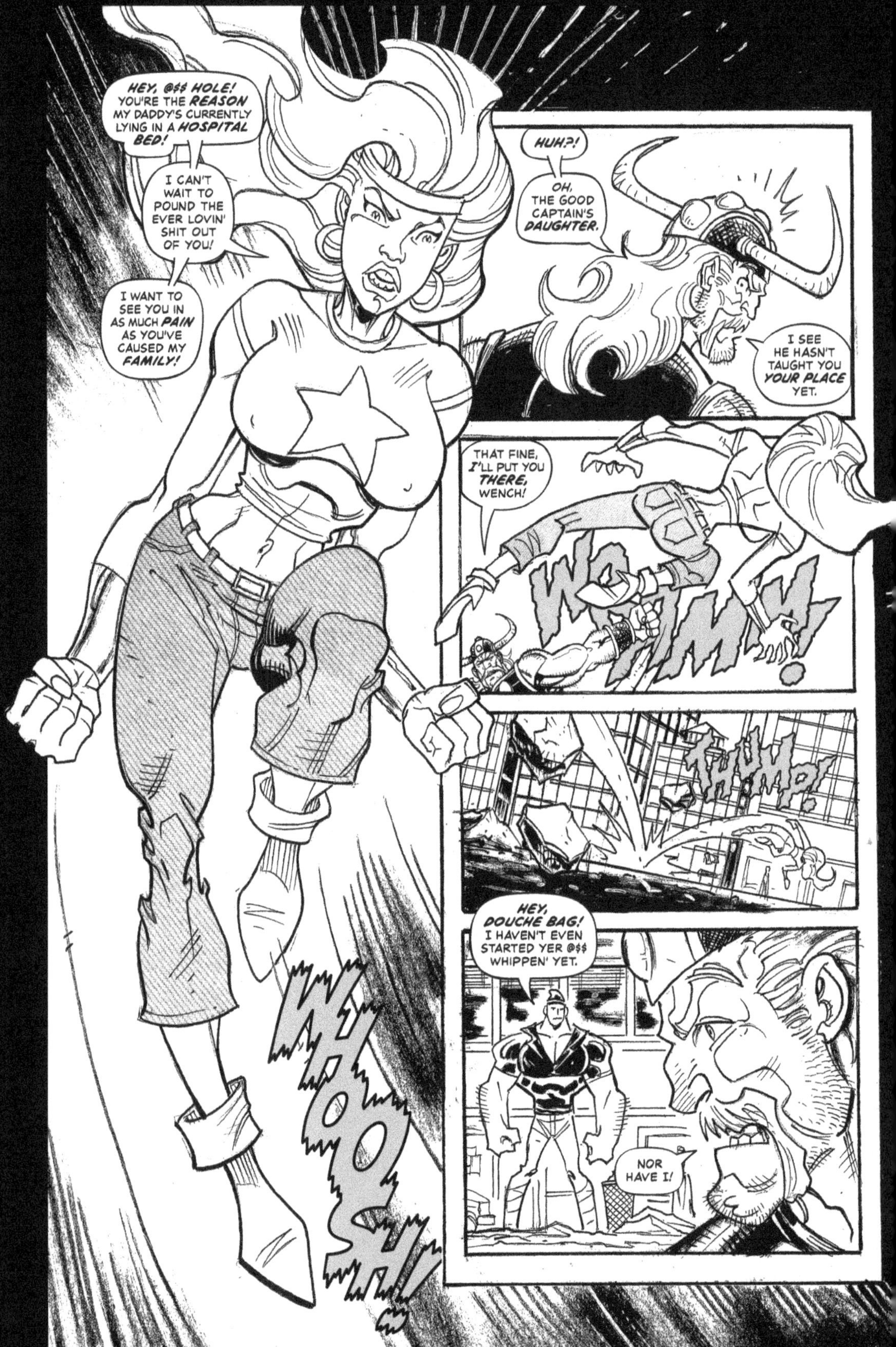
HEY, @$$ HOLE! YOU'RE THE REASON MY DADDY'S CURRENTLY LYING IN A HOSPITAL BED!
I CAN'T WAIT TO POUND THE EVER LOVIN' SHIT OUT OF YOU!
I WANT TO SEE YOU IN AS MUCH PAIN AS YOU'VE CAUSED MY FAMILY!
HUH?!
OH, THE GOOD CAPTAIN'S DAUGHTER.
I SEE HE HASN'T TAUGHT YOU YOUR PLACE YET.
THAT FINE, I'LL PUT YOU THERE, WENCH!
THUMP!
HEY, DOUCHE BAG! I HAVEN'T EVEN STARTED YER @$$ WHIPPEN' YET.
NOR HAVE I!
WHOOSH!

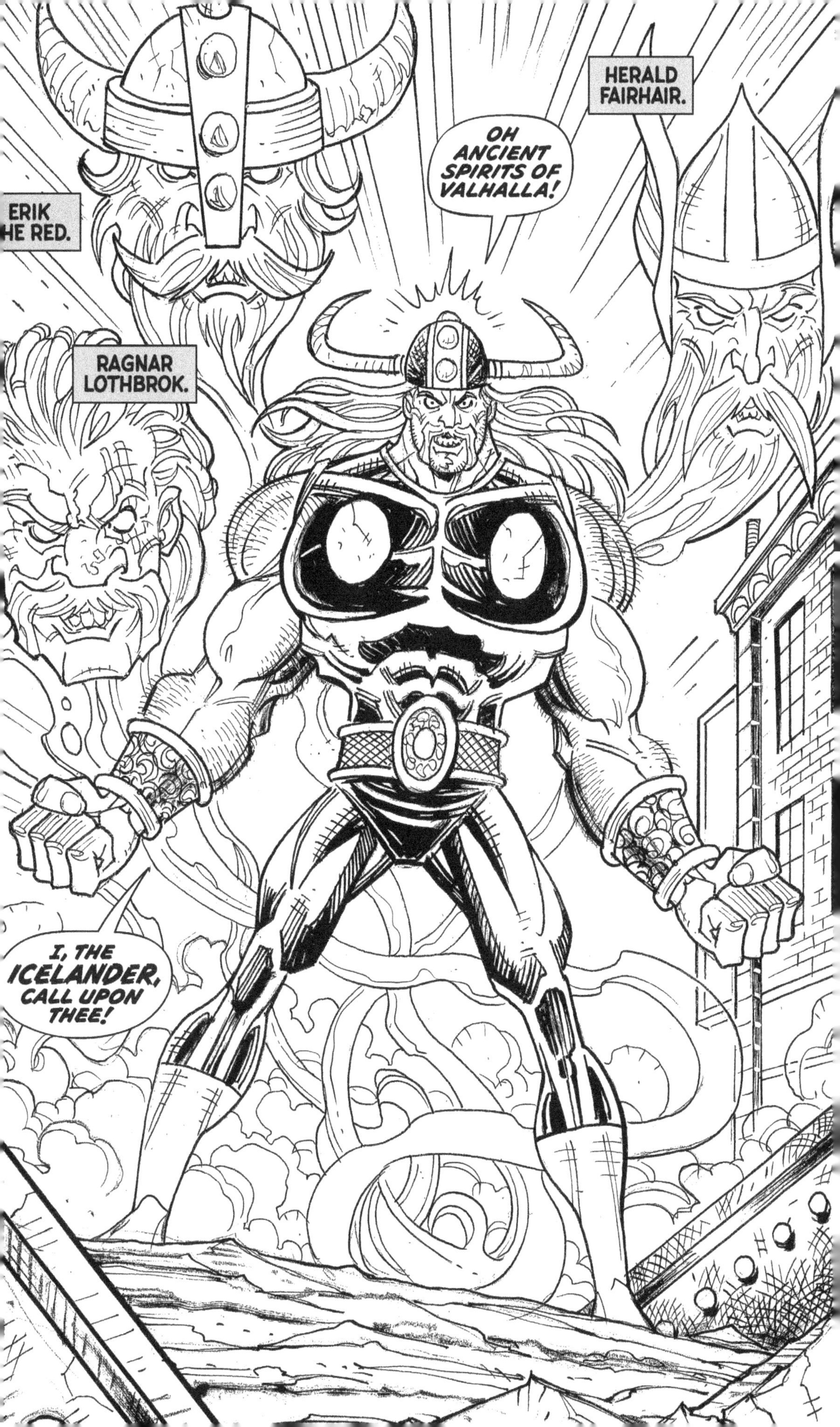
HERALD FAIRHAIR.
OH ANCIENT SPIRITS OF VALHALLA!
ERIK HE RED.
RAGNAR LOTHBROK.
I, THE ICELANDER, CALL UPON THEE!

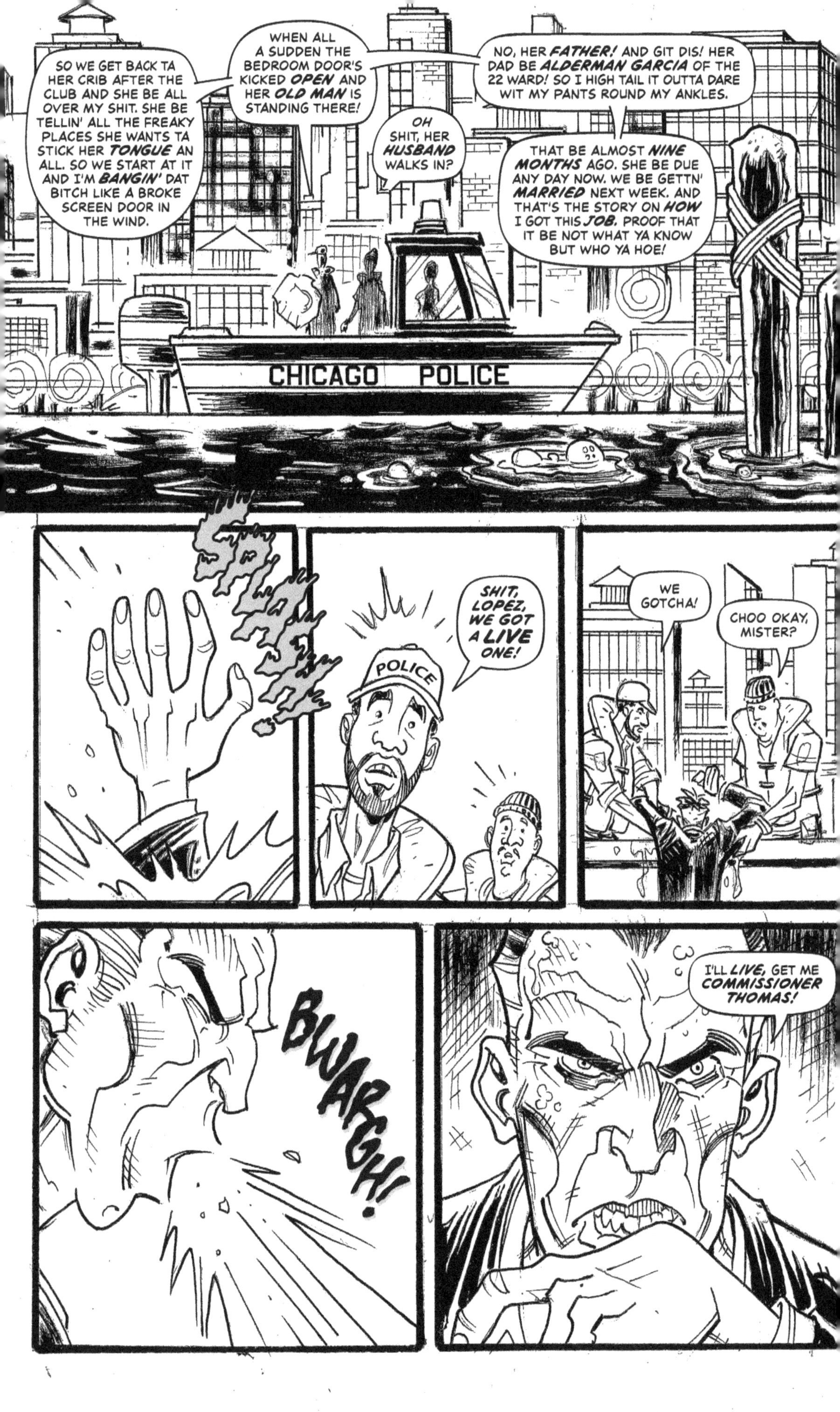
SO WE GET BACK TA HER CRIB AFTER THE CLUB AND SHE BE ALL OVER MY SHIT. SHE BE TELLIN' ALL THE FREAKY PLACES SHE WANTS TA STICK HER TONGUE AN ALL. SO WE START AT IT AND I'M BANGIN' DAT BITCH LIKE A BROKE SCREEN DOOR IN THE WIND.
WHEN ALL A SUDDEN THE BEDROOM DOOR'S KICKED OPEN AND HER OLD MAN IS STANDING THERE!
OH SHIT, HER HUSBAND WALKS IN?
NO, HER FATHER! AND GIT DIS! HER DAD BE ALDERMAN GARCIA OF THE 22 WARD! SO I HIGH TAIL IT OUTTA DARE WIT MY PANTS ROUND MY ANKLES.
THAT BE ALMOST NINE MONTHS AGO. SHE BE DUE ANY DAY NOW. WE BE GETTN' MARRIED NEXT WEEK. AND THAT'S THE STORY ON HOW I GOT THIS JOB. PROOF THAT IT BE NOT WHAT YA KNOW BUT WHO YA HOE!
CHICAGO POLICE
SPLASH
POLICE
SHIT, LOPEZ, WE GOT A LIVE ONE!
WE GOTCHA!
CHOO OKAY, MISTER?
BWARGH!
I'LL LIVE, GET ME COMMISSIONER THOMAS!

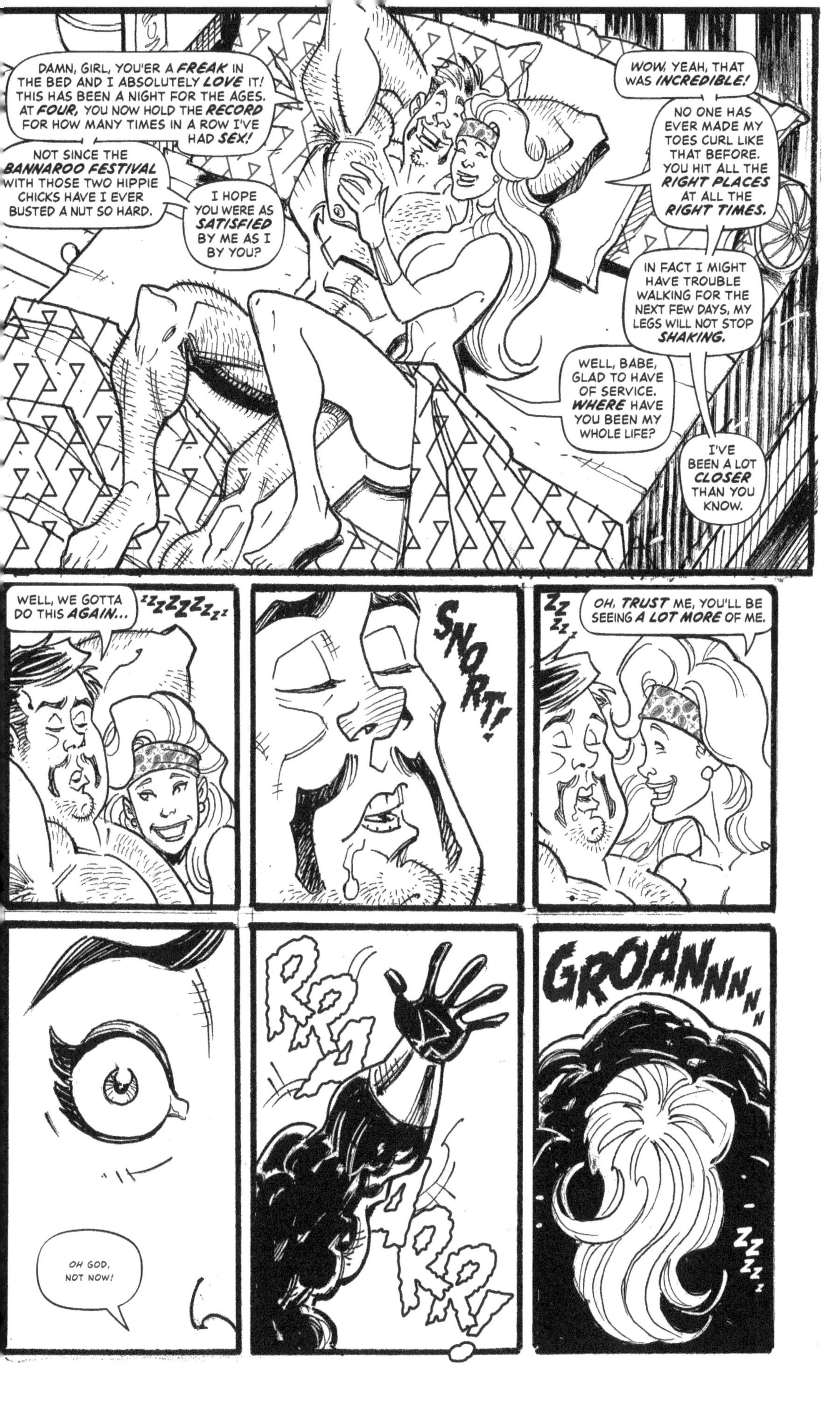
DAMN, GIRL, YOU'ER A FREAK IN THE BED AND I ABSOLUTELY LOVE IT! THIS HAS BEEN A NIGHT FOR THE AGES. AT FOUR, YOU NOW HOLD THE RECORD FOR HOW MANY TIMES IN A ROW I'VE HAD SEX!
NOT SINCE THE BANNAROO FESTIVAL WITH THOSE TWO HIPPIE CHICKS HAVE I EVER BUSTED A NUT SO HARD.
I HOPE YOU WERE AS SATISFIED BY ME AS I BY YOU?
WOW, YEAH, THAT WAS INCREDIBLE!
NO ONE HAS EVER MADE MY TOES CURL LIKE THAT BEFORE. YOU HIT ALL THE RIGHT PLACES AT ALL THE RIGHT TIMES.
IN FACT I MIGHT HAVE TROUBLE WALKING FOR THE NEXT FEW DAYS, MY LEGS WILL NOT STOP SHAKING.
WELL, BABE, GLAD TO HAVE OF SERVICE. WHERE HAVE YOU BEEN MY WHOLE LIFE?
I'VE BEEN A LOT CLOSER THAN YOU KNOW.
WELL, WE GOTTA DO THIS AGAIN...
ZZZZZZZZZ
SNORT!
ZZZZ
OH, TRUST ME, YOU'LL BE SEEING A LOT MORE OF ME.
OH GOD, NOT NOW!
GROANNNNN
ZZZZ

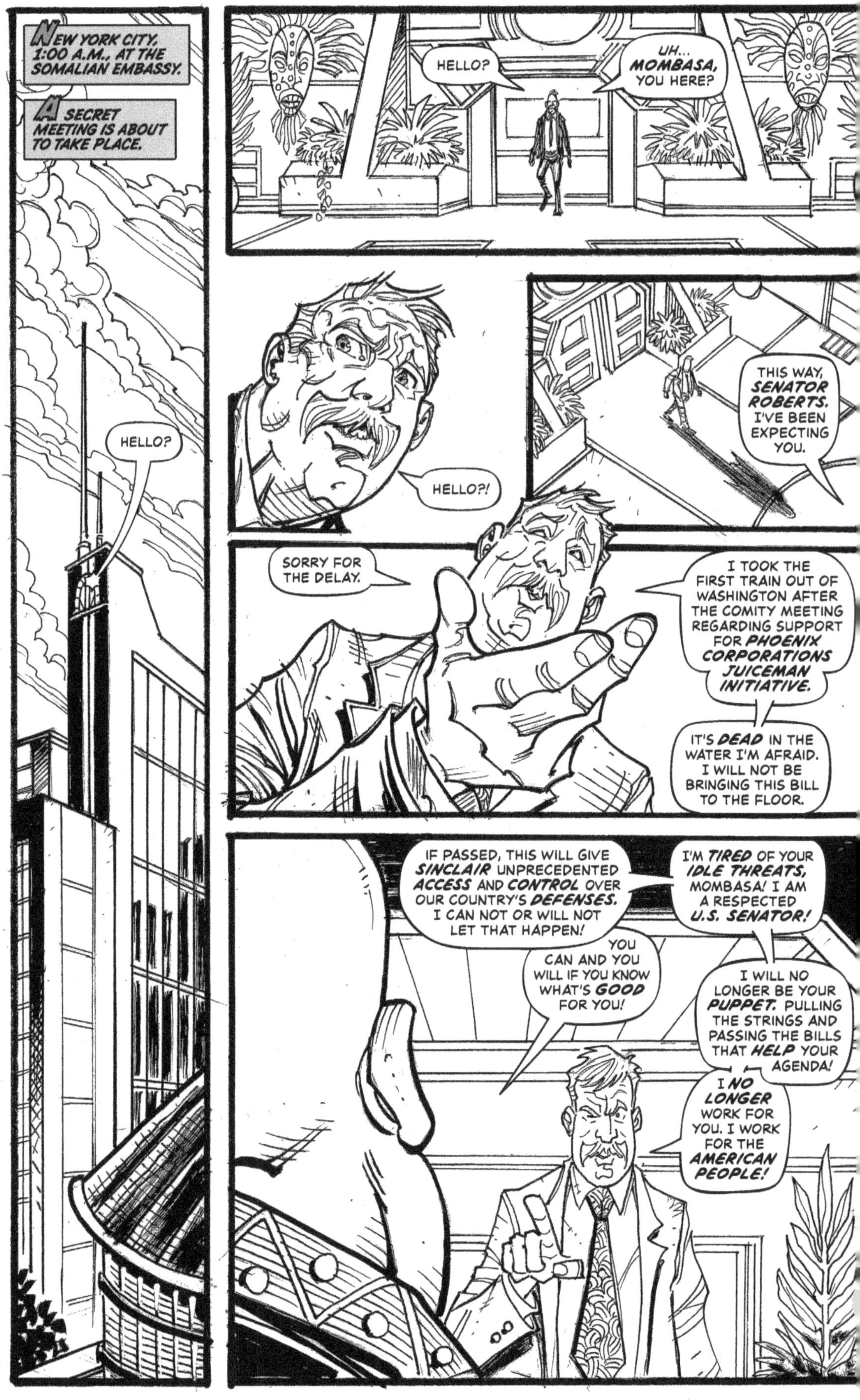
NEW YORK CITY, 1:00 A.M., AT THE SOMALIAN EMBASSY.
A SECRET MEETING IS ABOUT TO TAKE PLACE.
HELLO?
HELLO?
UH... MOMBASA, YOU HERE?
HELLO?!
THIS WAY, SENATOR ROBERTS. I'VE BEEN EXPECTING YOU.
SORRY FOR THE DELAY.
I TOOK THE FIRST TRAIN OUT OF WASHINGTON AFTER THE COMITY MEETING REGARDING SUPPORT FOR PHOENIX CORPORATIONS JUICEMAN INITIATIVE.
IT'S DEAD IN THE WATER I'M AFRAID. I WILL NOT BE BRINGING THIS BILL TO THE FLOOR.
IF PASSED, THIS WILL GIVE SINCLAIR UNPRECEDENTED ACCESS AND CONTROL OVER OUR COUNTRY'S DEFENSES. I CAN NOT OR WILL NOT LET THAT HAPPEN!
YOU CAN AND YOU WILL IF YOU KNOW WHAT'S GOOD FOR YOU!
I'M TIRED OF YOUR IDLE THREATS, MOMBASA! I AM A RESPECTED U.S. SENATOR!
I WILL NO LONGER BE YOUR PUPPET. PULLING THE STRINGS AND PASSING THE BILLS THAT HELP YOUR AGENDA!
I NO LONGER WORK FOR YOU. I WORK FOR THE AMERICAN PEOPLE!

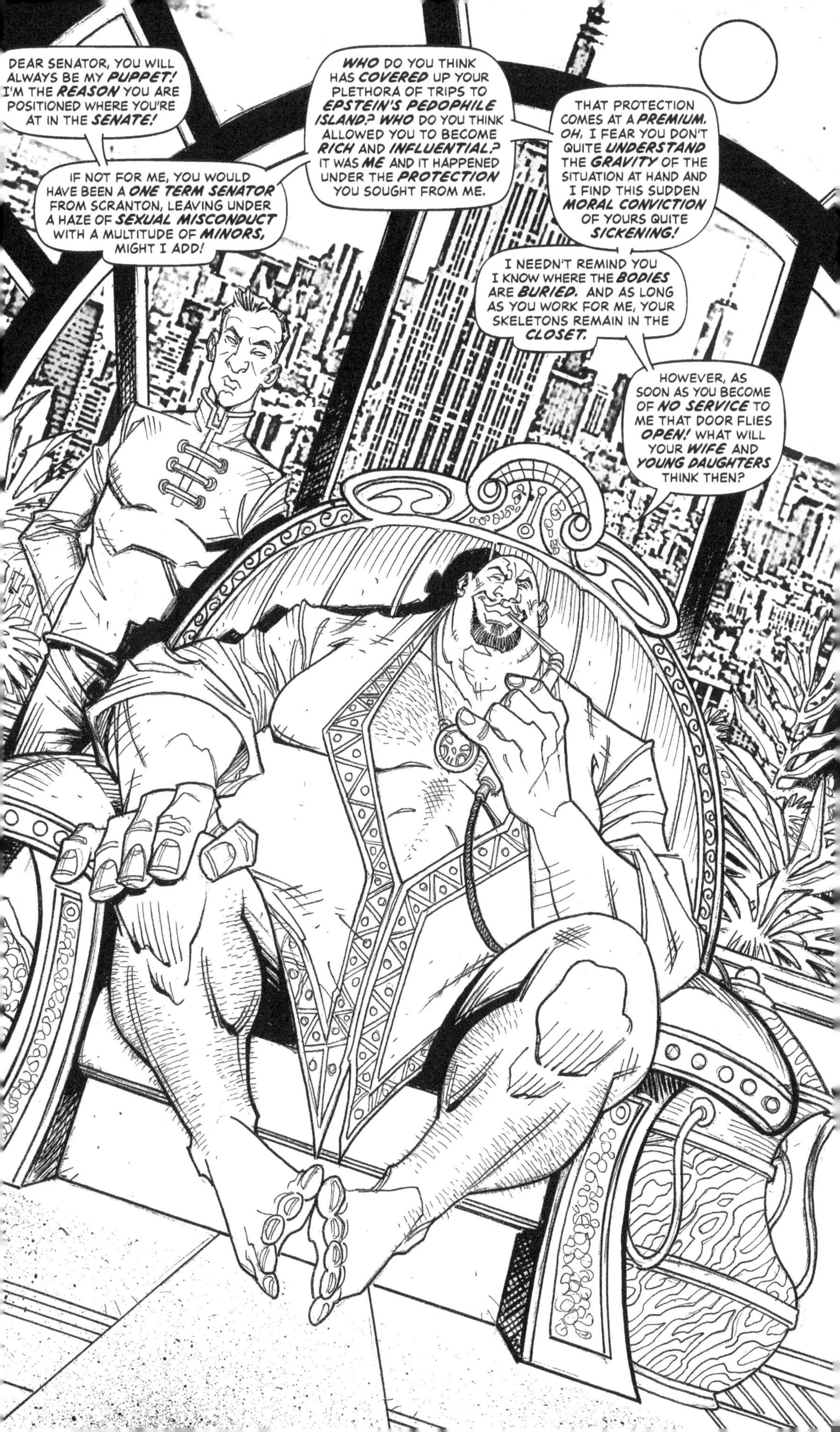
DEAR SENATOR, YOU WILL ALWAYS BE MY PUPPET! I'M THE REASON YOU ARE POSITIONED WHERE YOU'RE AT IN THE SENATE!
IF NOT FOR ME, YOU WOULD HAVE BEEN A ONE TERM SENATOR FROM SCRANTON, LEAVING UNDER A HAZE OF SEXUAL MISCONDUCT WITH A MULTITUDE OF MINORS, MIGHT I ADD!
WHO DO YOU THINK HAS COVERED UP YOUR PLETHORA OF TRIPS TO EPSTEIN'S PEDOPHILE ISLAND? WHO DO YOU THINK ALLOWED YOU TO BECOME RICH AND INFLUENTIAL? IT WAS ME AND IT HAPPENED UNDER THE PROTECTION YOU SOUGHT FROM ME.
THAT PROTECTION COMES AT A PREMIUM. OH, I FEAR YOU DON'T QUITE UNDERSTAND THE GRAVITY OF THE SITUATION AT HAND AND I FIND THIS SUDDEN MORAL CONVICTION OF YOURS QUITE SICKENING!
I NEEDN'T REMIND YOU I KNOW WHERE THE BODIES ARE BURIED. AND AS LONG AS YOU WORK FOR ME, YOUR SKELETONS REMAIN IN THE CLOSET.
HOWEVER, AS SOON AS YOU BECOME OF NO SERVICE TO ME THAT DOOR FLIES OPEN! WHAT WILL YOUR WIFE AND YOUNG DAUGHTERS THINK THEN?

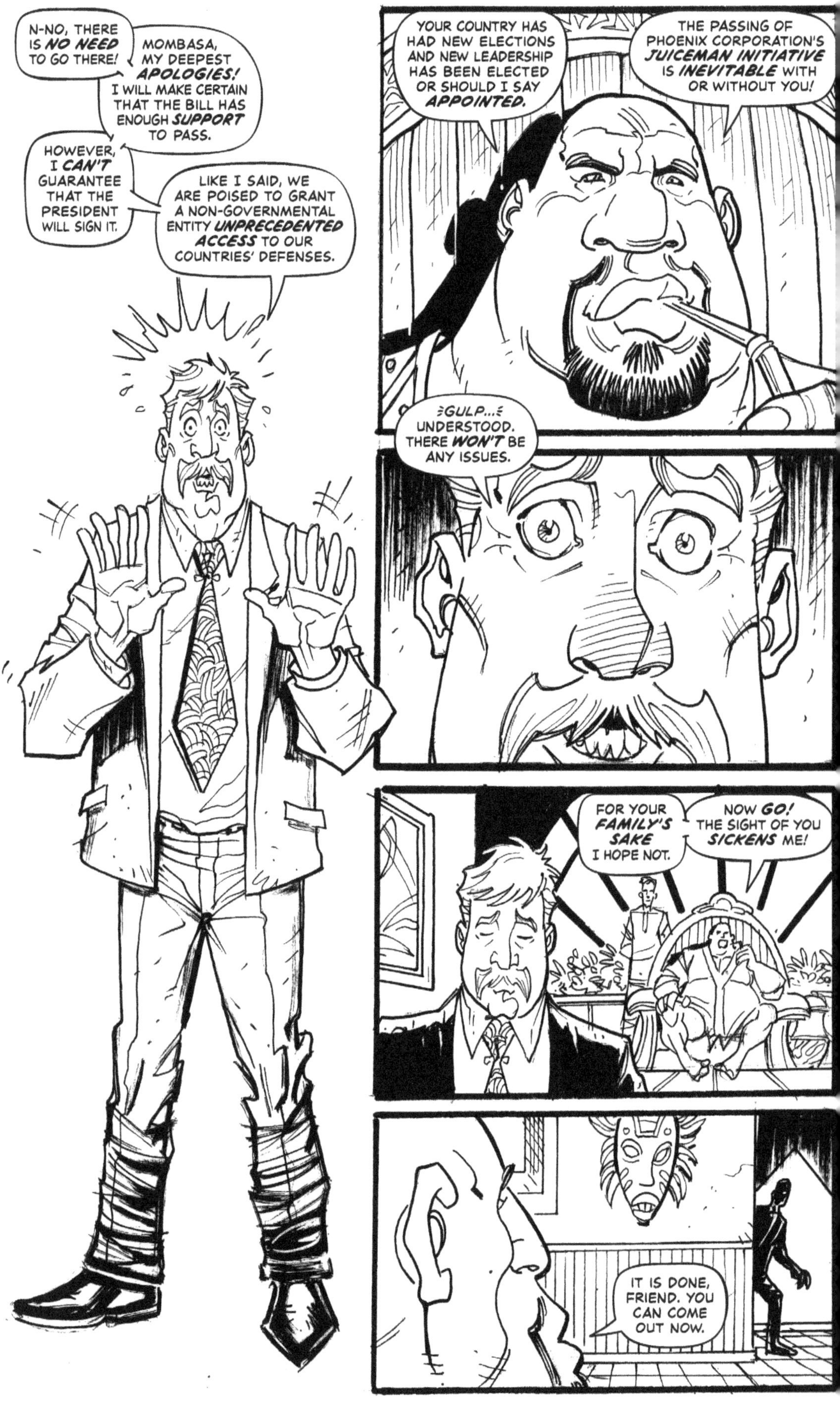
N-NO, THERE IS NO NEED TO GO THERE!
MOMBASA, MY DEEPEST APOLOGIES! I WILL MAKE CERTAIN THAT THE BILL HAS ENOUGH SUPPORT TO PASS.
HOWEVER, I CAN'T GUARANTEE THAT THE PRESIDENT WILL SIGN IT.
LIKE I SAID, WE ARE POISED TO GRANT A NON-GOVERNMENTAL ENTITY UNPRECEDENTED ACCESS TO OUR COUNTRIES' DEFENSES.
YOUR COUNTRY HAS HAD NEW ELECTIONS AND NEW LEADERSHIP HAS BEEN ELECTED OR SHOULD I SAY APPOINTED.
THE PASSING OF PHOENIX CORPORATION'S JUICEMAN INITIATIVE IS INEVITABLE WITH OR WITHOUT YOU!
GULP... UNDERSTOOD. THERE WON'T BE ANY ISSUES.
FOR YOUR FAMILY'S SAKE I HOPE NOT.
NOW GO! THE SIGHT OF YOU SICKENS ME!
IT IS DONE, FRIEND. YOU CAN COME OUT NOW.

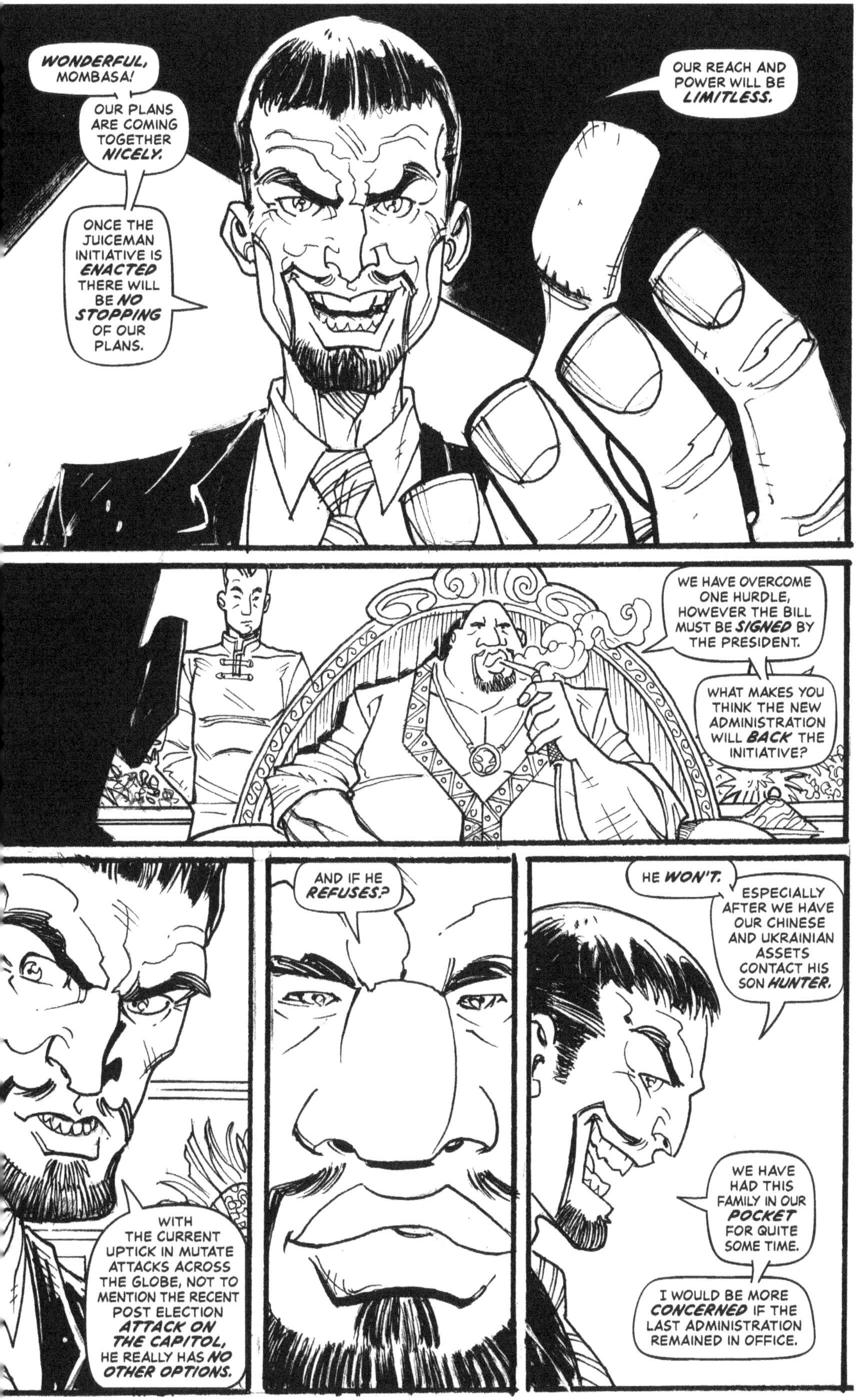
WONDERFUL, MOMBASA!
OUR PLANS ARE COMING TOGETHER NICELY.
ONCE THE JUICEMAN INITIATIVE IS ENACTED THERE WILL BE NO STOPPING OF OUR PLANS.
OUR REACH AND POWER WILL BE LIMITLESS.
WE HAVE OVERCOME ONE HURDLE, HOWEVER THE BILL MUST BE SIGNED BY THE PRESIDENT.
WHAT MAKES YOU THINK THE NEW ADMINISTRATION WILL BACK THE INITIATIVE?
WITH THE CURRENT UPTICK IN MUTATE ATTACKS ACROSS THE GLOBE, NOT TO MENTION THE RECENT POST ELECTION ATTACK ON THE CAPITOL, HE REALLY HAS NO OTHER OPTIONS.
AND IF HE REFUSES?
HE WON'T.
ESPECIALLY AFTER WE HAVE OUR CHINESE AND UKRAINIAN ASSETS CONTACT HIS SON HUNTER.
WE HAVE HAD THIS FAMILY IN OUR POCKET FOR QUITE SOME TIME.
I WOULD BE MORE CONCERNED IF THE LAST ADMINISTRATION REMAINED IN OFFICE.

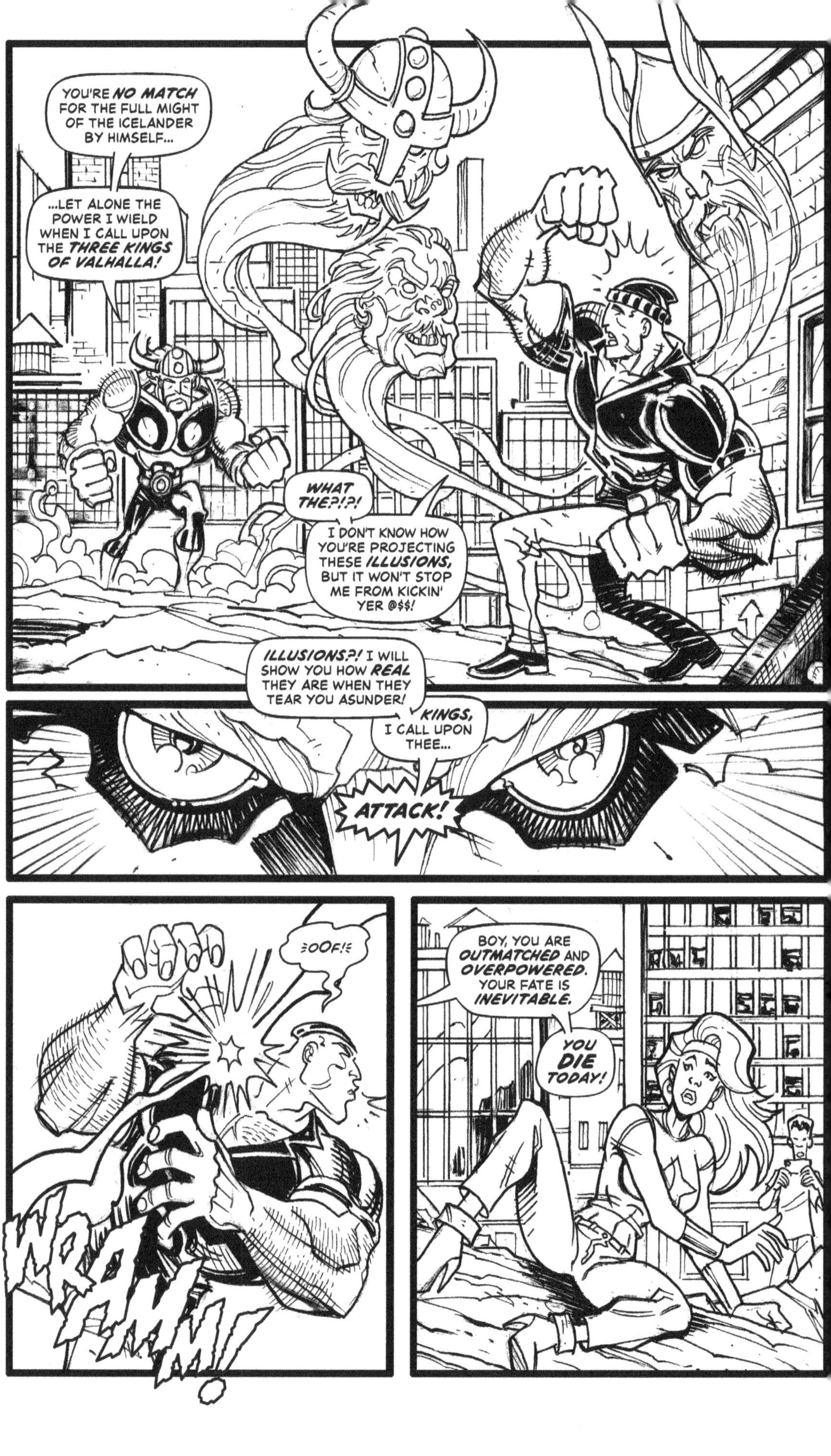
YOU'RE NO MATCH FOR THE FULL MIGHT OF THE ICELANDER BY HIMSELF...
...LET ALONE THE POWER I WIELD WHEN I CALL UPON THE THREE KINGS OF VALHALLA!
WHAT THE?!?!
I DON'T KNOW HOW YOU'RE PROJECTING THESE ILLUSIONS, BUT IT WON'T STOP ME FROM KICKIN' YER @$$!
ILLUSIONS?! I WILL SHOW YOU HOW REAL THEY ARE WHEN THEY TEAR YOU ASUNDER!
KINGS, I CALL UPON THEE...
ATTACK!
OOF!
WRAMM!
BOY, YOU ARE OUTMATCHED AND OVERPOWERED. YOUR FATE IS INEVITABLE.
YOU DIE TODAY!

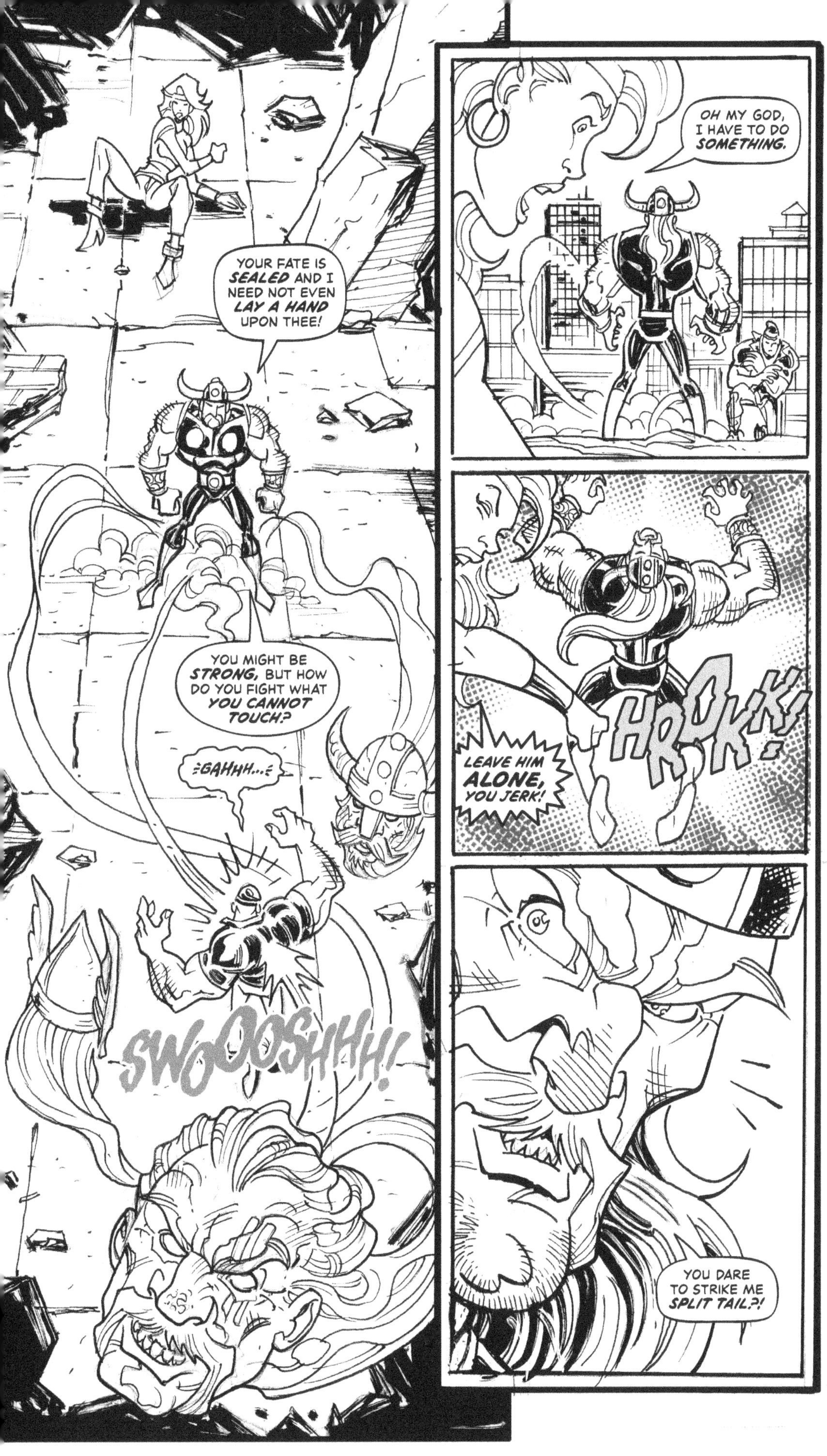
YOUR FATE IS SEALED AND I NEED NOT EVEN LAY A HAND UPON THEE!
YOU MIGHT BE STRONG, BUT HOW DO YOU FIGHT WHAT YOU CANNOT TOUCH?
GAHHH...
SWOOOSHHH!
OH MY GOD, I HAVE TO DO SOMETHING.
HROKK!
LEAVE HIM ALONE, YOU JERK!
YOU DARE TO STRIKE ME SPLIT TAIL?!

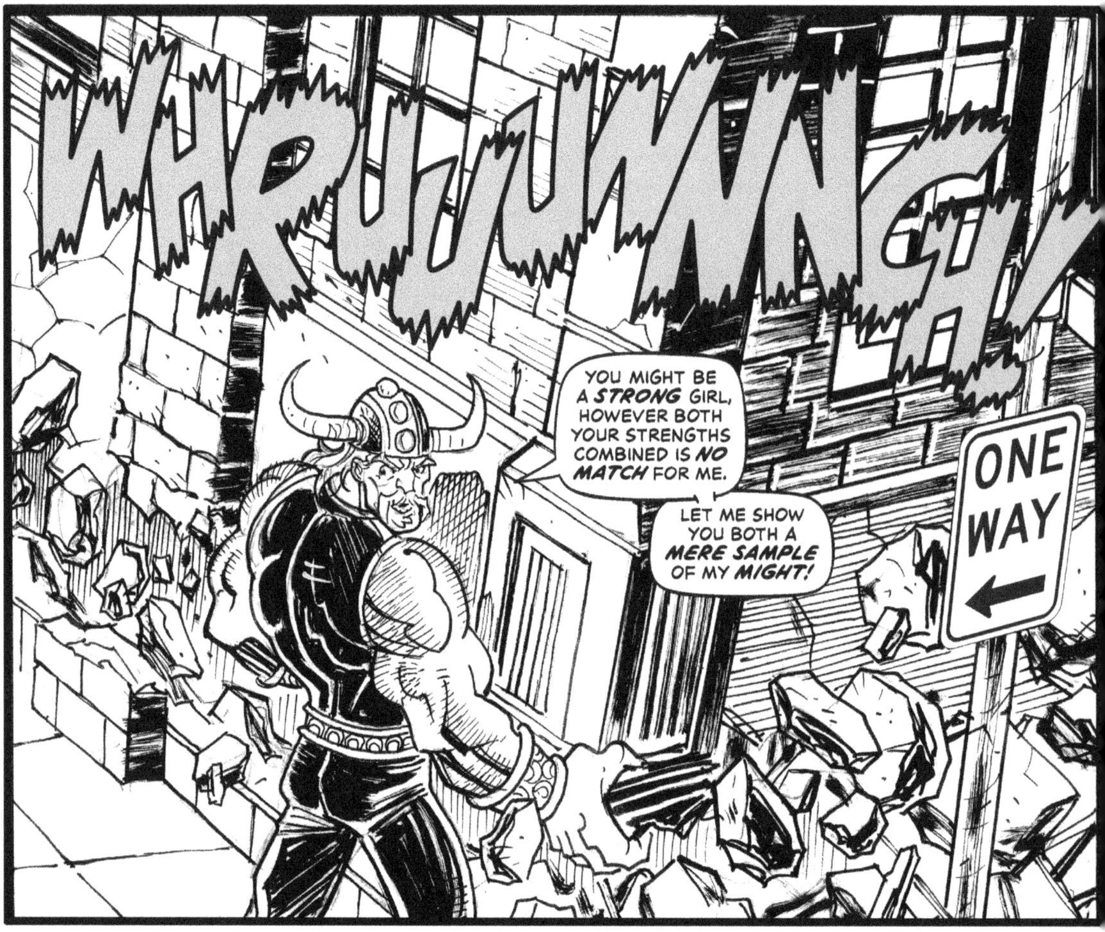
WHRUUWNGH!
YOU MIGHT BE A STRONG GIRL, HOWEVER BOTH YOUR STRENGTHS COMBINED IS NO MATCH FOR ME.
LET ME SHOW YOU BOTH A MERE SAMPLE OF MY MIGHT!
ONE WAY

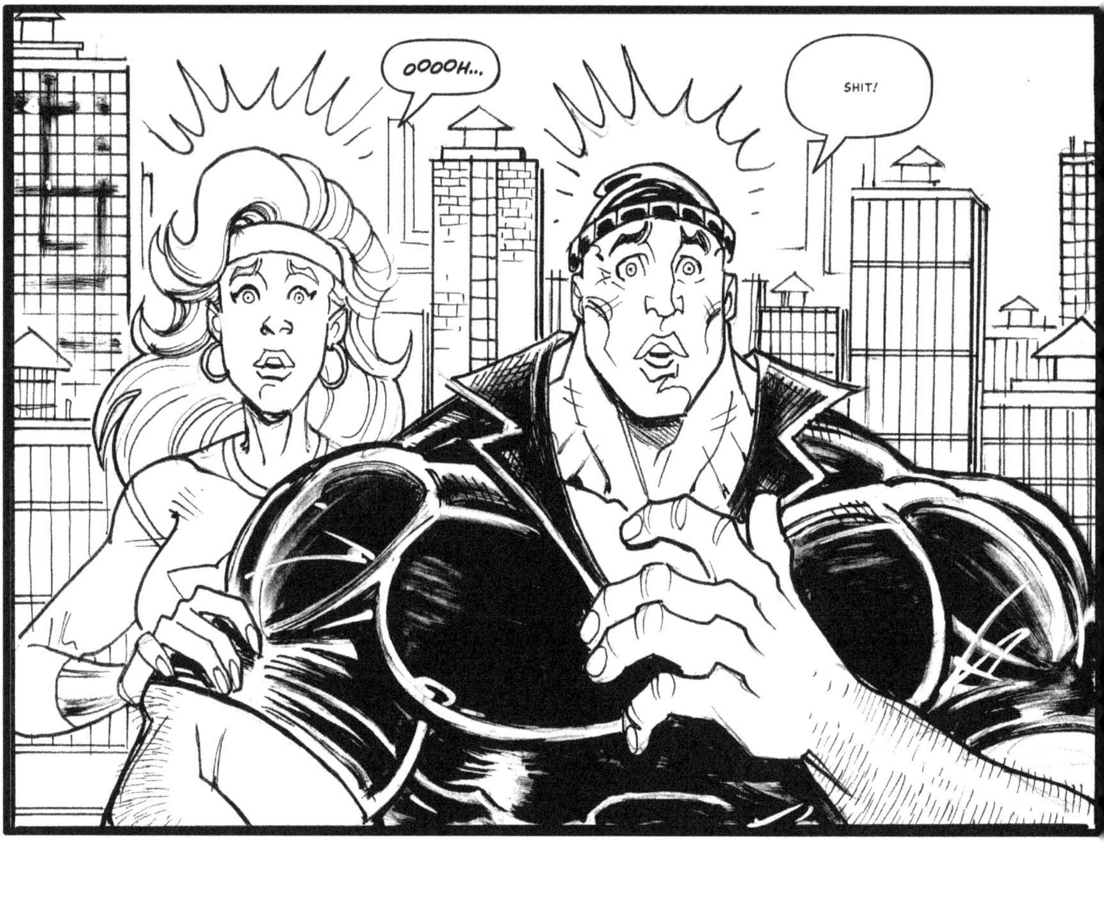
OOOOH...
SHIT!

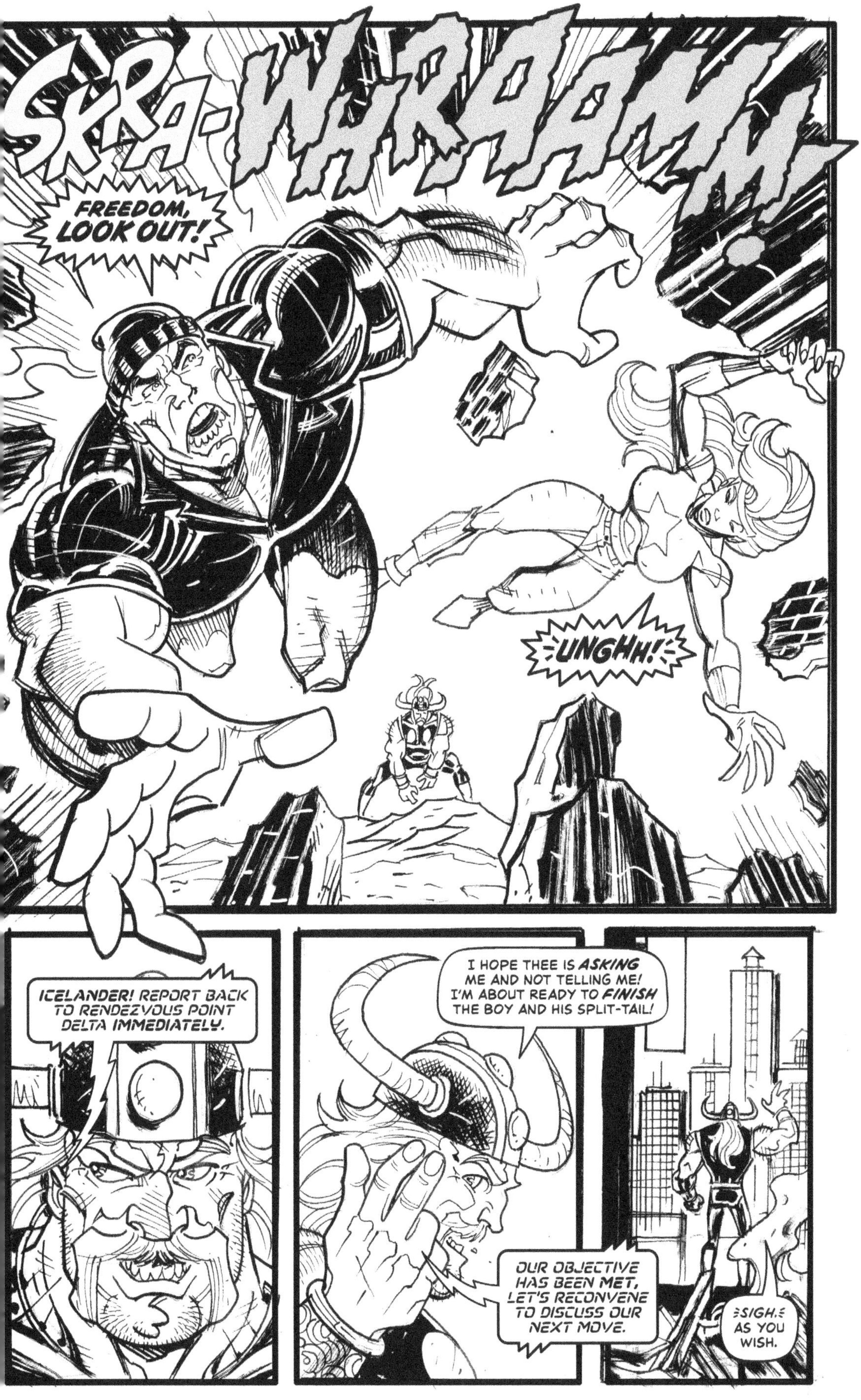

SKRA-WHRAAMM!
FREEDOM, LOOK OUT!
UNGHH!
ICELANDER! REPORT BACK TO RENDEZVOUS POINT DELTA IMMEDIATELY.
I HOPE THEE IS ASKING ME AND NOT TELLING ME! I'M ABOUT READY TO FINISH THE BOY AND HIS SPLIT-TAIL!
OUR OBJECTIVE HAS BEEN MET, LET'S RECONVENE TO DISCUSS OUR NEXT MOVE.
SIGH. AS YOU WISH.

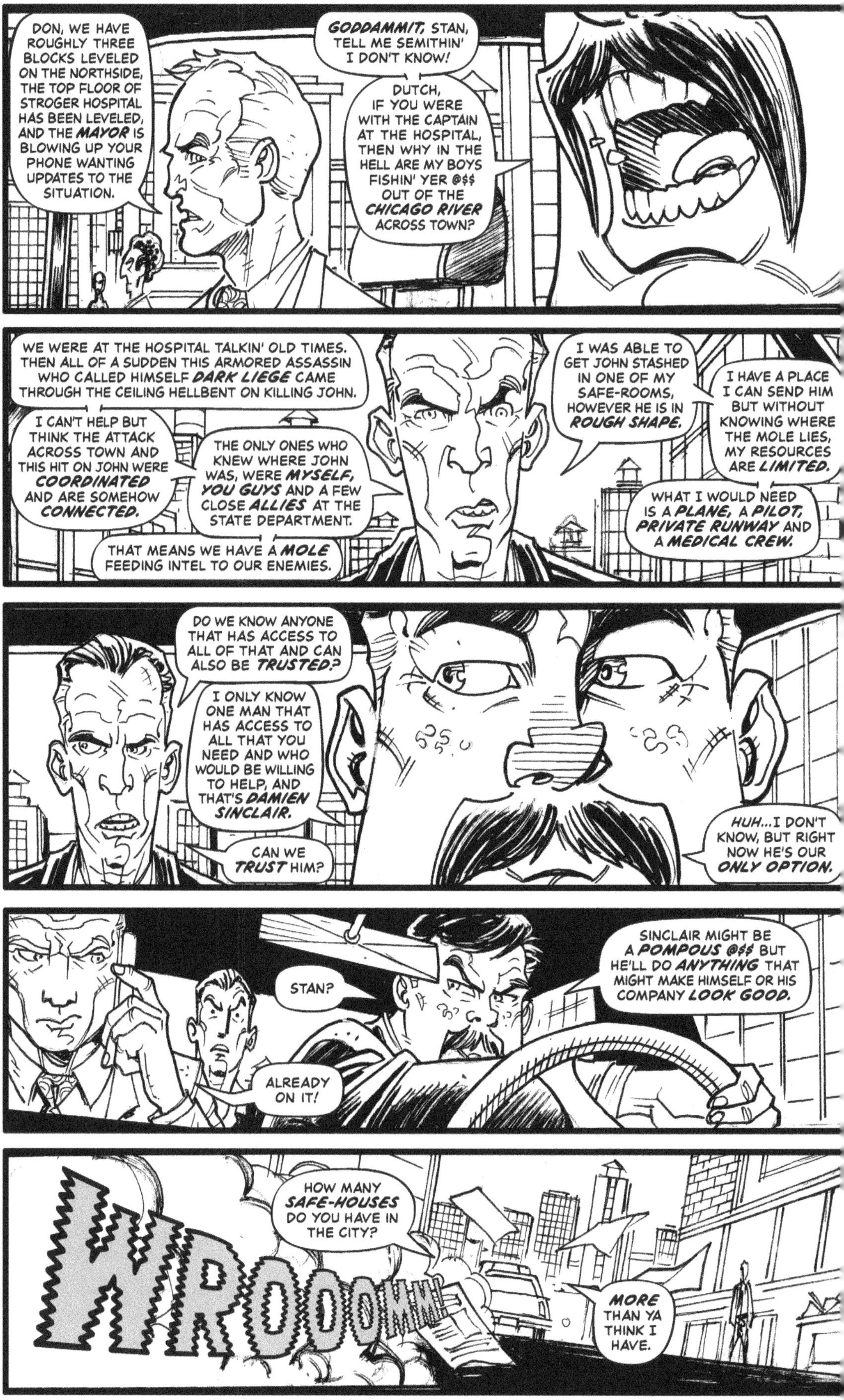
DON, WE HAVE ROUGHLY THREE BLOCKS LEVELED ON THE NORTHSIDE, THE TOP FLOOR OF STROGER HOSPITAL HAS BEEN LEVELED, AND THE MAYOR IS BLOWING UP YOUR PHONE WANTING UPDATES TO THE SITUATION.
GODDAMMIT, STAN, TELL ME SEMITHIN' I DON'T KNOW!
DUTCH, IF YOU WERE WITH THE CAPTAIN AT THE HOSPITAL, THEN WHY IN THE HELL ARE MY BOYS FISHIN' YER @$$ OUT OF THE CHICAGO RIVER ACROSS TOWN?
WE WERE AT THE HOSPITAL TALKIN' OLD TIMES. THEN ALL OF A SUDDEN THIS ARMORED ASSASSIN WHO CALLED HIMSELF DARK LIEGE CAME THROUGH THE CEILING HELLBENT ON KILLING JOHN.
I CAN'T HELP BUT THINK THE ATTACK ACROSS TOWN AND THIS HIT ON JOHN WERE COORDINATED AND ARE SOMEHOW CONNECTED.
THE ONLY ONES WHO KNEW WHERE JOHN WAS, WERE MYSELF, YOU GUYS AND A FEW CLOSE ALLIES AT THE STATE DEPARTMENT.
THAT MEANS WE HAVE A MOLE FEEDING INTEL TO OUR ENEMIES.
I WAS ABLE TO GET JOHN STASHED IN ONE OF MY SAFE-ROOMS, HOWEVER HE IS IN ROUGH SHAPE.
I HAVE A PLACE I CAN SEND HIM BUT WITHOUT KNOWING WHERE THE MOLE LIES, MY RESOURCES ARE LIMITED.
WHAT I WOULD NEED IS A PLANE, A PILOT, PRIVATE RUNWAY AND A MEDICAL CREW.
DO WE KNOW ANYONE THAT HAS ACCESS TO ALL OF THAT AND CAN ALSO BE TRUSTED?
I ONLY KNOW ONE MAN THAT HAS ACCESS TO ALL THAT YOU NEED AND WHO WOULD BE WILLING TO HELP, AND THAT'S DAMIEN SINCLAIR.
CAN WE TRUST HIM?
HUH...I DON'T KNOW, BUT RIGHT NOW HE'S OUR ONLY OPTION.
STAN?
ALREADY ON IT!
SINCLAIR MIGHT BE A POMPOUS @$$ BUT HE'LL DO ANYTHING THAT MIGHT MAKE HIMSELF OR HIS COMPANY LOOK GOOD.
WROOOMM
HOW MANY SAFE-HOUSES DO YOU HAVE IN THE CITY?
MORE THAN YA THINK I HAVE.

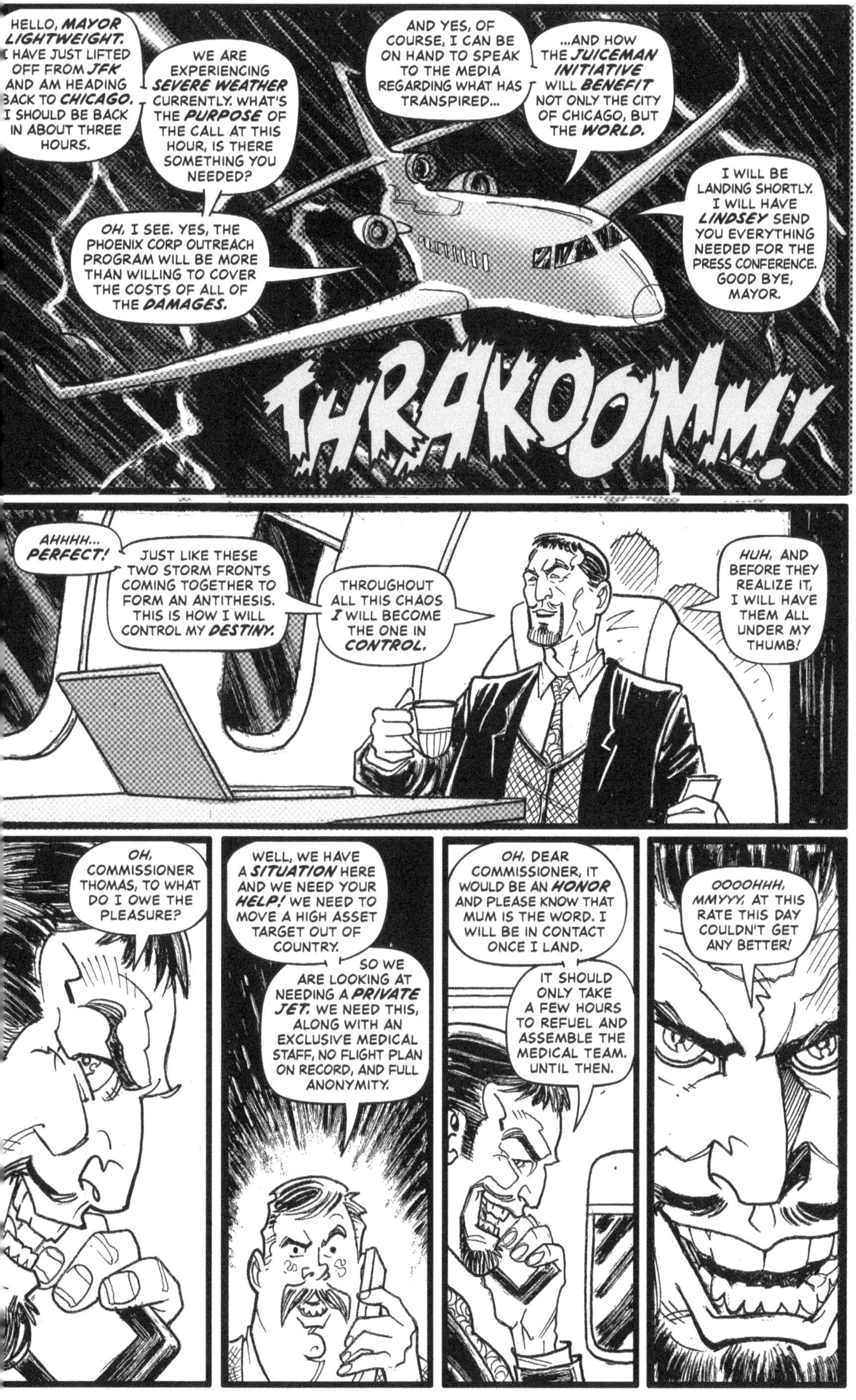
HELLO, MAYOR LIGHTWEIGHT. I HAVE JUST LIFTED OFF FROM JFK AND AM HEADING BACK TO CHICAGO. I SHOULD BE BACK IN ABOUT THREE HOURS.
WE ARE EXPERIENCING SEVERE WEATHER CURRENTLY. WHAT'S THE PURPOSE OF THE CALL AT THIS HOUR, IS THERE SOMETHING YOU NEEDED?
OH, I SEE. YES, THE PHOENIX CORP OUTREACH PROGRAM WILL BE MORE THAN WILLING TO COVER THE COSTS OF ALL OF THE DAMAGES.
AND YES, OF COURSE, I CAN BE ON HAND TO SPEAK TO THE MEDIA REGARDING WHAT HAS TRANSPIRED...
...AND HOW THE JUICEMAN INITIATIVE WILL BENEFIT NOT ONLY THE CITY OF CHICAGO, BUT THE WORLD.
I WILL BE LANDING SHORTLY. I WILL HAVE LINDSEY SEND YOU EVERYTHING NEEDED FOR THE PRESS CONFERENCE. GOOD BYE, MAYOR.
THRAKOOMM!
AHHHH... PERFECT!
JUST LIKE THESE TWO STORM FRONTS COMING TOGETHER TO FORM AN ANTITHESIS. THIS IS HOW I WILL CONTROL MY DESTINY.
THROUGHOUT ALL THIS CHAOS I WILL BECOME THE ONE IN CONTROL.
HUH, AND BEFORE THEY REALIZE IT, I WILL HAVE THEM ALL UNDER MY THUMB!
OH, COMMISSIONER THOMAS, TO WHAT DO I OWE THE PLEASURE?
WELL, WE HAVE A SITUATION HERE AND WE NEED YOUR HELP! WE NEED TO MOVE A HIGH ASSET TARGET OUT OF COUNTRY.
SO WE ARE LOOKING AT NEEDING A PRIVATE JET. WE NEED THIS, ALONG WITH AN EXCLUSIVE MEDICAL STAFF, NO FLIGHT PLAN ON RECORD, AND FULL ANONYMITY.
OH, DEAR COMMISSIONER, IT WOULD BE AN HONOR AND PLEASE KNOW THAT MUM IS THE WORD. I WILL BE IN CONTACT ONCE I LAND.
IT SHOULD ONLY TAKE A FEW HOURS TO REFUEL AND ASSEMBLE THE MEDICAL TEAM. UNTIL THEN.
OOOOHHH, MMYYY, AT THIS RATE THIS DAY COULDN'T GET ANY BETTER!

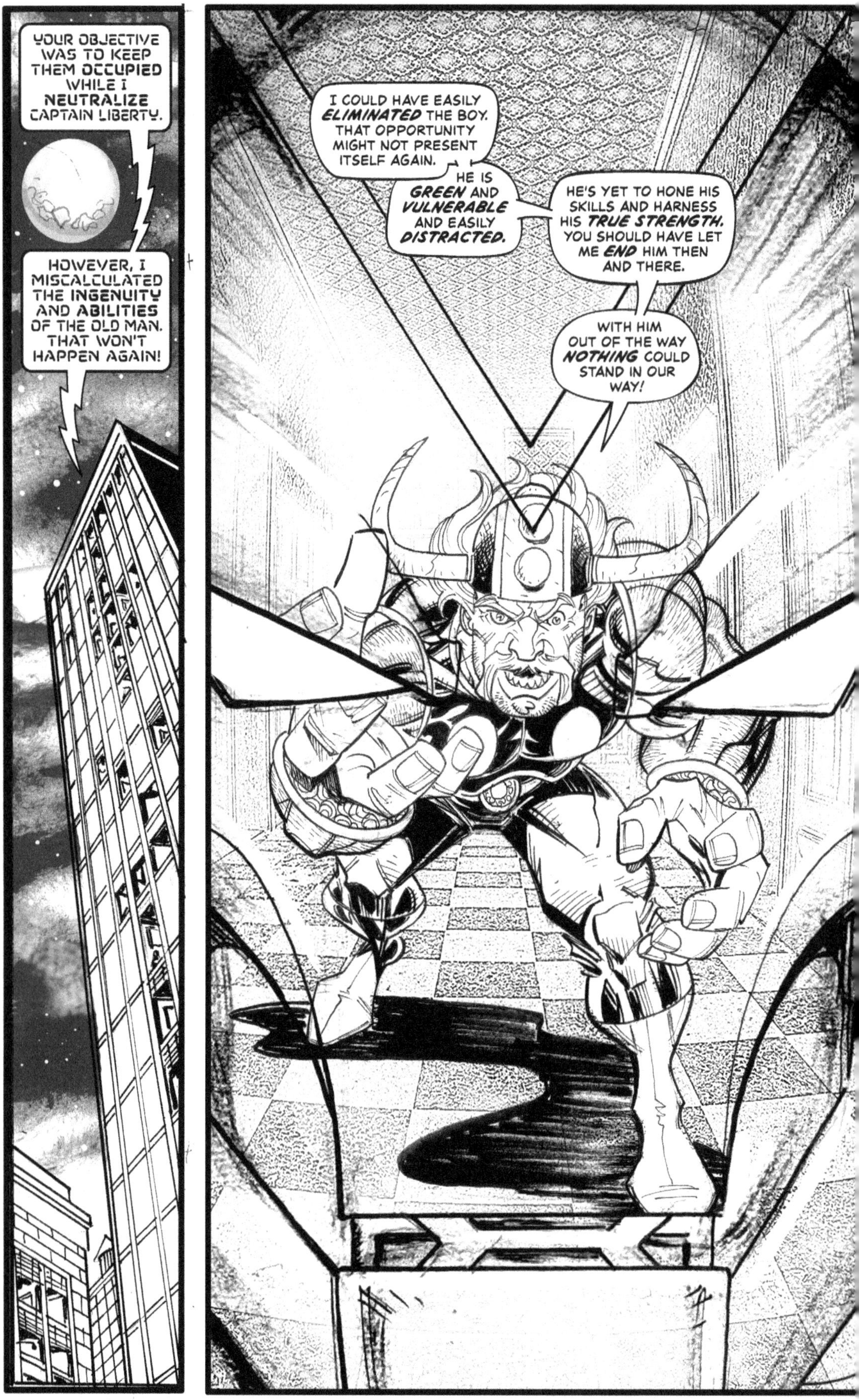
YOUR OBJECTIVE WAS TO KEEP THEM OCCUPIED WHILE I NEUTRALIZE CAPTAIN LIBERTY.
HOWEVER, I MISCALCULATED THE INGENUITY AND ABILITIES OF THE OLD MAN. THAT WON'T HAPPEN AGAIN!
I COULD HAVE EASILY ELIMINATED THE BOY. THAT OPPORTUNITY MIGHT NOT PRESENT ITSELF AGAIN.
HE IS GREEN AND VULNERABLE AND EASILY DISTRACTED.
HE'S YET TO HONE HIS SKILLS AND HARNESS HIS TRUE STRENGTH. YOU SHOULD HAVE LET ME END HIM THEN AND THERE.
WITH HIM OUT OF THE WAY NOTHING COULD STAND IN OUR WAY!

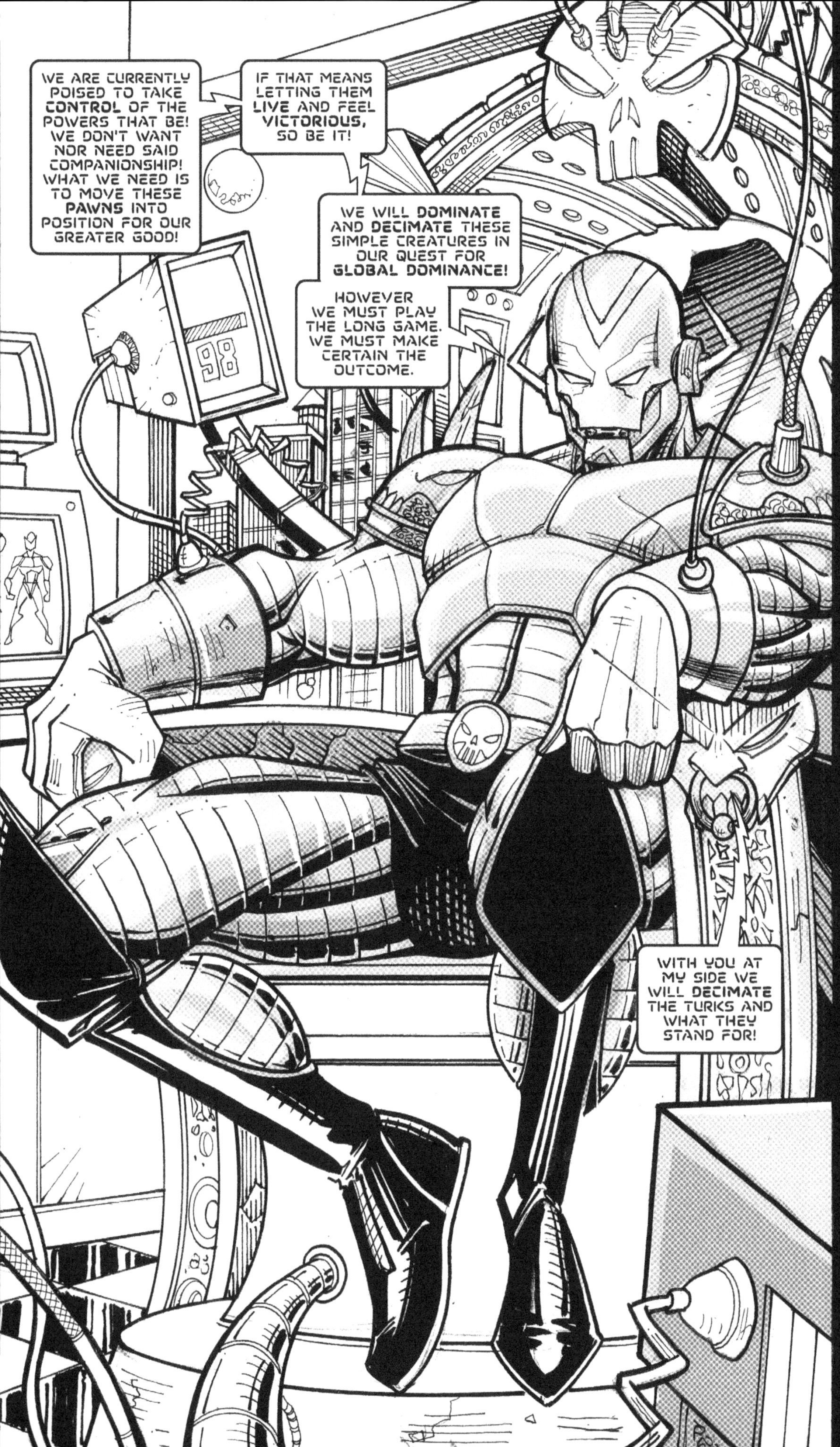

WE ARE CURRENTLY POISED TO TAKE **CONTROL** OF THE POWERS THAT BE! WE DON'T WANT NOR NEED SAID COMPANIONSHIP! WHAT WE NEED IS TO MOVE THESE **PAWNS** INTO POSITION FOR OUR GREATER GOOD!
IF THAT MEANS LETTING THEM **LIVE** AND FEEL **VICTORIOUS,** SO BE IT!
WE WILL **DOMINATE** AND **DECIMATE** THESE SIMPLE CREATURES IN OUR QUEST FOR **GLOBAL DOMINANCE!**
HOWEVER WE MUST PLAY THE LONG GAME. WE MUST MAKE CERTAIN THE OUTCOME.
98
WITH YOU AT MY SIDE WE WILL **DECIMATE** THE TURKS AND WHAT THEY STAND FOR!

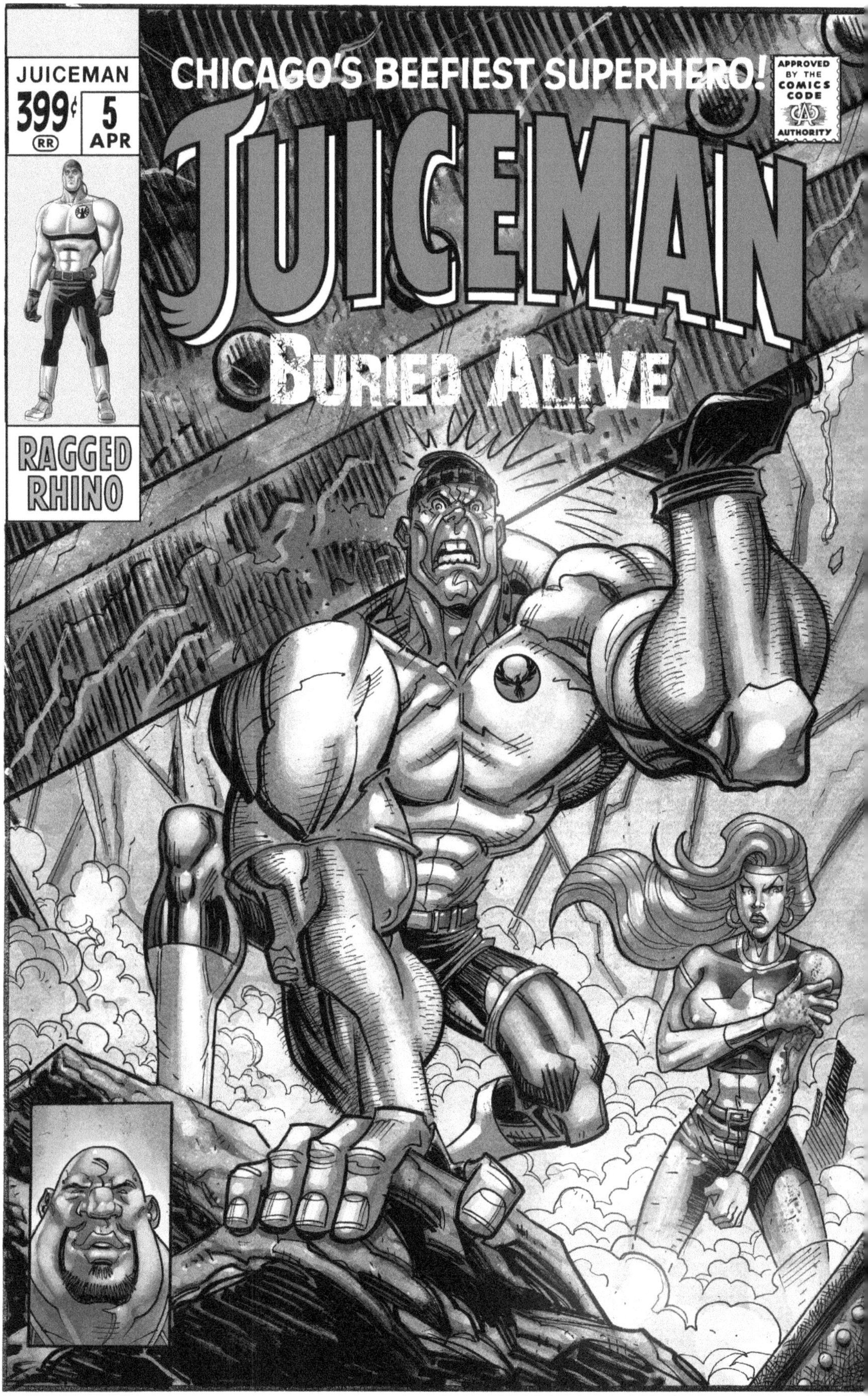
JUICEMAN
399¢
RR
5
APR
RAGGED RHINO
CHICAGO'S BEEFIEST SUPERHERO!
APPROVED BY THE COMICS CODE AUTHORITY
JUICEMAN
BURIED ALIVE

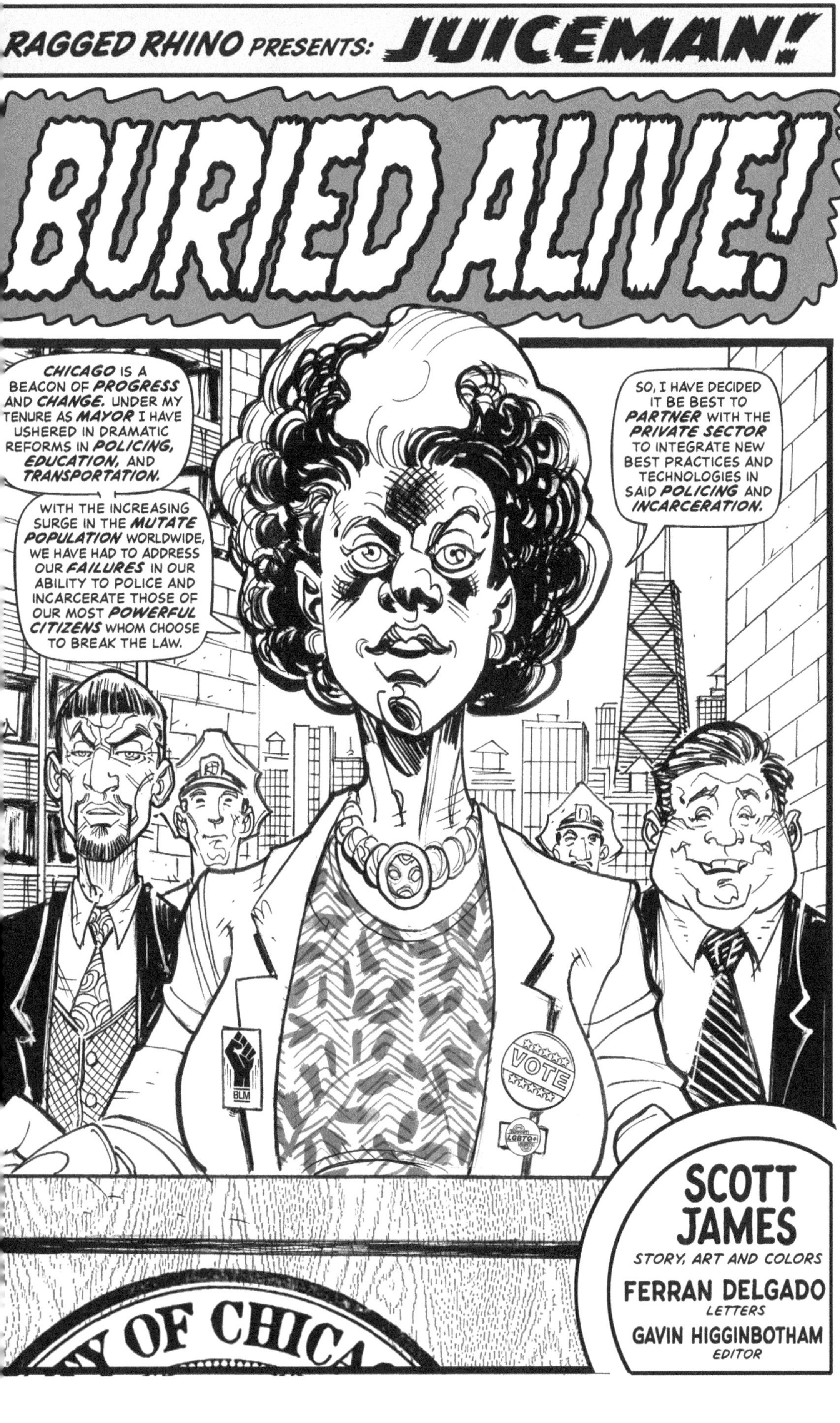
RAGGED RHINO PRESENTS: JUICEMAN!
BURIED ALIVE!
CHICAGO IS A BEACON OF PROGRESS AND CHANGE. UNDER MY TENURE AS MAYOR I HAVE USHERED IN DRAMATIC REFORMS IN POLICING, EDUCATION, AND TRANSPORTATION.
WITH THE INCREASING SURGE IN THE MUTATE POPULATION WORLDWIDE, WE HAVE HAD TO ADDRESS OUR FAILURES IN OUR ABILITY TO POLICE AND INCARCERATE THOSE OF OUR MOST POWERFUL CITIZENS WHOM CHOOSE TO BREAK THE LAW.
SO, I HAVE DECIDED IT BE BEST TO PARTNER WITH THE PRIVATE SECTOR TO INTEGRATE NEW BEST PRACTICES AND TECHNOLOGIES IN SAID POLICING AND INCARCERATION.
BLM
VOTE
LGBTQ+
OF CHICA
SCOTT JAMES
STORY, ART AND COLORS
FERRAN DELGADO
LETTERS
GAVIN HIGGINBOTHAM
EDITOR

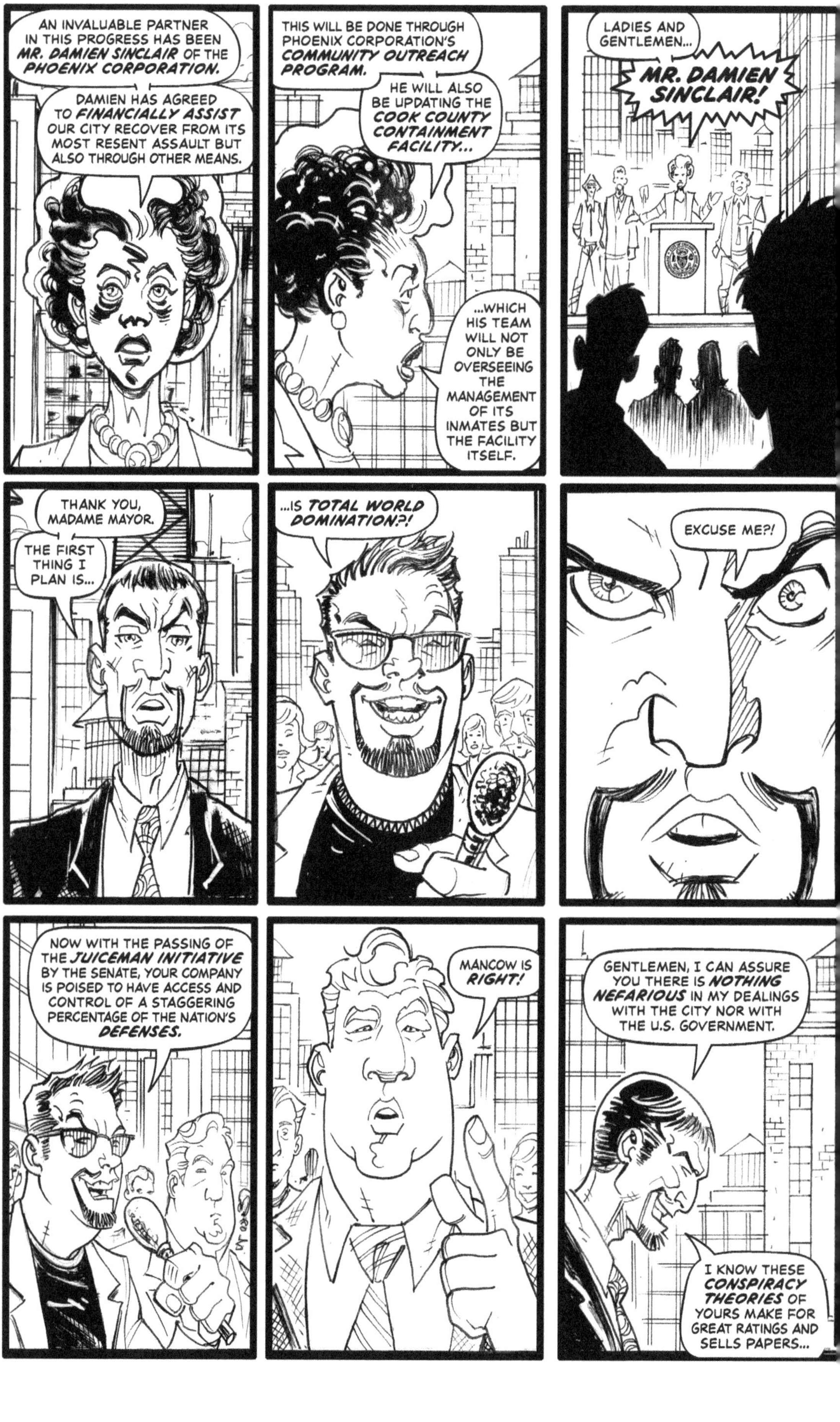
AN INVALUABLE PARTNER IN THIS PROGRESS HAS BEEN MR. DAMIEN SINCLAIR OF THE PHOENIX CORPORATION.
DAMIEN HAS AGREED TO FINANCIALLY ASSIST OUR CITY RECOVER FROM ITS MOST RESENT ASSAULT BUT ALSO THROUGH OTHER MEANS.
THIS WILL BE DONE THROUGH PHOENIX CORPORATION'S COMMUNITY OUTREACH PROGRAM.
HE WILL ALSO BE UPDATING THE COOK COUNTY CONTAINMENT FACILITY...
...WHICH HIS TEAM WILL NOT ONLY BE OVERSEEING THE MANAGEMENT OF ITS INMATES BUT THE FACILITY ITSELF.
LADIES AND GENTLEMEN...
MR. DAMIEN SINCLAIR!
THANK YOU, MADAME MAYOR.
THE FIRST THING I PLAN IS...
...IS TOTAL WORLD DOMINATION?!
EXCUSE ME?!
NOW WITH THE PASSING OF THE JUICEMAN INITIATIVE BY THE SENATE, YOUR COMPANY IS POISED TO HAVE ACCESS AND CONTROL OF A STAGGERING PERCENTAGE OF THE NATION'S DEFENSES.
MANCOW IS RIGHT!
GENTLEMEN, I CAN ASSURE YOU THERE IS NOTHING NEFARIOUS IN MY DEALINGS WITH THE CITY NOR WITH THE U.S. GOVERNMENT.
I KNOW THESE CONSPIRACY THEORIES OF YOURS MAKE FOR GREAT RATINGS AND SELLS PAPERS...

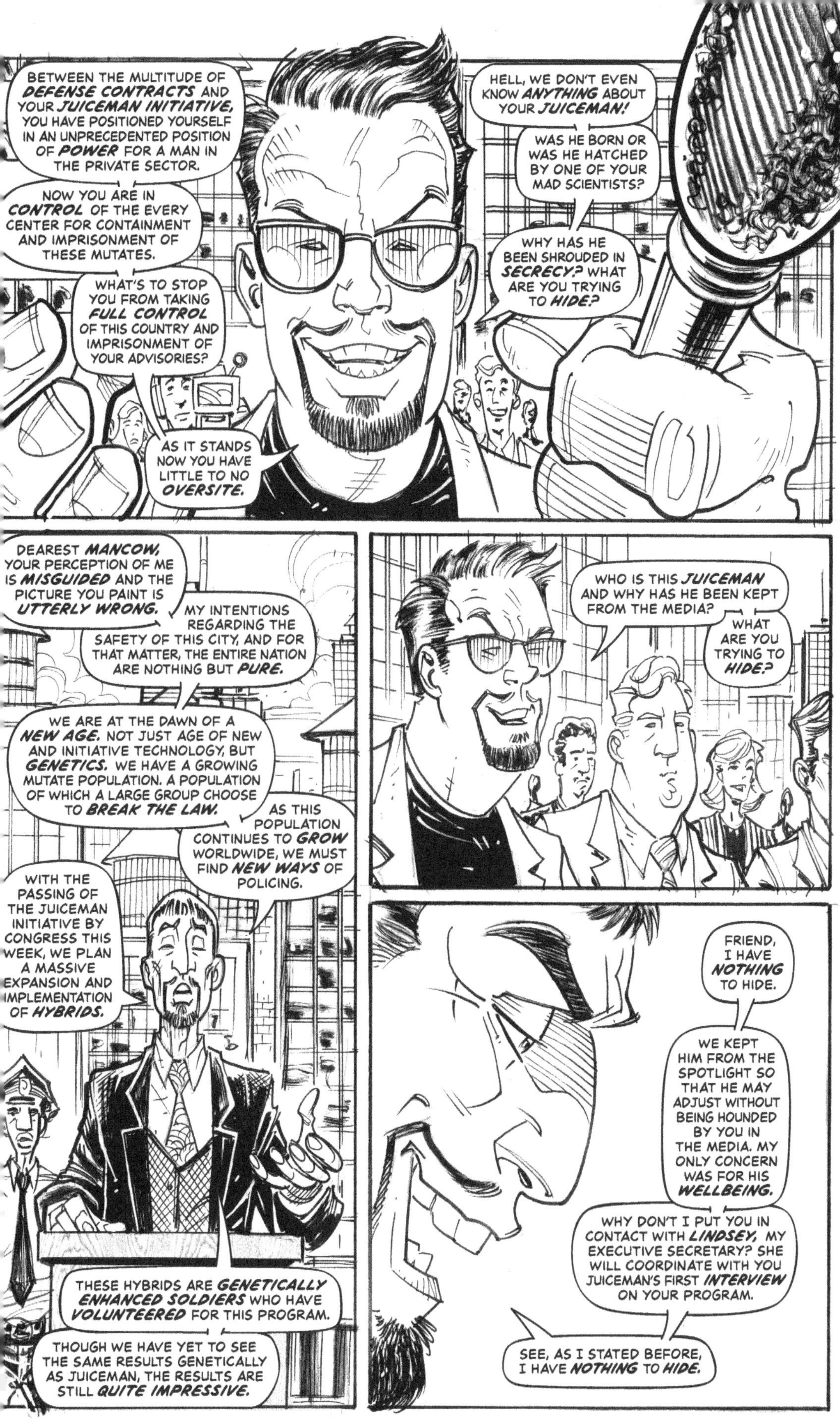
BETWEEN THE MULTITUDE OF DEFENSE CONTRACTS AND YOUR JUICEMAN INITIATIVE, YOU HAVE POSITIONED YOURSELF IN AN UNPRECEDENTED POSITION OF POWER FOR A MAN IN THE PRIVATE SECTOR.
NOW YOU ARE IN CONTROL OF THE EVERY CENTER FOR CONTAINMENT AND IMPRISONMENT OF THESE MUTATES.
WHAT'S TO STOP YOU FROM TAKING FULL CONTROL OF THIS COUNTRY AND IMPRISONMENT OF YOUR ADVISORIES?
AS IT STANDS NOW YOU HAVE LITTLE TO NO OVERSITE.
HELL, WE DON'T EVEN KNOW ANYTHING ABOUT YOUR JUICEMAN!
WAS HE BORN OR WAS HE HATCHED BY ONE OF YOUR MAD SCIENTISTS?
WHY HAS HE BEEN SHROUDED IN SECRECY? WHAT ARE YOU TRYING TO HIDE?
DEAREST MANCOW, YOUR PERCEPTION OF ME IS MISGUIDED AND THE PICTURE YOU PAINT IS UTTERLY WRONG.
MY INTENTIONS REGARDING THE SAFETY OF THIS CITY, AND FOR THAT MATTER, THE ENTIRE NATION ARE NOTHING BUT PURE.
WE ARE AT THE DAWN OF A NEW AGE. NOT JUST AGE OF NEW AND INITIATIVE TECHNOLOGY, BUT GENETICS. WE HAVE A GROWING MUTATE POPULATION. A POPULATION OF WHICH A LARGE GROUP CHOOSE TO BREAK THE LAW.
AS THIS POPULATION CONTINUES TO GROW WORLDWIDE, WE MUST FIND NEW WAYS OF POLICING.
WITH THE PASSING OF THE JUICEMAN INITIATIVE BY CONGRESS THIS WEEK, WE PLAN A MASSIVE EXPANSION AND IMPLEMENTATION OF HYBRIDS.
THESE HYBRIDS ARE GENETICALLY ENHANCED SOLDIERS WHO HAVE VOLUNTEERED FOR THIS PROGRAM.
THOUGH WE HAVE YET TO SEE THE SAME RESULTS GENETICALLY AS JUICEMAN, THE RESULTS ARE STILL QUITE IMPRESSIVE.
WHO IS THIS JUICEMAN AND WHY HAS HE BEEN KEPT FROM THE MEDIA?
WHAT ARE YOU TRYING TO HIDE?
FRIEND, I HAVE NOTHING TO HIDE.
WE KEPT HIM FROM THE SPOTLIGHT SO THAT HE MAY ADJUST WITHOUT BEING HOUNDED BY YOU IN THE MEDIA. MY ONLY CONCERN WAS FOR HIS WELLBEING.
WHY DON'T I PUT YOU IN CONTACT WITH LINDSEY, MY EXECUTIVE SECRETARY? SHE WILL COORDINATE WITH YOU JUICEMAN'S FIRST INTERVIEW ON YOUR PROGRAM.
SEE, AS I STATED BEFORE, I HAVE NOTHING TO HIDE.

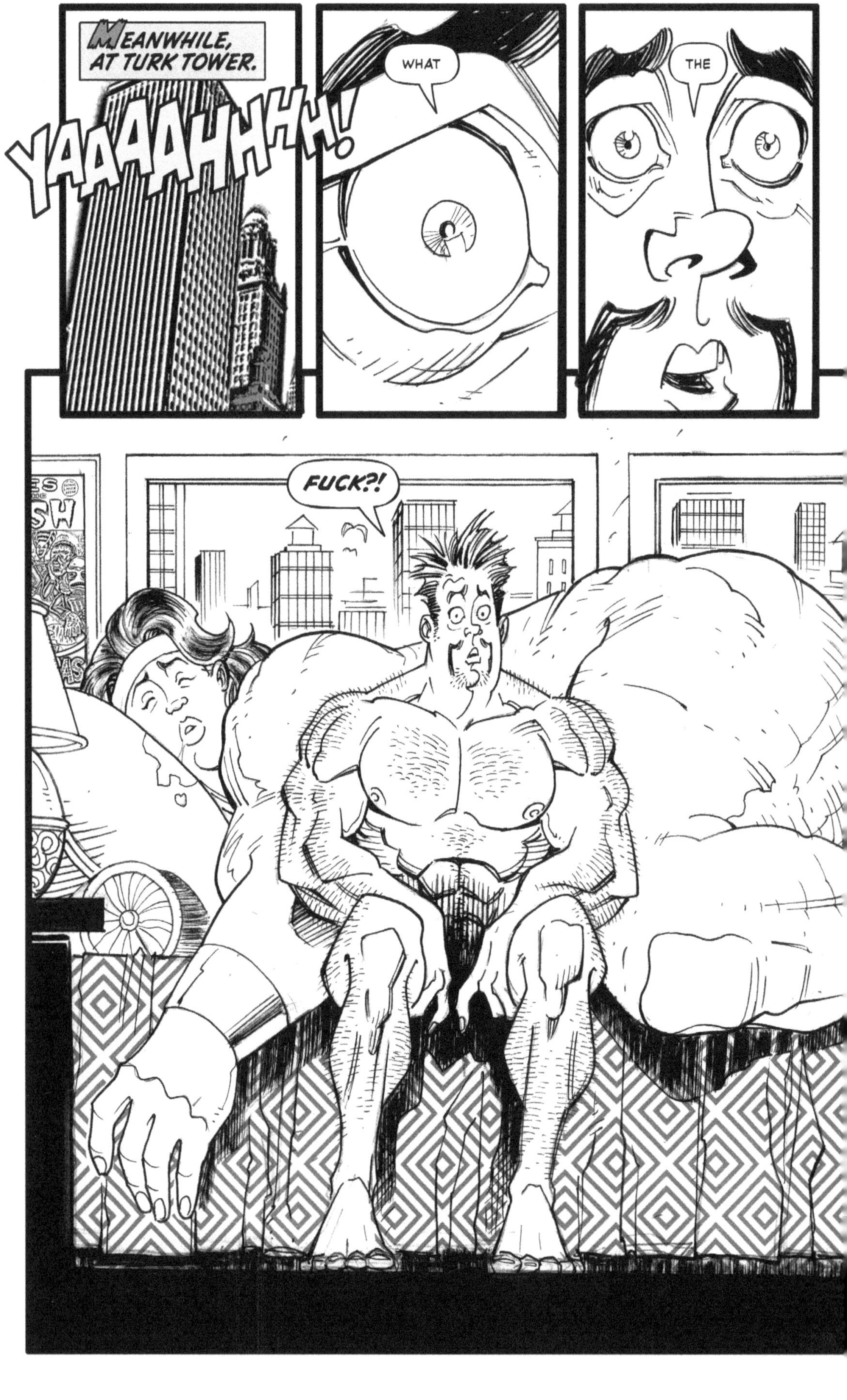
MEANWHILE, AT TURK TOWER.
YAAAAHHHH!
WHAT
THE
FUCK?!

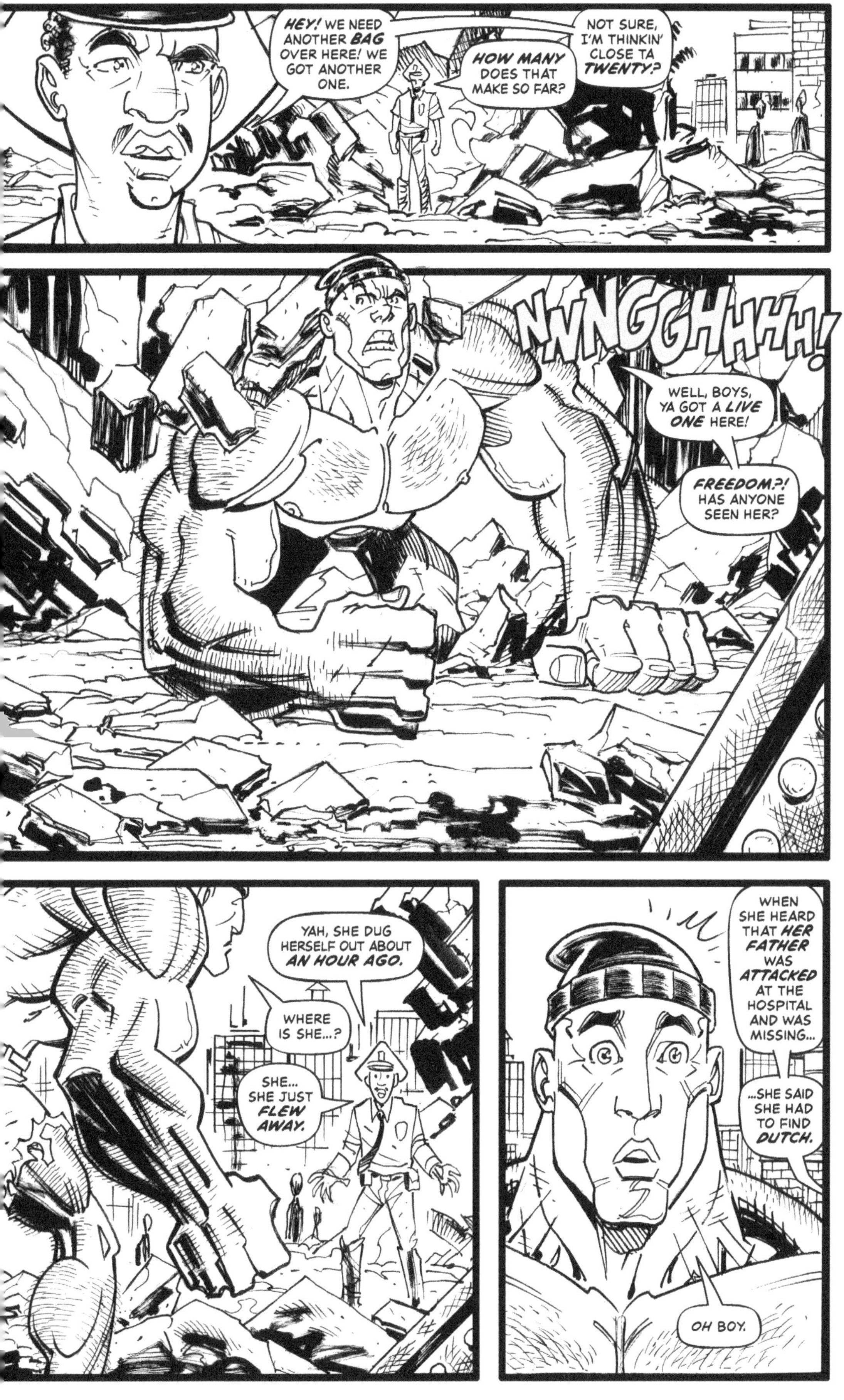
HEY! WE NEED ANOTHER BAG OVER HERE! WE GOT ANOTHER ONE.
HOW MANY DOES THAT MAKE SO FAR?
NOT SURE, I'M THINKIN' CLOSE TA TWENTY?
NNNGGHHHH!
WELL, BOYS, YA GOT A LIVE ONE HERE!
FREEDOM?! HAS ANYONE SEEN HER?
YAH, SHE DUG HERSELF OUT ABOUT AN HOUR AGO.
WHERE IS SHE...?
SHE... SHE JUST FLEW AWAY.
WHEN SHE HEARD THAT HER FATHER WAS ATTACKED AT THE HOSPITAL AND WAS MISSING...
...SHE SAID SHE HAD TO FIND DUTCH.
OH BOY.

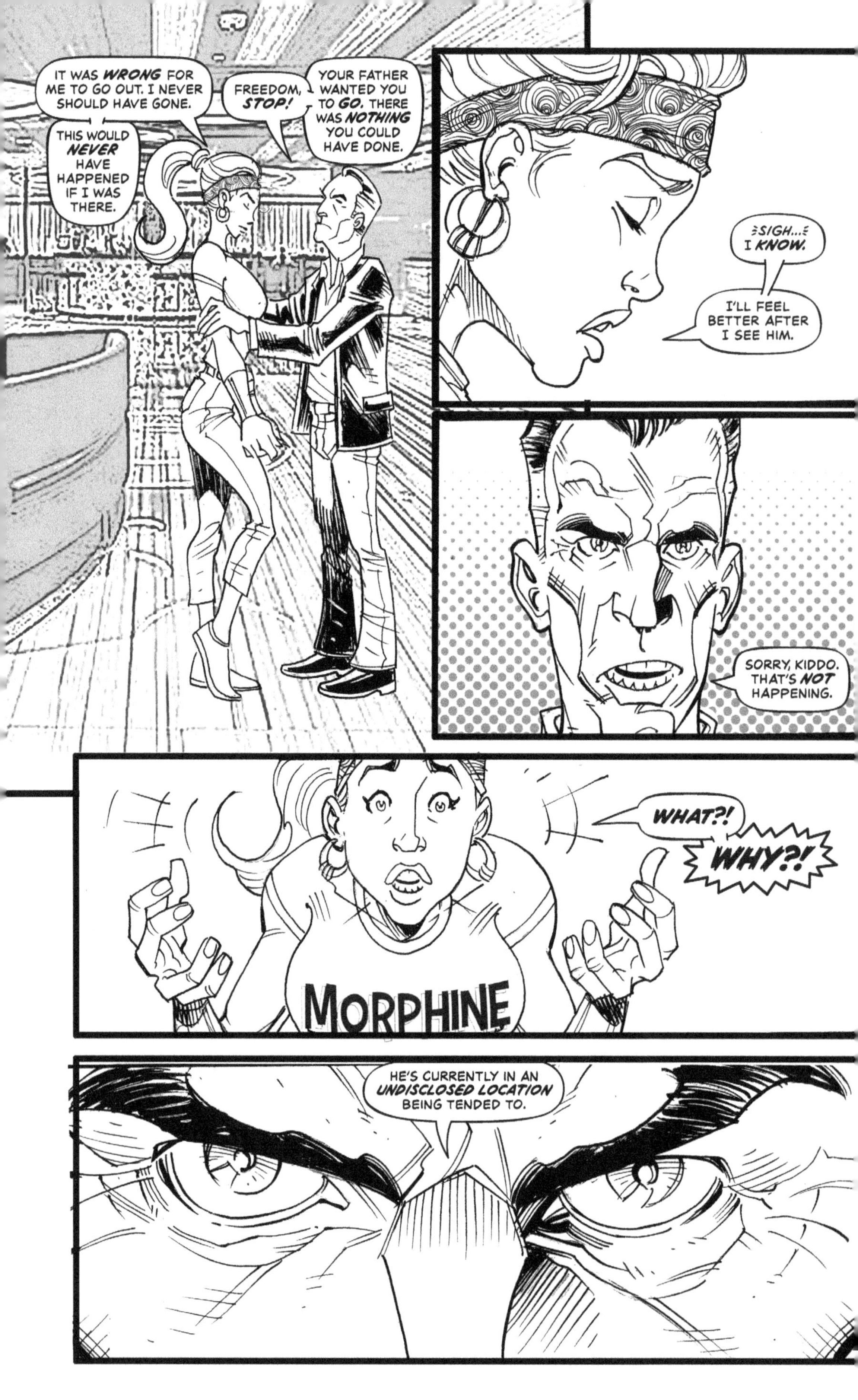
IT WAS WRONG FOR ME TO GO OUT. I NEVER SHOULD HAVE GONE.
THIS WOULD NEVER HAVE HAPPENED IF I WAS THERE.
FREEDOM, STOP!
YOUR FATHER WANTED YOU TO GO. THERE WAS NOTHING YOU COULD HAVE DONE.
SIGH... I KNOW.
I'LL FEEL BETTER AFTER I SEE HIM.
SORRY, KIDDO. THAT'S NOT HAPPENING.
WHAT?!
WHY?!
MORPHINE
HE'S CURRENTLY IN AN UNDISCLOSED LOCATION BEING TENDED TO.

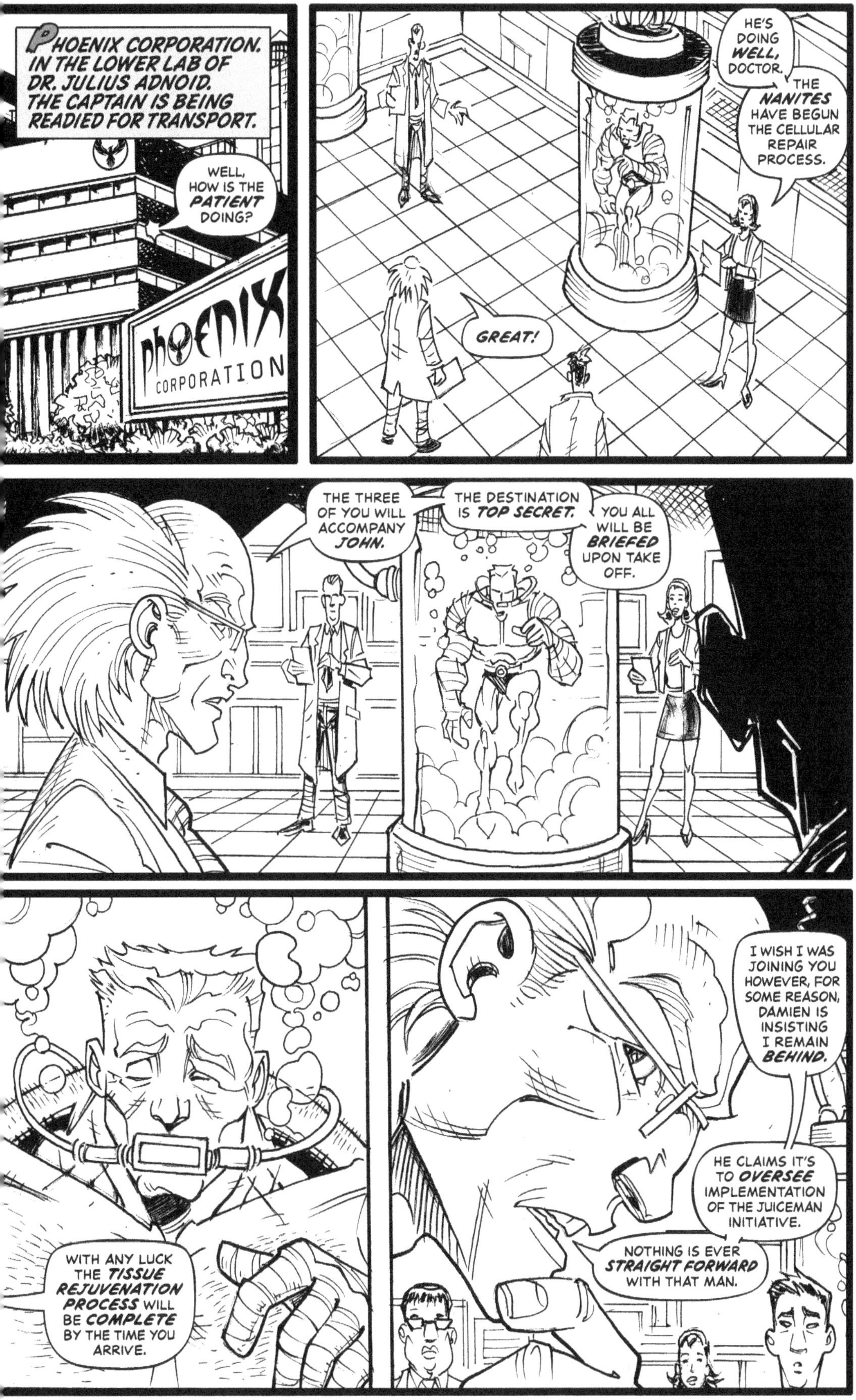

PHOENIX CORPORATION. IN THE LOWER LAB OF DR. JULIUS ADNOID. THE CAPTAIN IS BEING READIED FOR TRANSPORT.
PHOENIX CORPORATION
WELL, HOW IS THE PATIENT DOING?
HE'S DOING WELL, DOCTOR.
THE NANITES HAVE BEGUN THE CELLULAR REPAIR PROCESS.
GREAT!
THE THREE OF YOU WILL ACCOMPANY JOHN.
THE DESTINATION IS TOP SECRET.
YOU ALL WILL BE BRIEFED UPON TAKE OFF.
WITH ANY LUCK THE TISSUE REJUVENATION PROCESS WILL BE COMPLETE BY THE TIME YOU ARRIVE.
I WISH I WAS JOINING YOU HOWEVER, FOR SOME REASON, DAMIEN IS INSISTING I REMAIN BEHIND.
HE CLAIMS IT'S TO OVERSEE IMPLEMENTATION OF THE JUICEMAN INITIATIVE.
NOTHING IS EVER STRAIGHT FORWARD WITH THAT MAN.

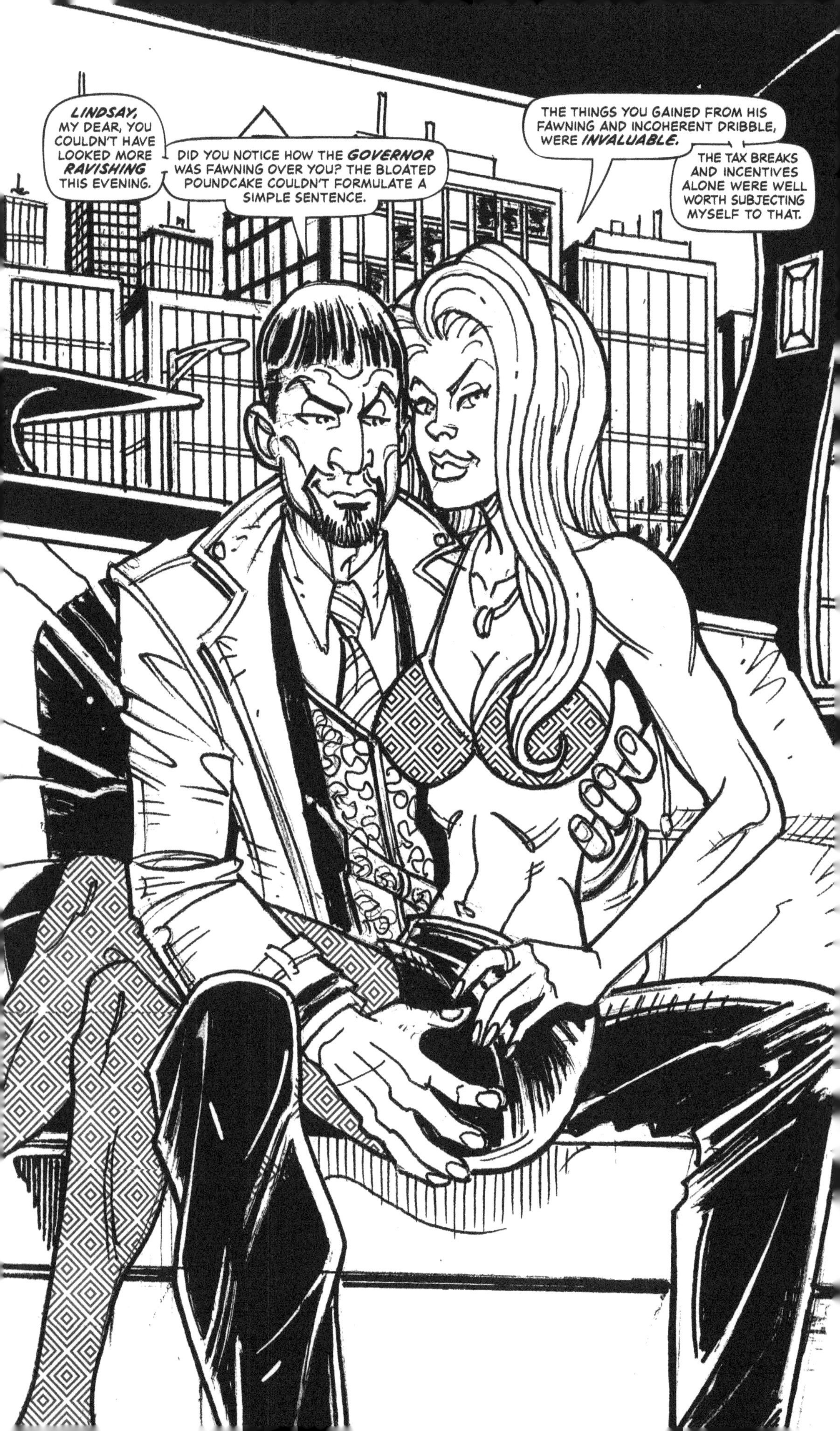
LINDSAY, MY DEAR, YOU COULDN'T HAVE LOOKED MORE RAVISHING THIS EVENING.
DID YOU NOTICE HOW THE GOVERNOR WAS FAWNING OVER YOU? THE BLOATED POUNDCAKE COULDN'T FORMULATE A SIMPLE SENTENCE.
THE THINGS YOU GAINED FROM HIS FAWNING AND INCOHERENT DRIBBLE, WERE INVALUABLE.
THE TAX BREAKS AND INCENTIVES ALONE WERE WELL WORTH SUBJECTING MYSELF TO THAT.

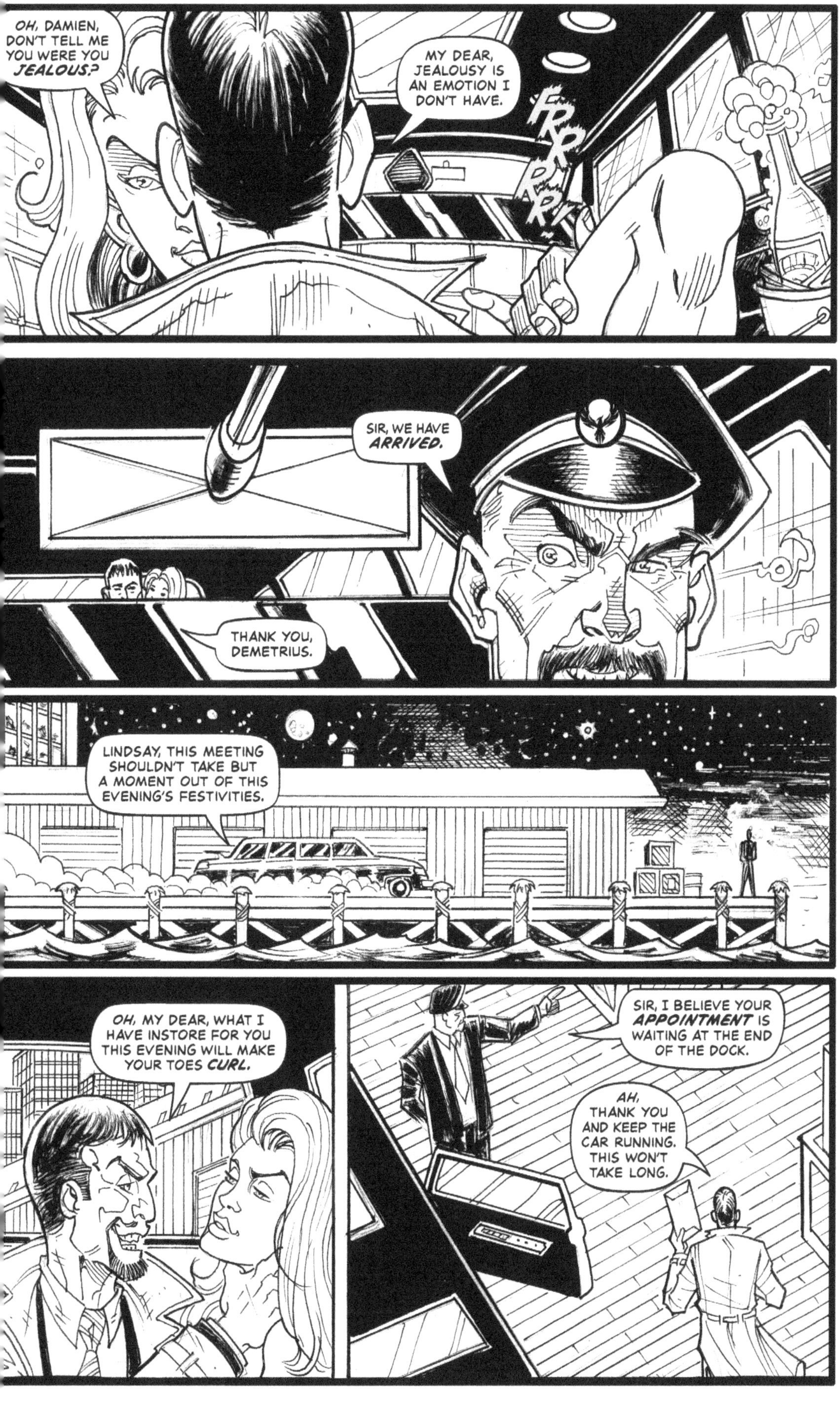
OH, DAMIEN, DON'T TELL ME YOU WERE YOU JEALOUS?
MY DEAR, JEALOUSY IS AN EMOTION I DON'T HAVE.
FRRRRR!
SIR, WE HAVE ARRIVED.
THANK YOU, DEMETRIUS.
LINDSAY, THIS MEETING SHOULDN'T TAKE BUT A MOMENT OUT OF THIS EVENING'S FESTIVITIES.
OH, MY DEAR, WHAT I HAVE INSTORE FOR YOU THIS EVENING WILL MAKE YOUR TOES CURL.
SIR, I BELIEVE YOUR APPOINTMENT IS WAITING AT THE END OF THE DOCK.
AH, THANK YOU AND KEEP THE CAR RUNNING. THIS WON'T TAKE LONG.

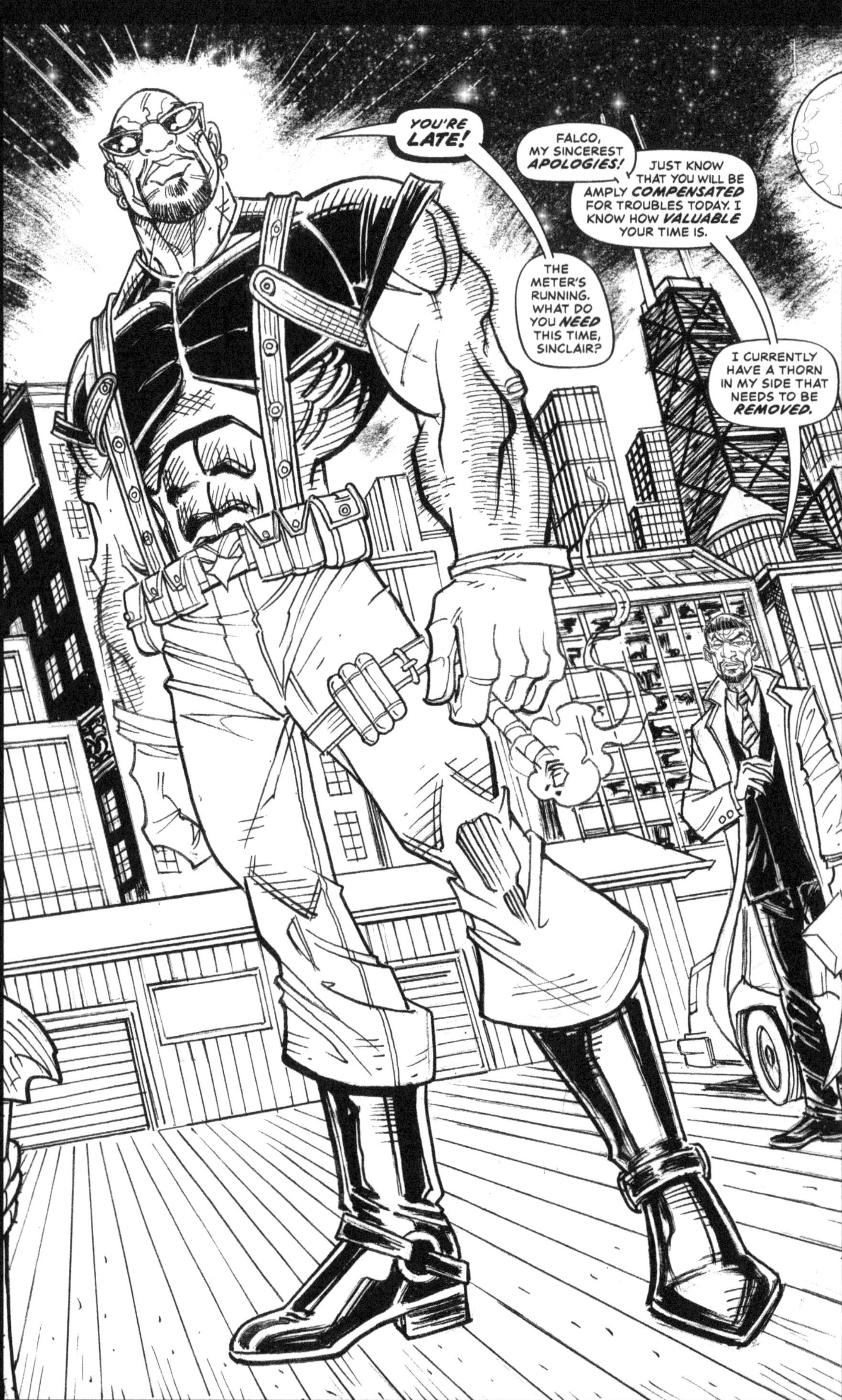
YOU'RE LATE!
THE METER'S RUNNING. WHAT DO YOU NEED THIS TIME, SINCLAIR?
FALCO, MY SINCEREST APOLOGIES!
JUST KNOW THAT YOU WILL BE AMPLY COMPENSATED FOR TROUBLES TODAY. I KNOW HOW VALUABLE YOUR TIME IS.
I CURRENTLY HAVE A THORN IN MY SIDE THAT NEEDS TO BE REMOVED.

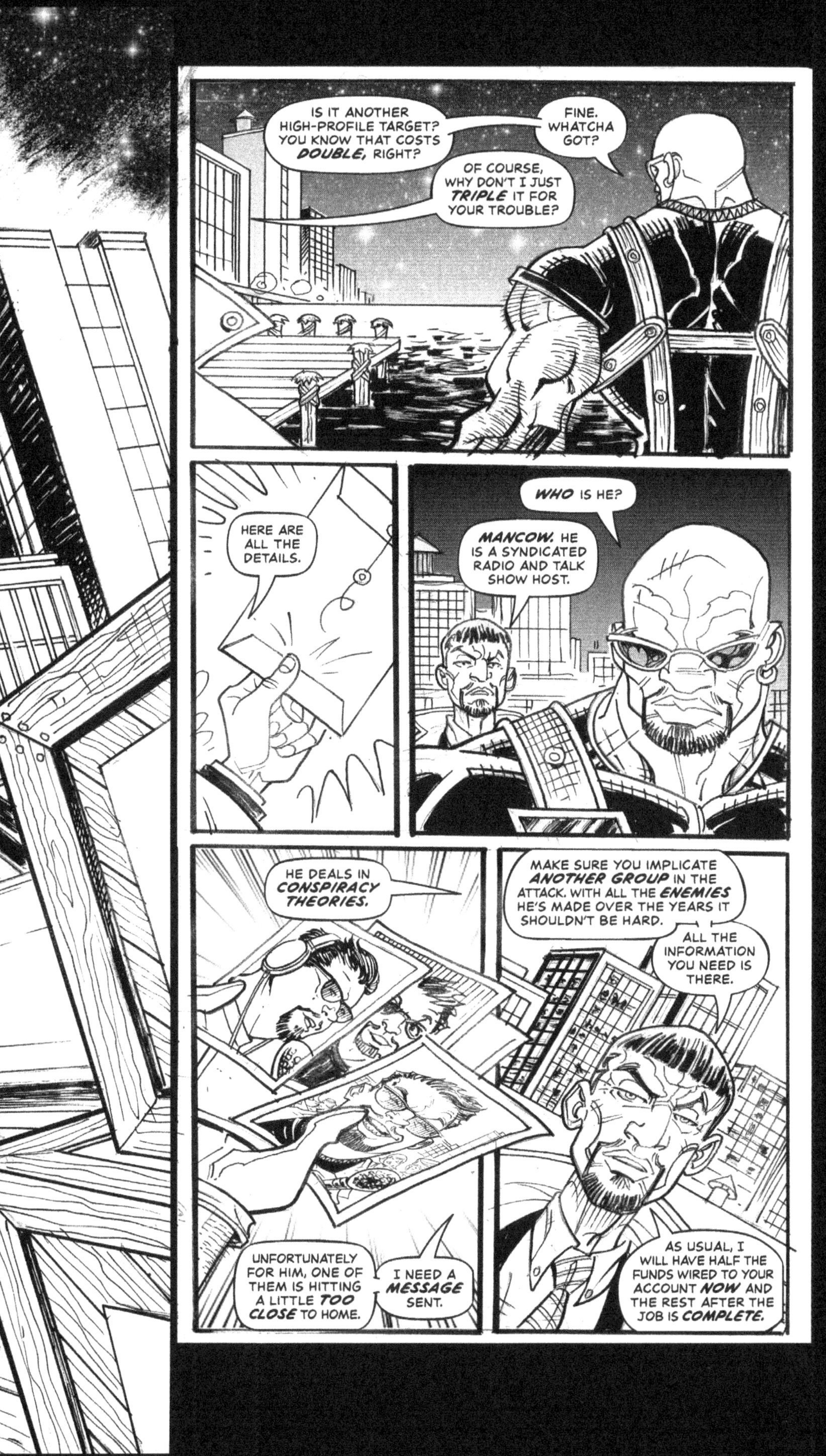

IS IT ANOTHER HIGH-PROFILE TARGET? YOU KNOW THAT COSTS DOUBLE, RIGHT?
FINE. WHATCHA GOT?
OF COURSE, WHY DON'T I JUST TRIPLE IT FOR YOUR TROUBLE?
HERE ARE ALL THE DETAILS.
WHO IS HE?
MANCOW. HE IS A SYNDICATED RADIO AND TALK SHOW HOST.
HE DEALS IN CONSPIRACY THEORIES.
UNFORTUNATELY FOR HIM, ONE OF THEM IS HITTING A LITTLE TOO CLOSE TO HOME.
I NEED A MESSAGE SENT.
MAKE SURE YOU IMPLICATE ANOTHER GROUP IN THE ATTACK. WITH ALL THE ENEMIES HE'S MADE OVER THE YEARS IT SHOULDN'T BE HARD.
ALL THE INFORMATION YOU NEED IS THERE.
AS USUAL, I WILL HAVE HALF THE FUNDS WIRED TO YOUR ACCOUNT NOW AND THE REST AFTER THE JOB IS COMPLETE.

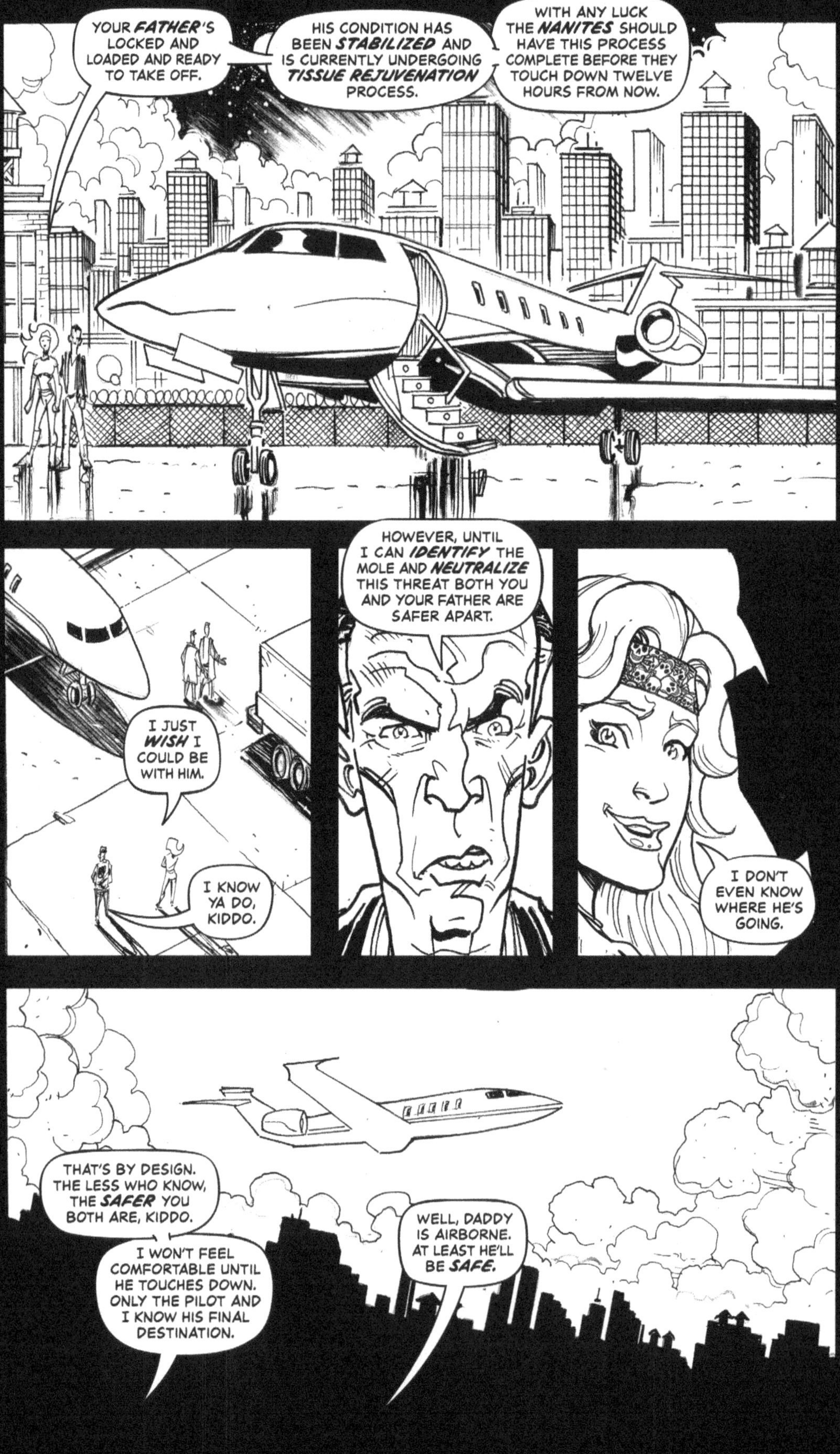
YOUR FATHER'S LOCKED AND LOADED AND READY TO TAKE OFF.
HIS CONDITION HAS BEEN STABILIZED AND IS CURRENTLY UNDERGOING TISSUE REJUVENATION PROCESS.
WITH ANY LUCK THE NANITES SHOULD HAVE THIS PROCESS COMPLETE BEFORE THEY TOUCH DOWN TWELVE HOURS FROM NOW.
I JUST WISH I COULD BE WITH HIM.
I KNOW YA DO, KIDDO.
HOWEVER, UNTIL I CAN IDENTIFY THE MOLE AND NEUTRALIZE THIS THREAT BOTH YOU AND YOUR FATHER ARE SAFER APART.
I DON'T EVEN KNOW WHERE HE'S GOING.
THAT'S BY DESIGN. THE LESS WHO KNOW, THE SAFER YOU BOTH ARE, KIDDO.
I WON'T FEEL COMFORTABLE UNTIL HE TOUCHES DOWN. ONLY THE PILOT AND I KNOW HIS FINAL DESTINATION.
WELL, DADDY IS AIRBORNE. AT LEAST HE'LL BE SAFE.

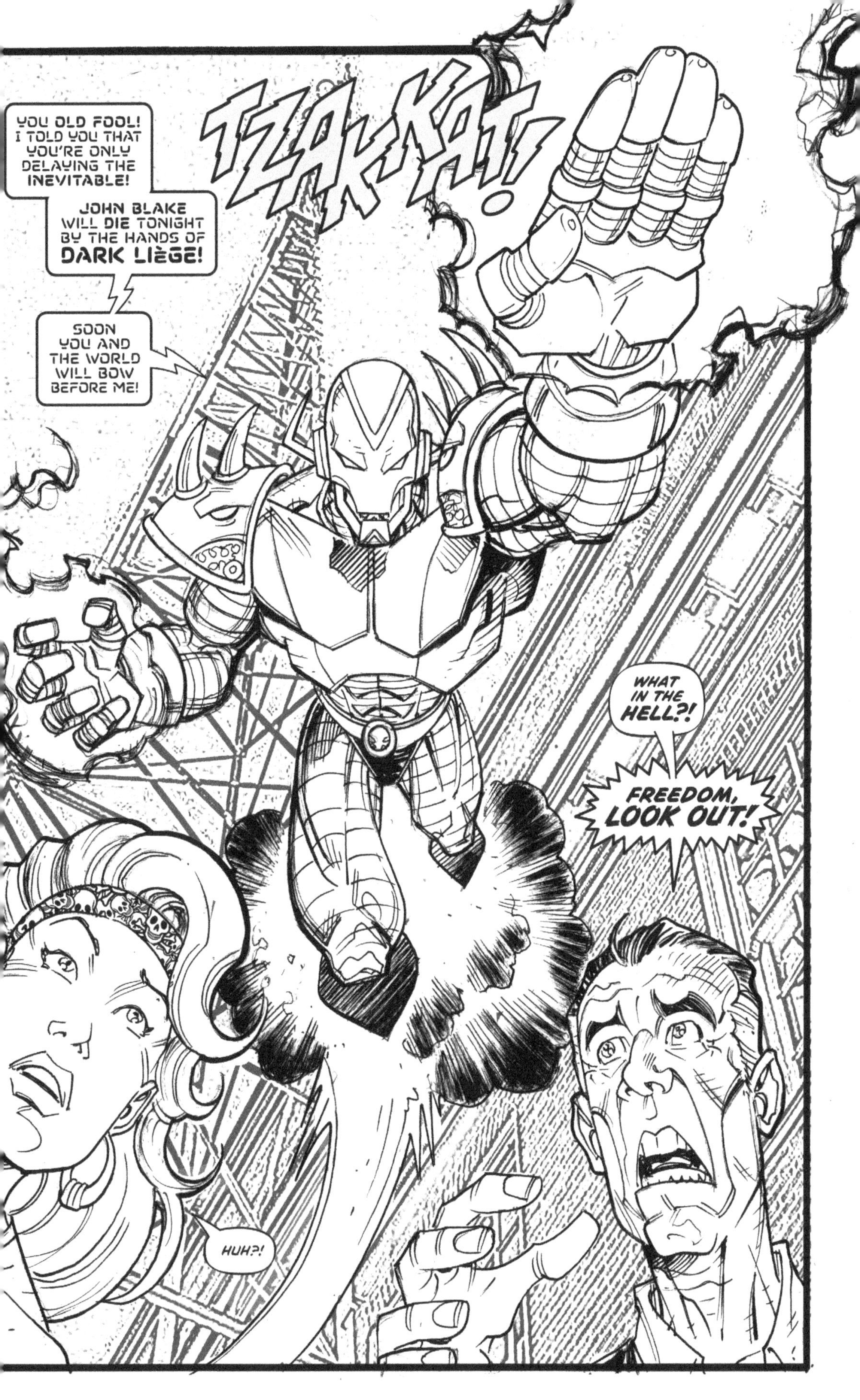

YOU OLD FOOL! I TOLD YOU THAT YOU'RE ONLY DELAYING THE INEVITABLE!
JOHN BLAKE WILL DIE TONIGHT BY THE HANDS OF DARK LIÈGE!
SOON YOU AND THE WORLD WILL BOW BEFORE ME!
TZAKKAT!
WHAT IN THE HELL?!
FREEDOM, LOOK OUT!
HUH?!

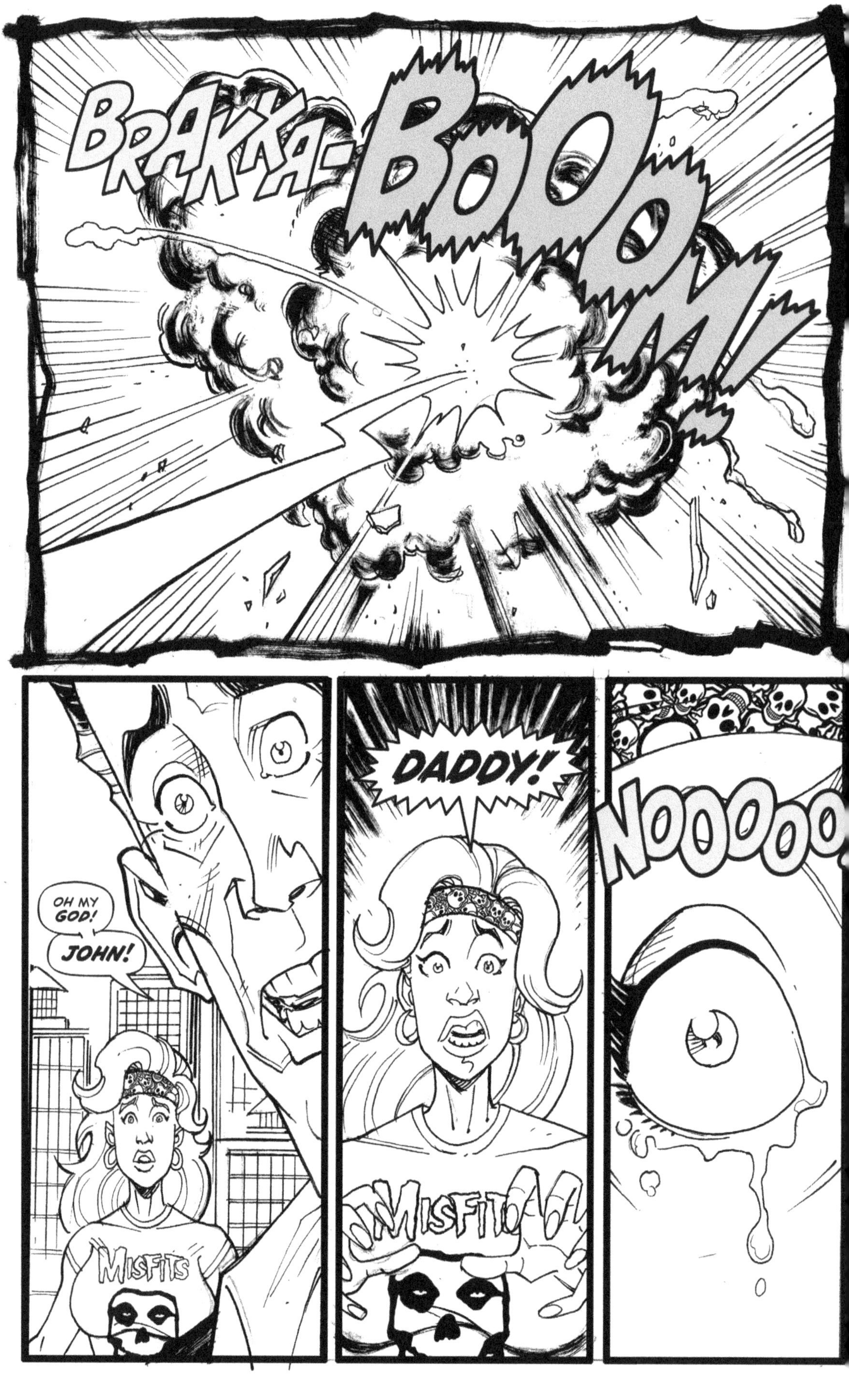
BRAKKA-BOOOM!
OH MY GOD!
JOHN!
DADDY!
NOOOOO
MISFITS
MISFITS

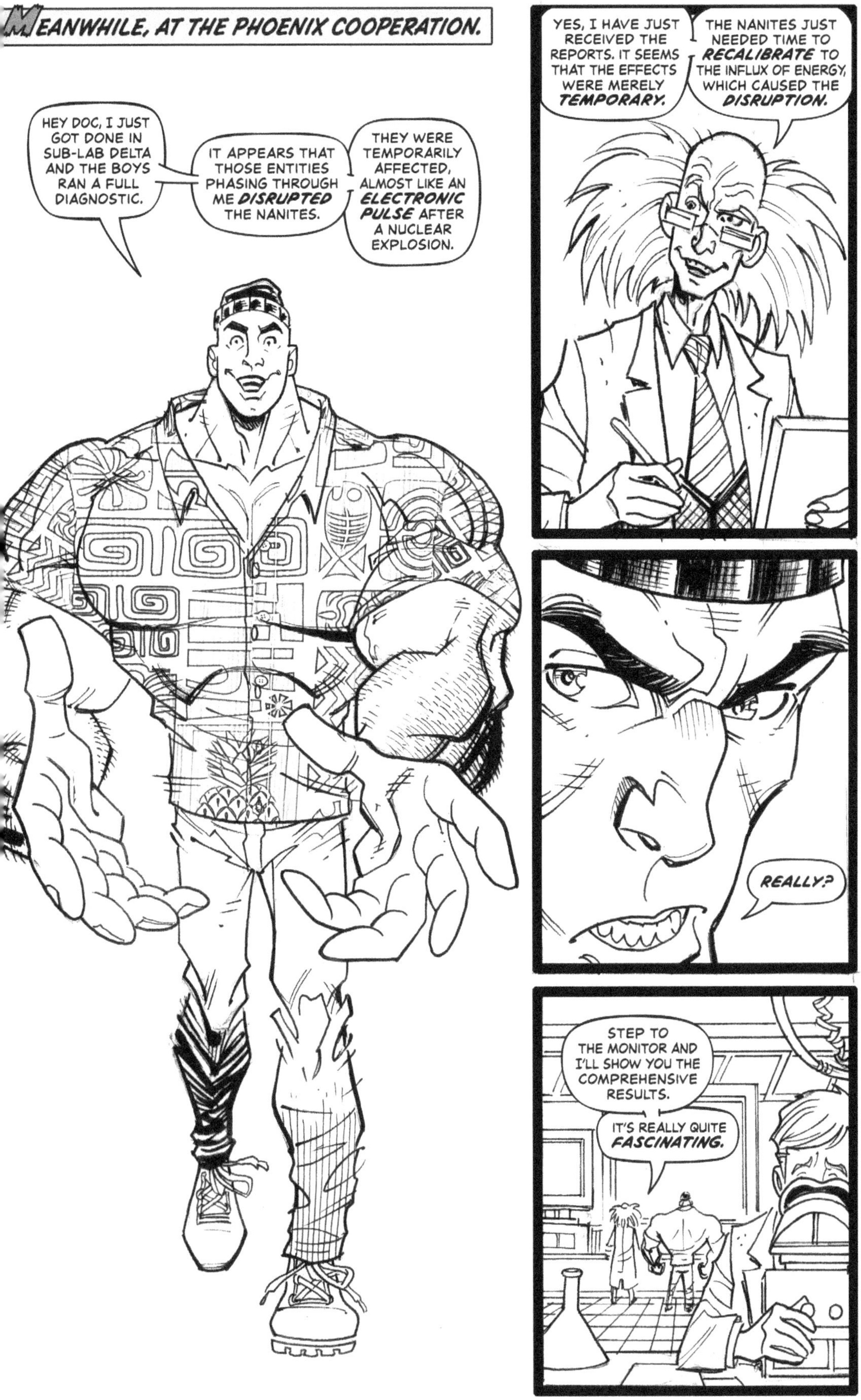
MEANWHILE, AT THE PHOENIX COOPERATION.
HEY DOC, I JUST GOT DONE IN SUB-LAB DELTA AND THE BOYS RAN A FULL DIAGNOSTIC.
IT APPEARS THAT THOSE ENTITIES PHASING THROUGH ME DISRUPTED THE NANITES.
THEY WERE TEMPORARILY AFFECTED, ALMOST LIKE AN ELECTRONIC PULSE AFTER A NUCLEAR EXPLOSION.
YES, I HAVE JUST RECEIVED THE REPORTS. IT SEEMS THAT THE EFFECTS WERE MERELY TEMPORARY.
THE NANITES JUST NEEDED TIME TO RECALIBRATE TO THE INFLUX OF ENERGY, WHICH CAUSED THE DISRUPTION.
REALLY?
STEP TO THE MONITOR AND I'LL SHOW YOU THE COMPREHENSIVE RESULTS.
IT'S REALLY QUITE FASCINATING.

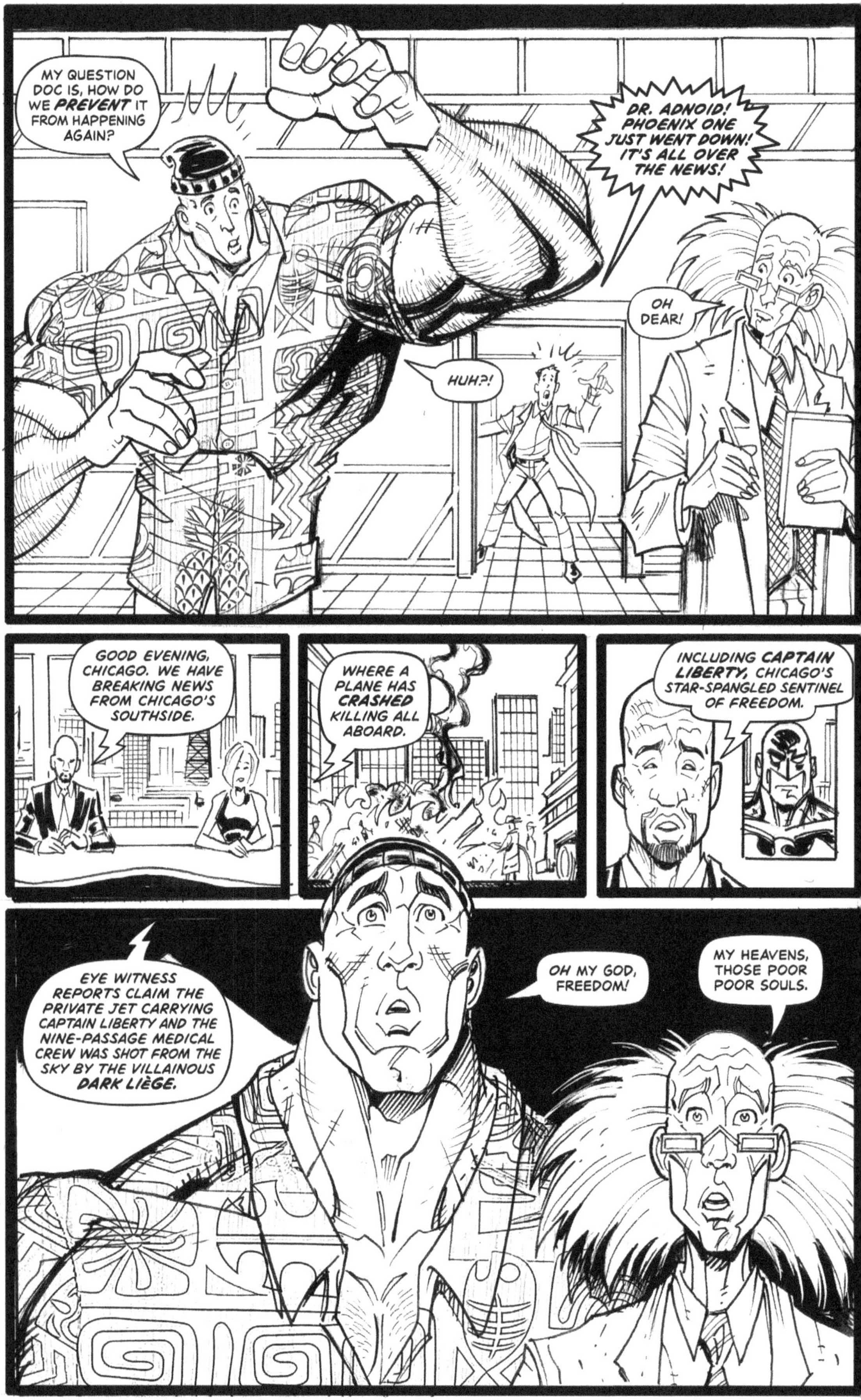
MY QUESTION DOC IS, HOW DO WE PREVENT IT FROM HAPPENING AGAIN?
DR. ADNOID! PHOENIX ONE JUST WENT DOWN! IT'S ALL OVER THE NEWS!
HUH?!
OH DEAR!
GOOD EVENING, CHICAGO. WE HAVE BREAKING NEWS FROM CHICAGO'S SOUTHSIDE.
WHERE A PLANE HAS CRASHED KILLING ALL ABOARD.
INCLUDING CAPTAIN LIBERTY, CHICAGO'S STAR-SPANGLED SENTINEL OF FREEDOM.
EYE WITNESS REPORTS CLAIM THE PRIVATE JET CARRYING CAPTAIN LIBERTY AND THE NINE-PASSAGE MEDICAL CREW WAS SHOT FROM THE SKY BY THE VILLAINOUS DARK LIÈGE.
OH MY GOD, FREEDOM!
MY HEAVENS, THOSE POOR POOR SOULS.

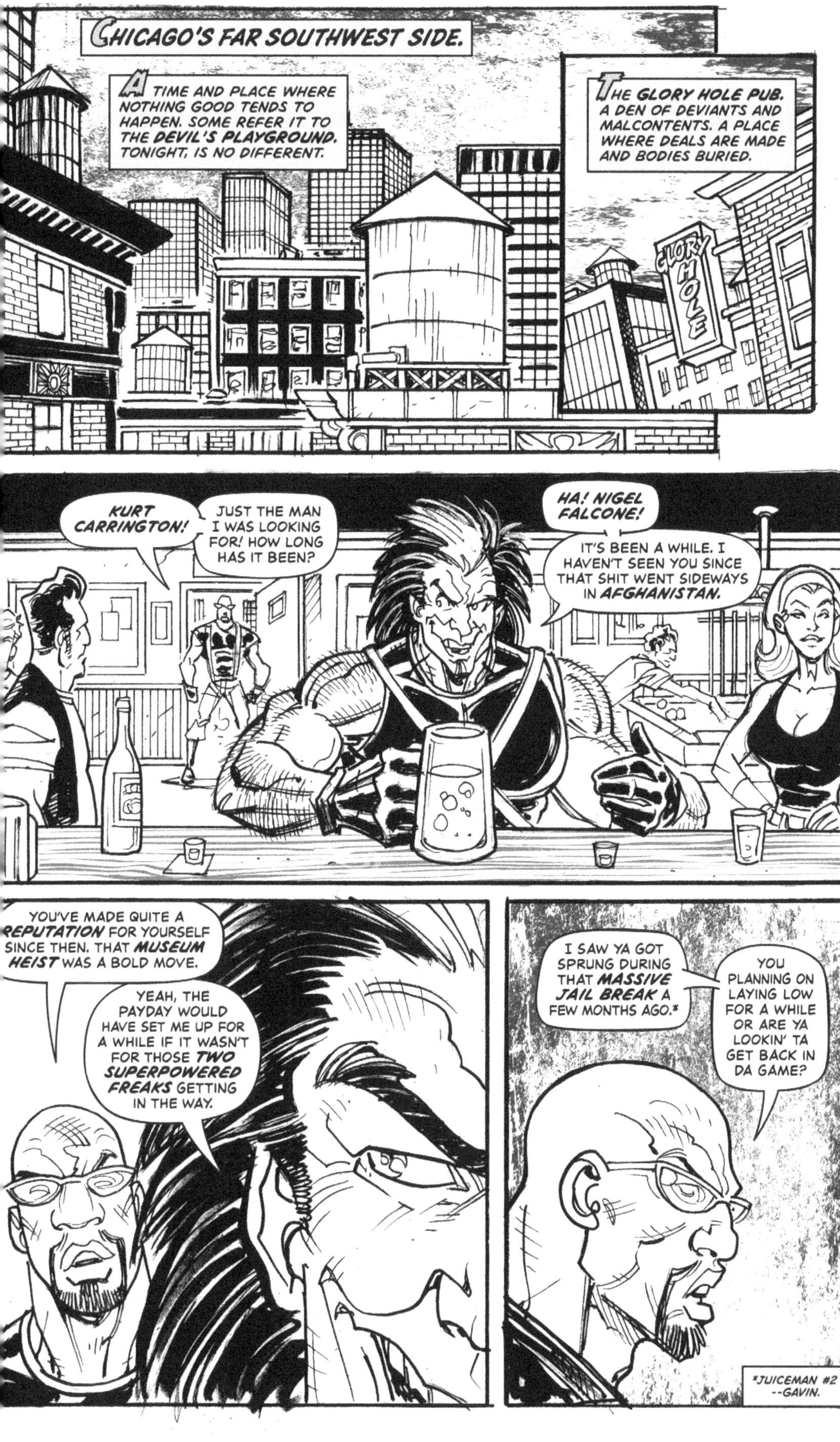

CHICAGO'S FAR SOUTHWEST SIDE.
A TIME AND PLACE WHERE NOTHING GOOD TENDS TO HAPPEN. SOME REFER IT TO THE DEVIL'S PLAYGROUND. TONIGHT, IS NO DIFFERENT.
THE GLORY HOLE PUB. A DEN OF DEVIANTS AND MALCONTENTS. A PLACE WHERE DEALS ARE MADE AND BODIES BURIED.
GLORY HOLE
KURT CARRINGTON!
JUST THE MAN I WAS LOOKING FOR! HOW LONG HAS IT BEEN?
HA! NIGEL FALCONE!
IT'S BEEN A WHILE. I HAVEN'T SEEN YOU SINCE THAT SHIT WENT SIDEWAYS IN AFGHANISTAN.
YOU'VE MADE QUITE A REPUTATION FOR YOURSELF SINCE THEN. THAT MUSEUM HEIST WAS A BOLD MOVE.
YEAH, THE PAYDAY WOULD HAVE SET ME UP FOR A WHILE IF IT WASN'T FOR THOSE TWO SUPERPOWERED FREAKS GETTING IN THE WAY.
I SAW YA GOT SPRUNG DURING THAT MASSIVE JAIL BREAK A FEW MONTHS AGO.*
YOU PLANNING ON LAYING LOW FOR A WHILE OR ARE YA LOOKIN' TA GET BACK IN DA GAME?
*JUICEMAN #2 --GAVIN.

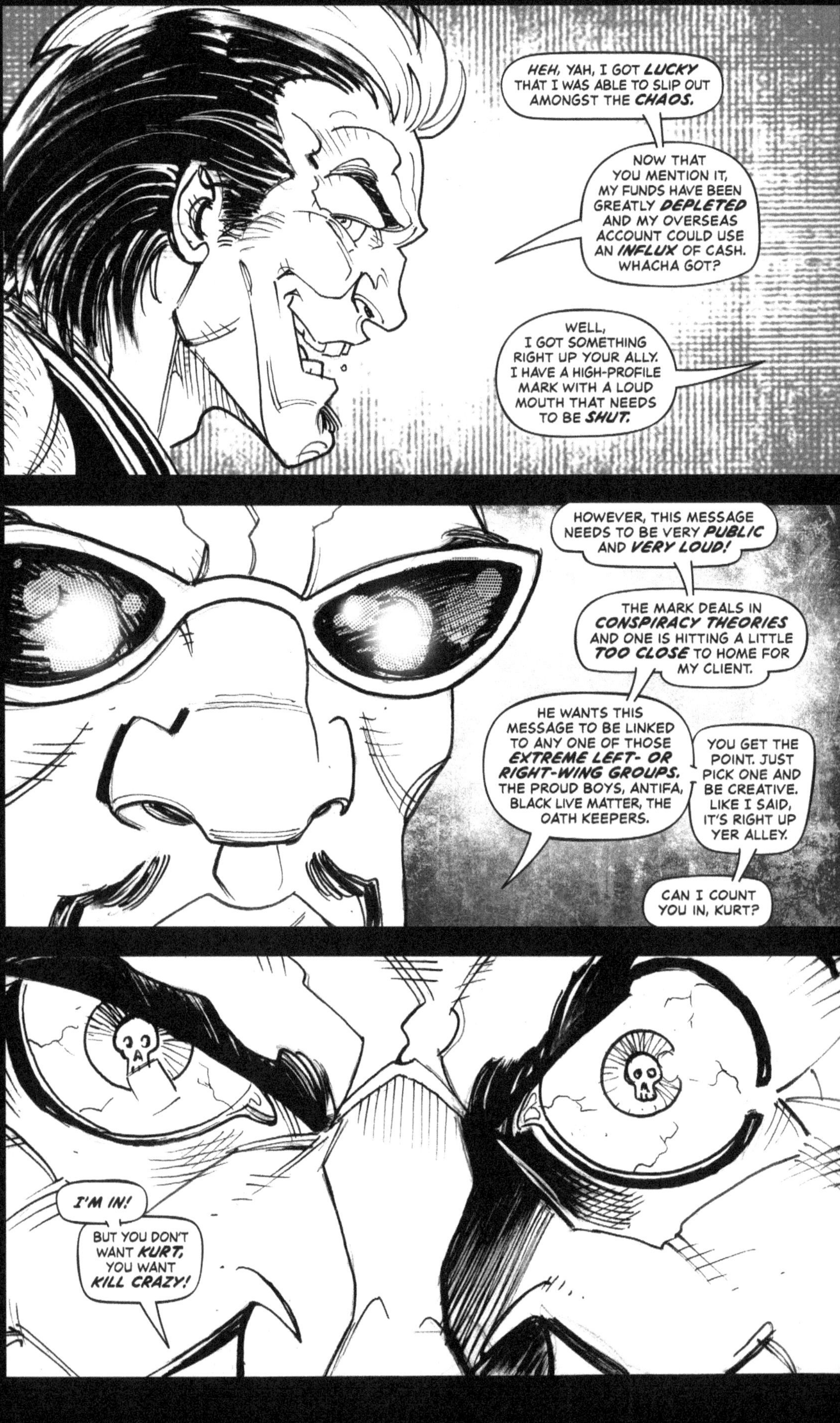
HEH, YAH, I GOT LUCKY THAT I WAS ABLE TO SLIP OUT AMONGST THE CHAOS.
NOW THAT YOU MENTION IT, MY FUNDS HAVE BEEN GREATLY DEPLETED AND MY OVERSEAS ACCOUNT COULD USE AN INFLUX OF CASH. WHACHA GOT?
WELL, I GOT SOMETHING RIGHT UP YOUR ALLY. I HAVE A HIGH-PROFILE MARK WITH A LOUD MOUTH THAT NEEDS TO BE SHUT.
HOWEVER, THIS MESSAGE NEEDS TO BE VERY PUBLIC AND VERY LOUD!
THE MARK DEALS IN CONSPIRACY THEORIES AND ONE IS HITTING A LITTLE TOO CLOSE TO HOME FOR MY CLIENT.
HE WANTS THIS MESSAGE TO BE LINKED TO ANY ONE OF THOSE EXTREME LEFT- OR RIGHT-WING GROUPS. THE PROUD BOYS, ANTIFA, BLACK LIVE MATTER, THE OATH KEEPERS.
YOU GET THE POINT. JUST PICK ONE AND BE CREATIVE. LIKE I SAID, IT'S RIGHT UP YER ALLEY.
CAN I COUNT YOU IN, KURT?
I'M IN!
BUT YOU DON'T WANT KURT, YOU WANT KILL CRAZY!

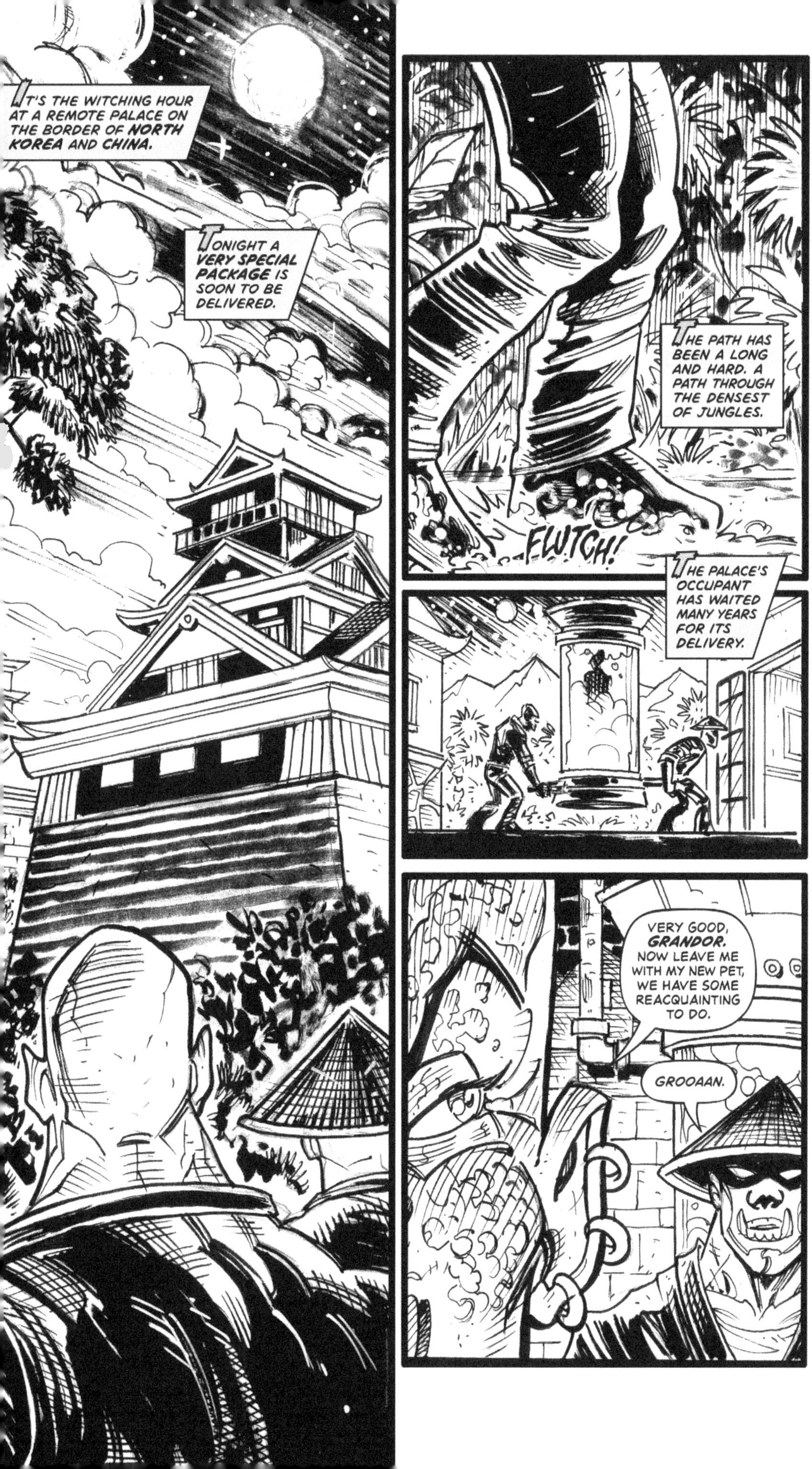
IT'S THE WITCHING HOUR AT A REMOTE PALACE ON THE BORDER OF NORTH KOREA AND CHINA.
TONIGHT A VERY SPECIAL PACKAGE IS SOON TO BE DELIVERED.
THE PATH HAS BEEN A LONG AND HARD. A PATH THROUGH THE DENSEST OF JUNGLES.
FLUTCH!
THE PALACE'S OCCUPANT HAS WAITED MANY YEARS FOR ITS DELIVERY.
VERY GOOD, GRANDOR. NOW LEAVE ME WITH MY NEW PET, WE HAVE SOME REACQUAINTING TO DO.
GROOAAN.

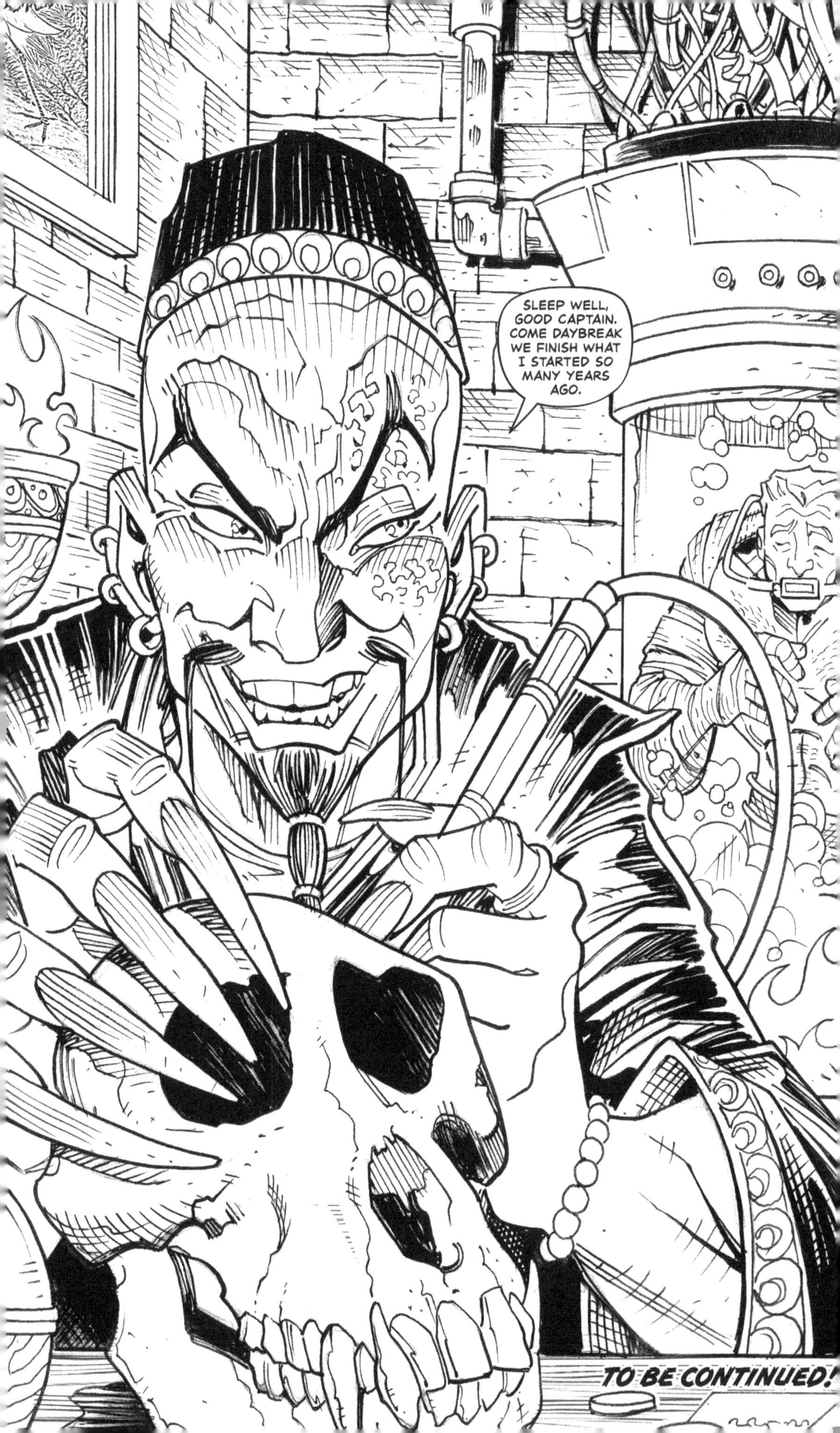
SLEEP WELL, GOOD CAPTAIN. COME DAYBREAK WE FINISH WHAT I STARTED SO MANY YEARS AGO.
TO BE CONTINUED!

THE JUICEBOX

Juiceman was the creation of an art school student with a love of comics. He was conceived one day in art class. A fellow classmate and I joked about all of the guys on campus that forgot leg day at the gym. I called them Juice men and the name stuck. I found the proportions fun to draw. So I littered my sketchbook with Juiceman and the rest of the would-be cast. Soon Freedom, Badger, Cass (She-Blob), Kid Comet, Dutch, and Captain Liberty were born along with a whole slew of bad guys as well.

Next came the hard part. I had the designs, I just needed an origin. Why did Juice have these proportions? I thought of those who were wheelchair-bound and how their legs often suffered severe atrophy. So I came up with that Zach (Juiceman) was paralyzed in high school and turned to his academics. He was awarded a science scholarship and subsequent internship with the Phoenix Corporation working under Dr. Julius Adnoid. Dr. Adnoid had developed a super serum with tissue rejuvenating properties. Zach saw a chance to regain the use of his legs in the hope to regain his life. Only it was more than he bargained for. He doesn't regain his old life, but starts a whole new one! Here is his story and here are my original charater sketches from 1991. Some have changed, However most have stayed true to the original design!

As a creator I have been fortunate to work with a multitude of talented artists. Some have been so gracious to include Juiceman into their independent projects. Raven Perez has been one of those whom have champione my work and projects.

I met Raven through our mutual love of Savage Dragon. He, James Purcell, and Craig Olsen produce the Savage Fincast. A podcast dedicated to all things Savage Dragon! I met the guys through doing a plethora of Savage Dragon work for Erik Larsen. I had done so many back-ups for the book they ask me to cohost from time to time.

For those not famillair with Ravens work here is a page from His Raven's DoJo featuring Juiceman! You can find his work on the inter-web at https://ravensdojo.com/

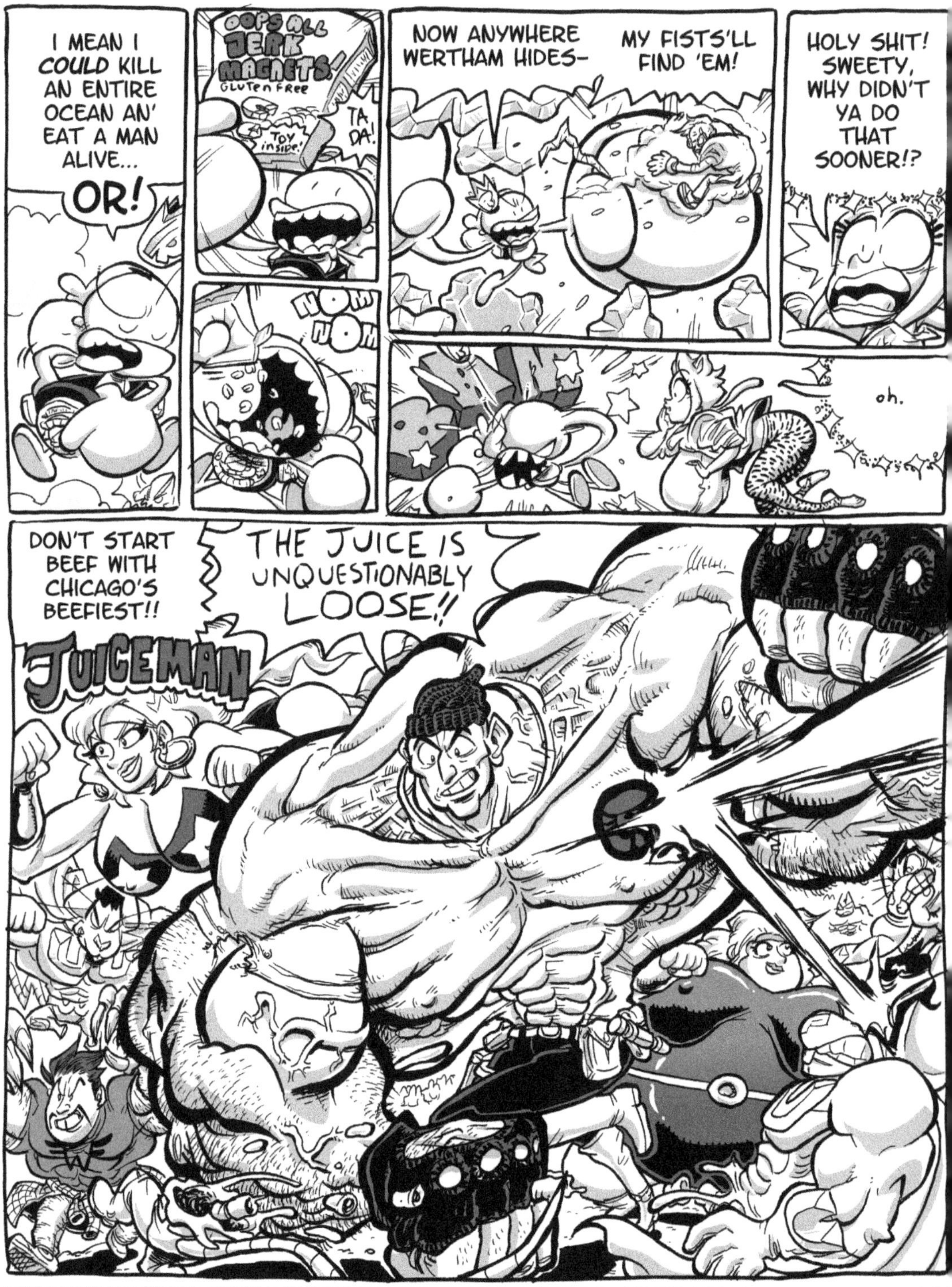

I MEAN I COULD KILL AN ENTIRE OCEAN AN' EAT A MAN ALIVE...
OR!
OOPS ALL JERK MAGNETS! GLUTEN FREE
TOY INSIDE!
TA DA!
NOM NOM
NOW ANYWHERE WERTHAM HIDES–
MY FISTS'LL FIND 'EM!
HOLY SHIT! SWEETY, WHY DIDN'T YA DO THAT SOONER!?
oh.
DON'T START BEEF WITH CHICAGO'S BEEFIEST!!
THE JUICE IS UNQUESTIONABLY LOOSE!!
JUICEMAN

As I have said before I have been blessed to have work with some great tallent! Chritopher Kloiber is one such talent. He publishes Tracht Man and has started publishing Juiceman in Germany! Juiceman has even made a breif appearance in his book! Here is a small snippet of that appearance.

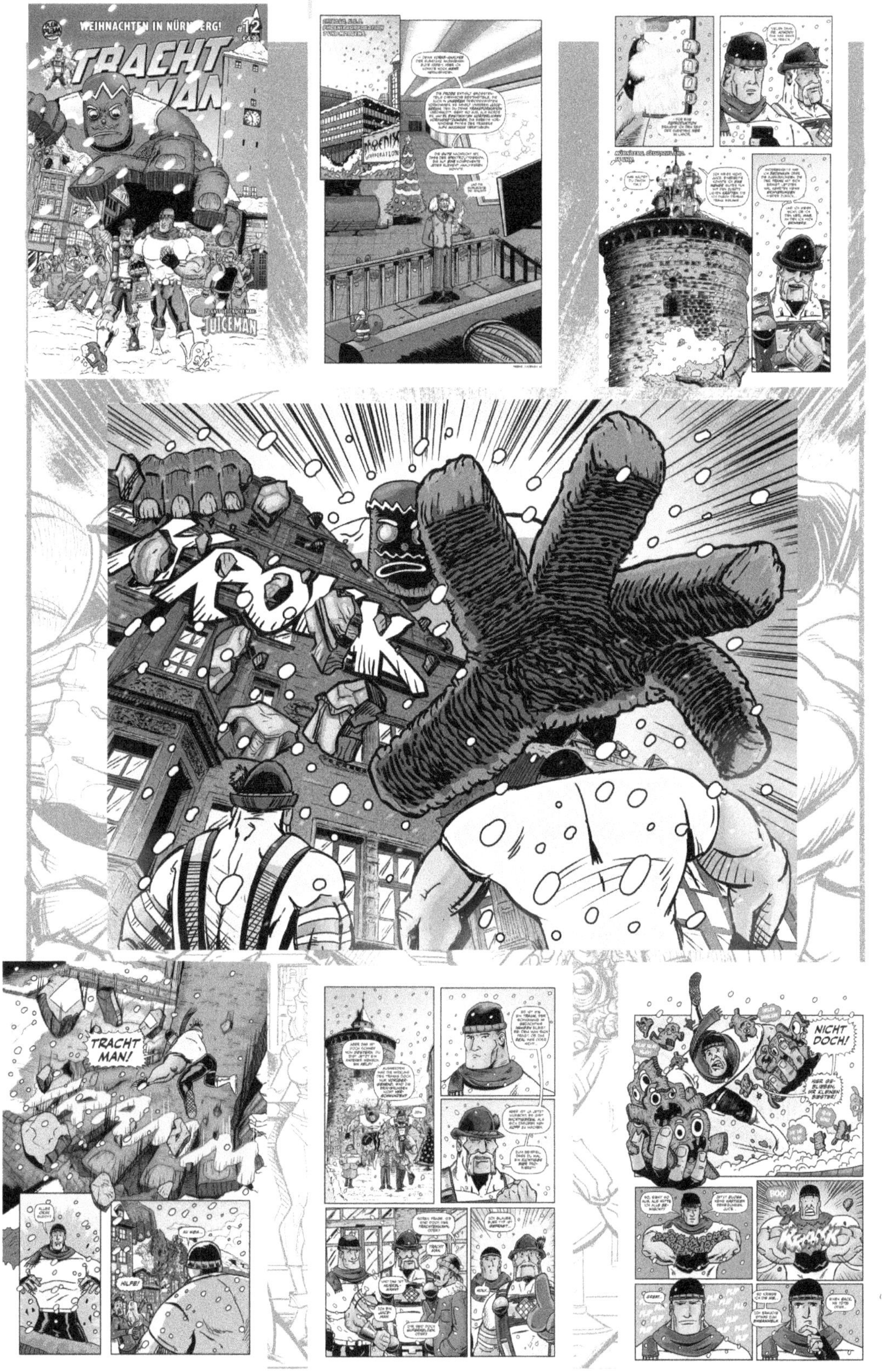

TRACHT MAN
#12
JUICEMAN
TRACHT MAN!
NICHT DOCH!

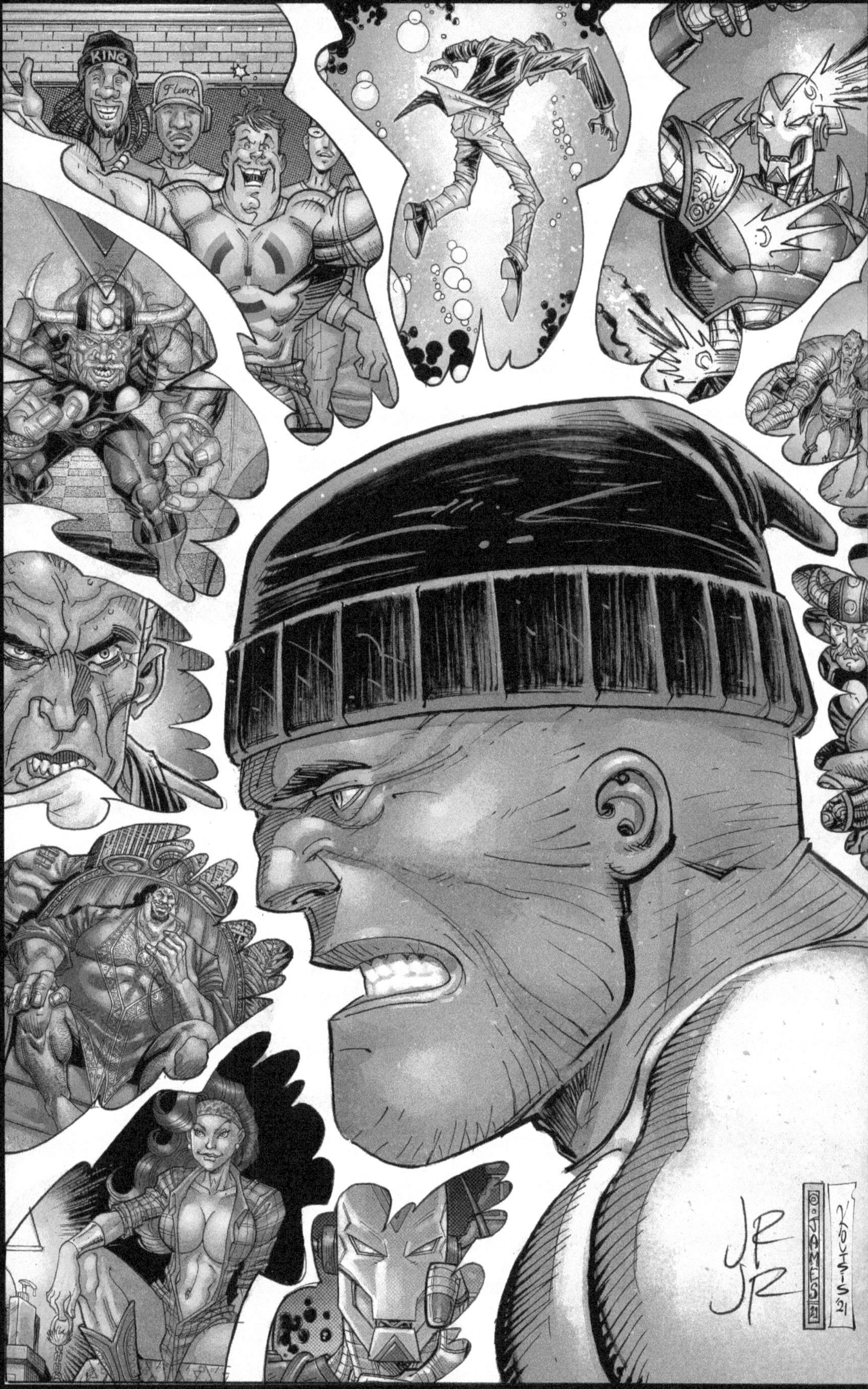
KING

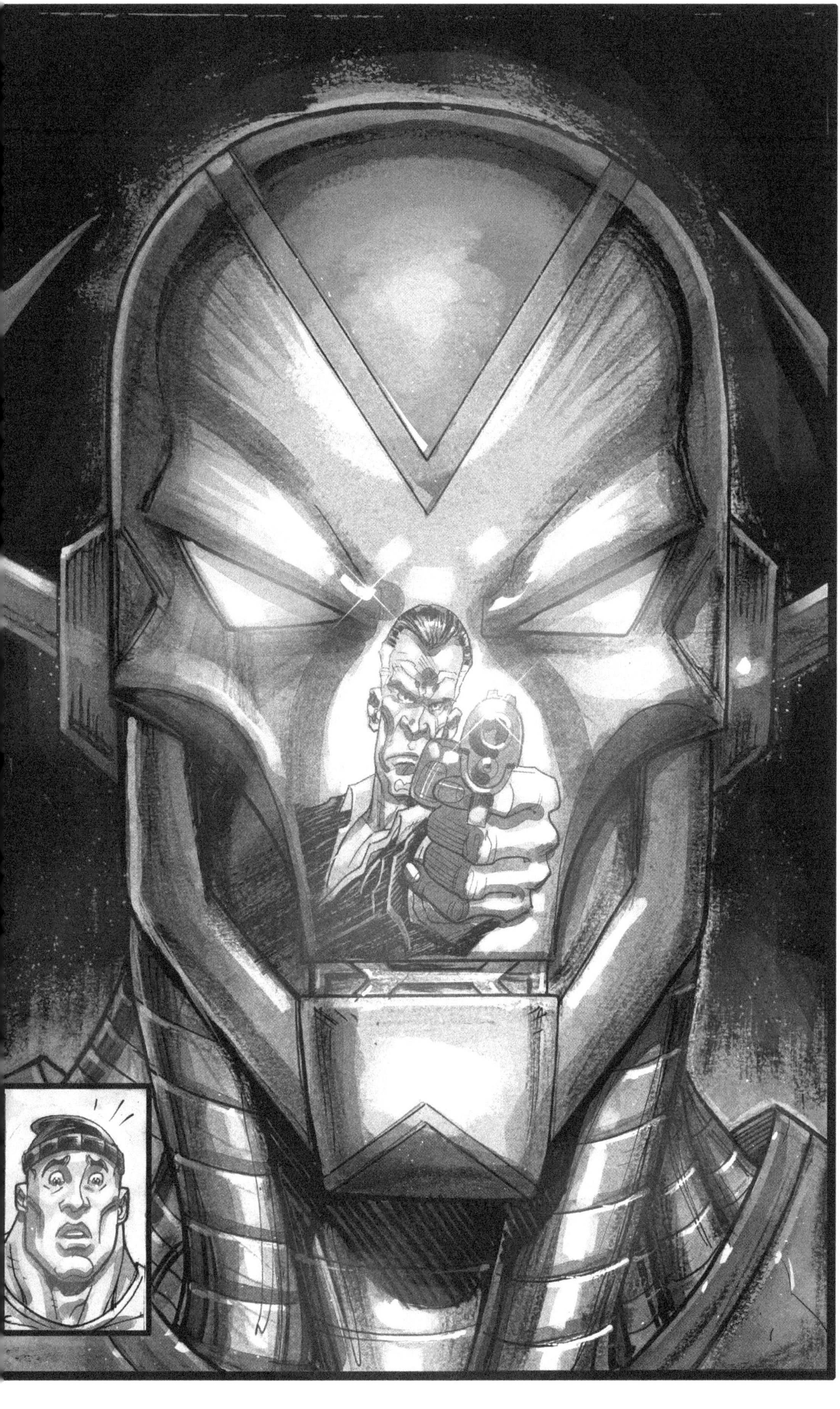

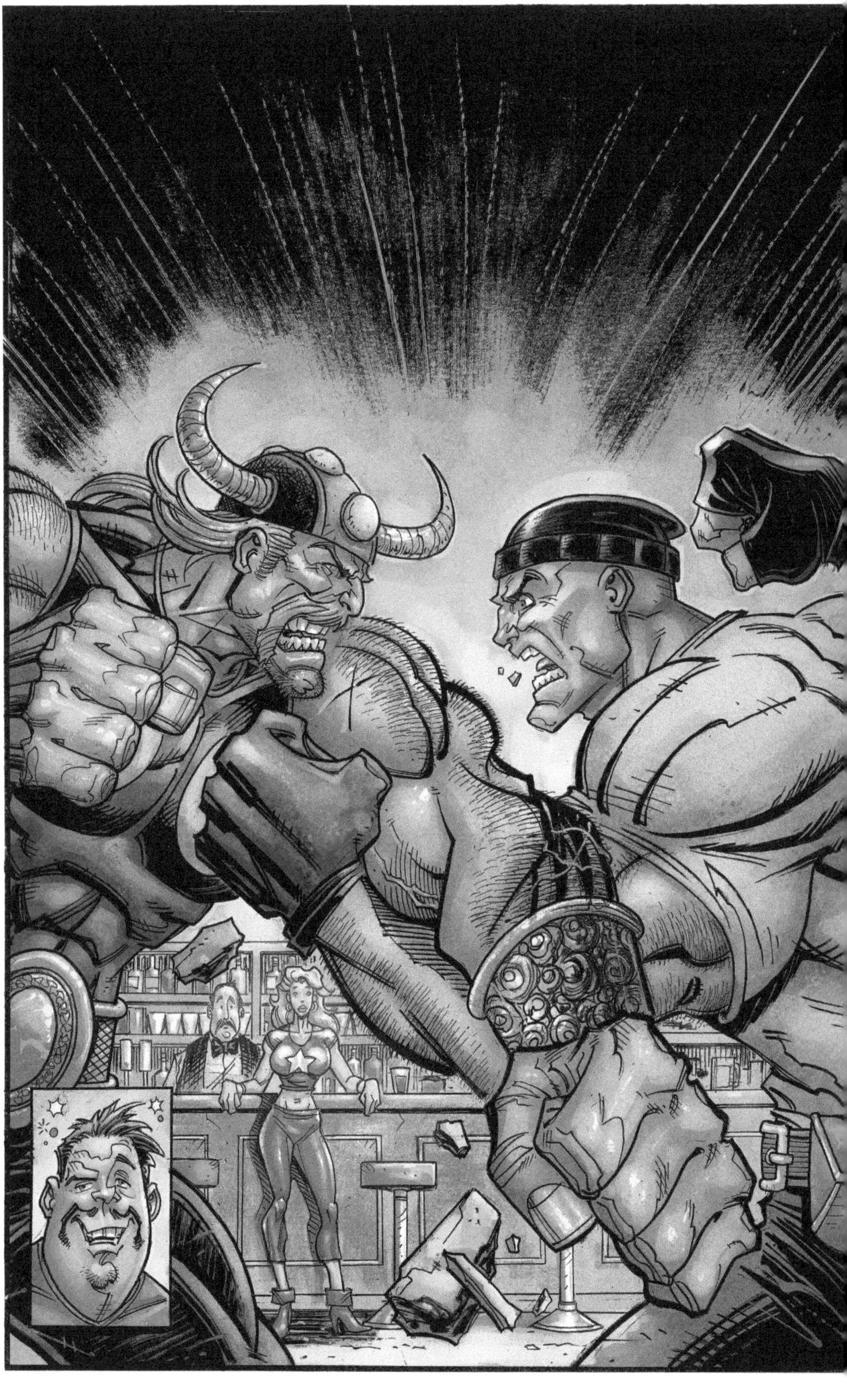

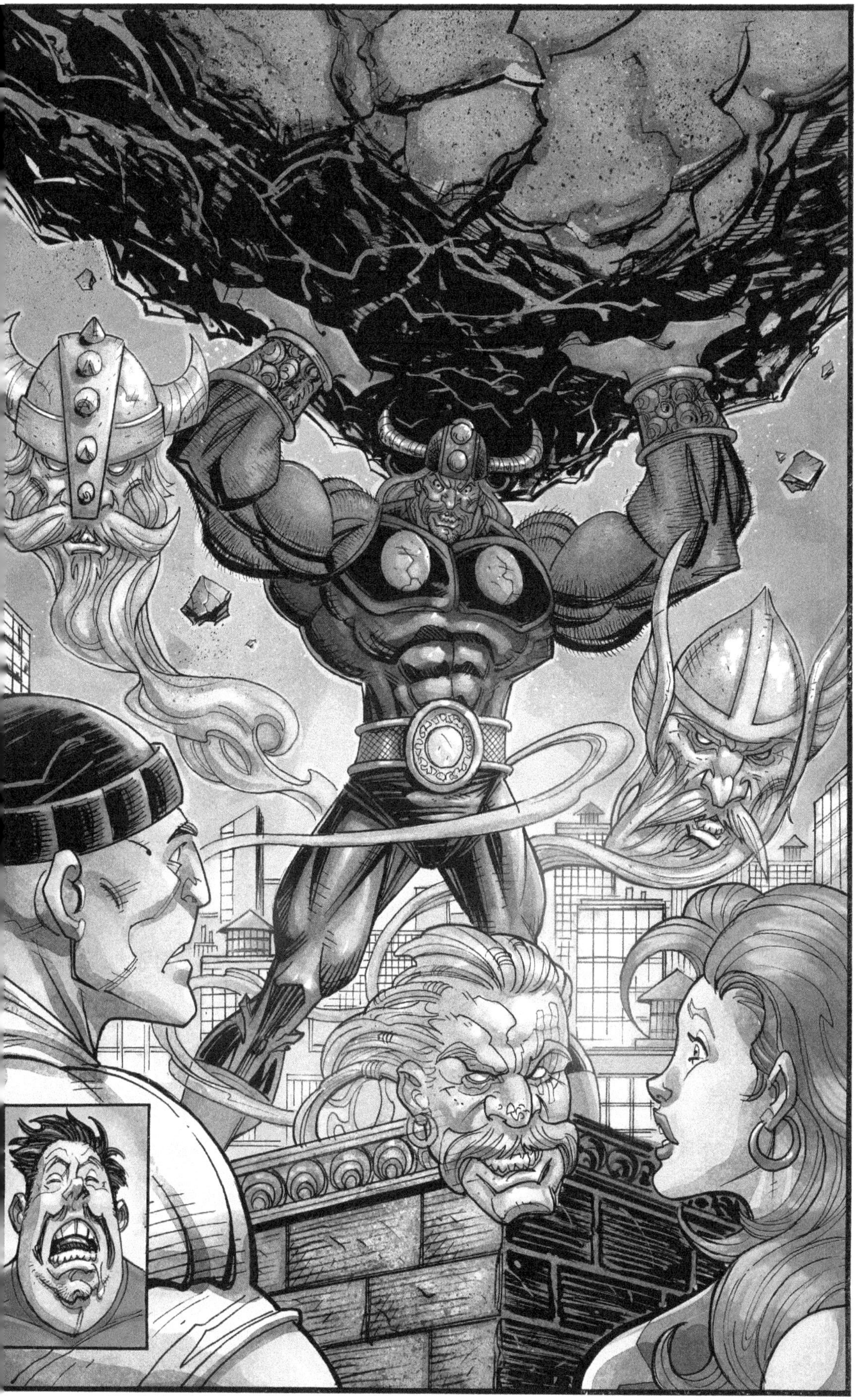

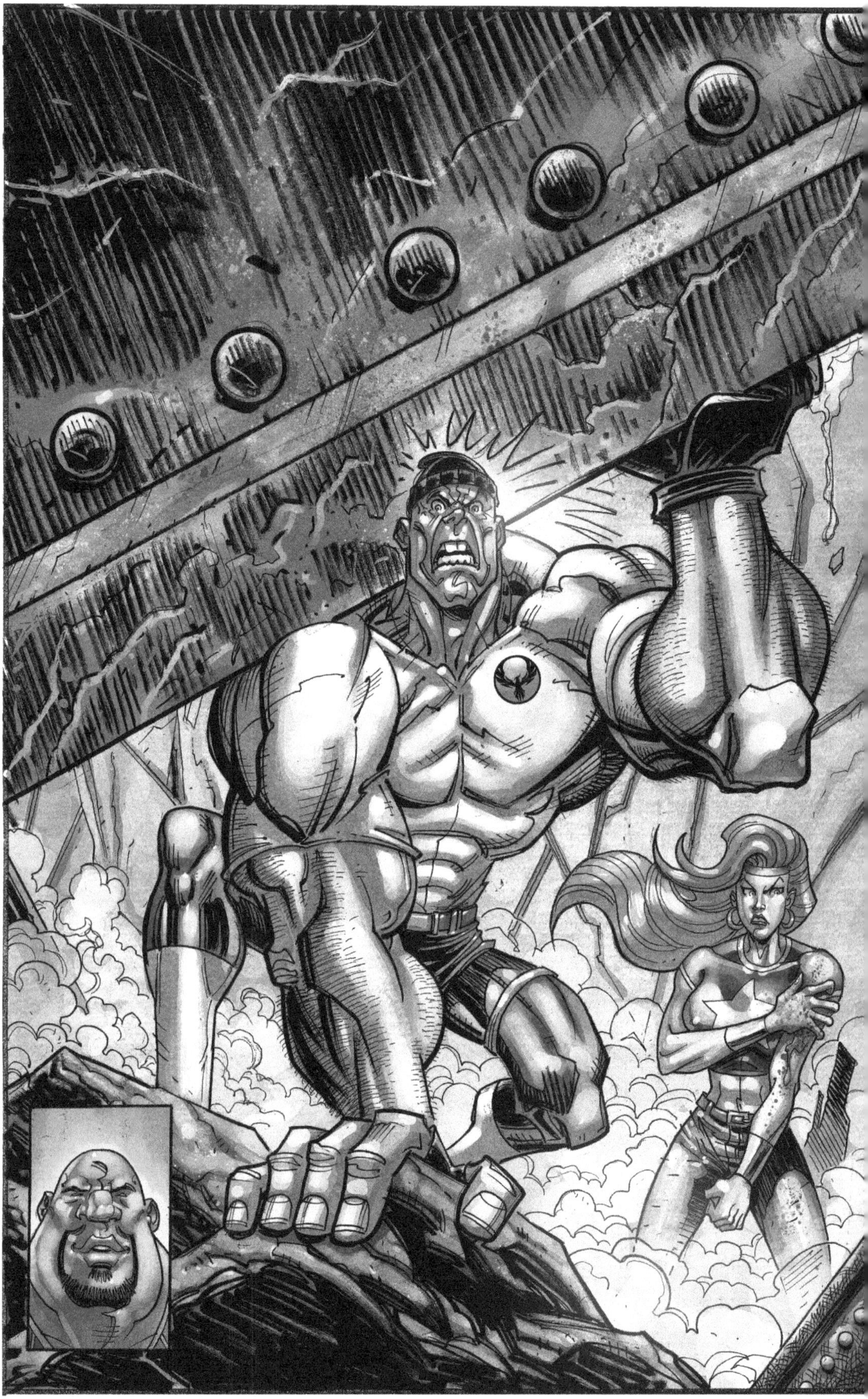

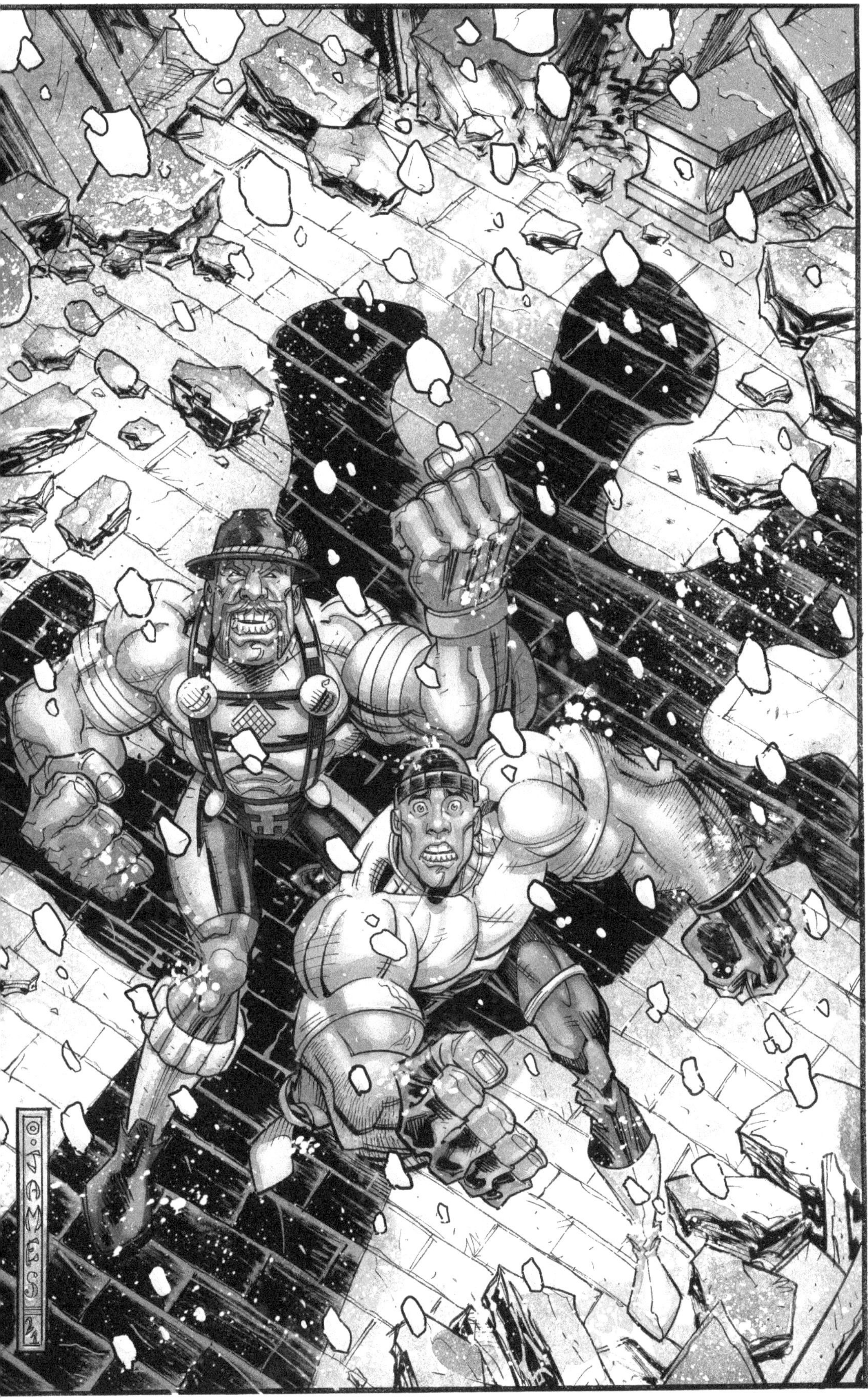

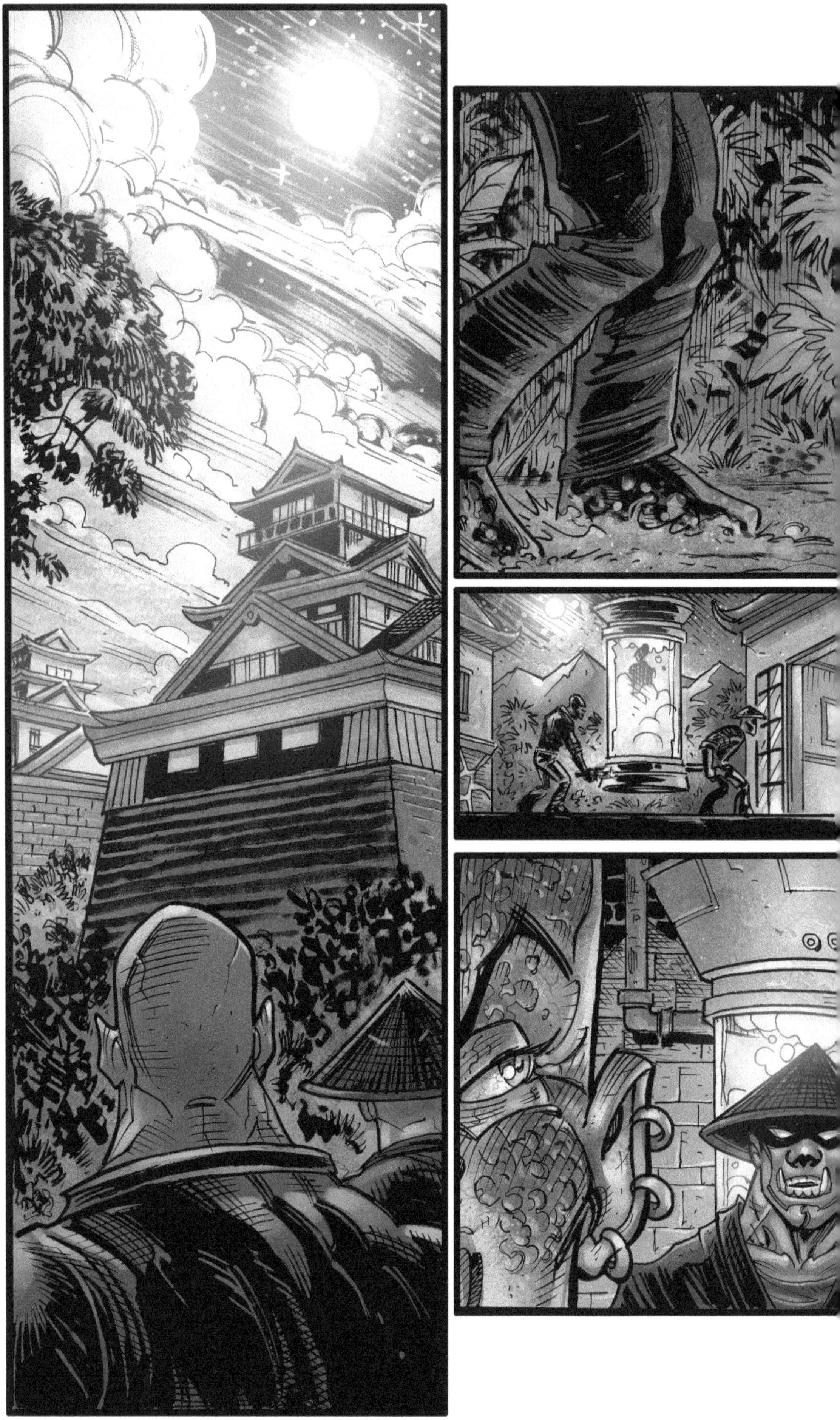

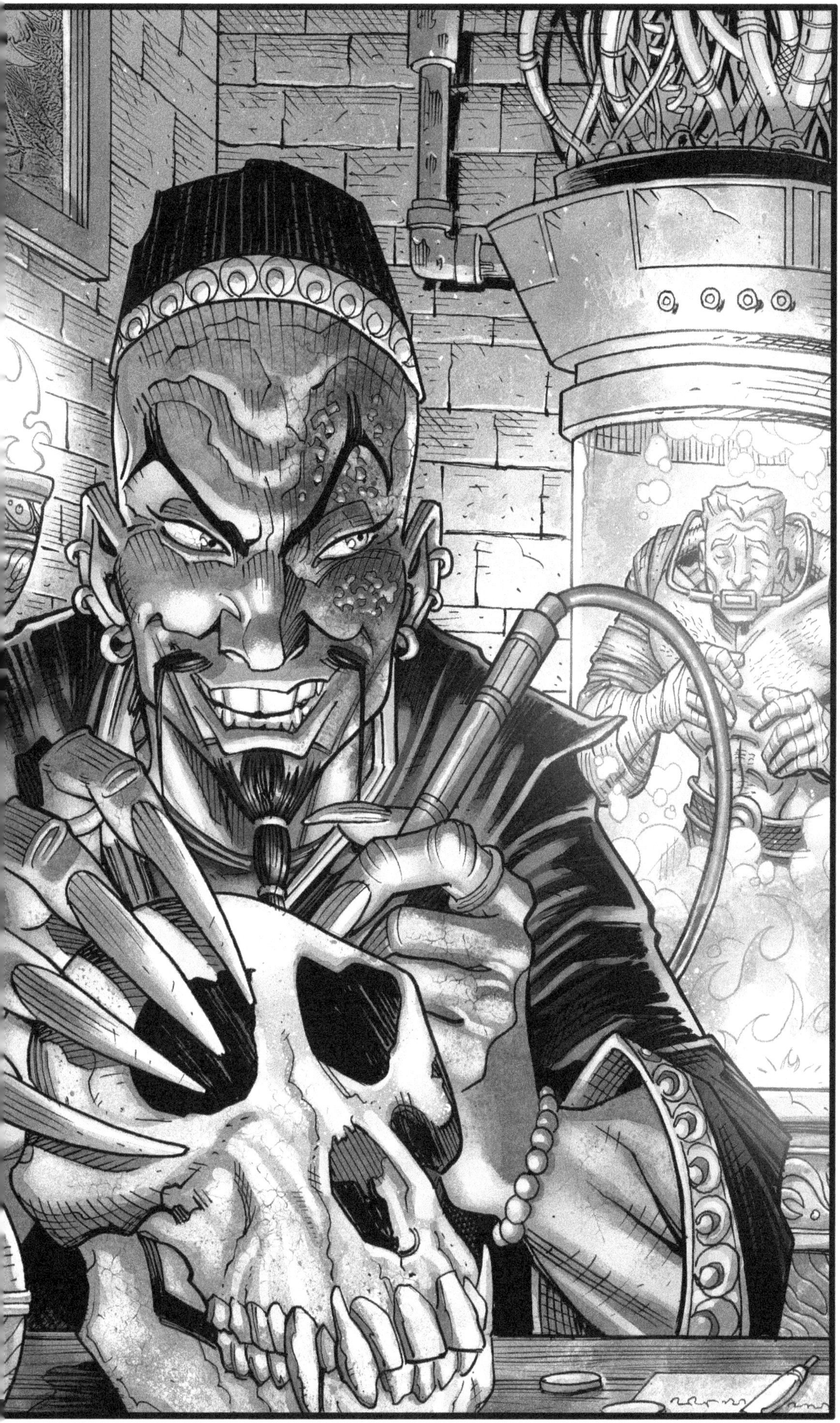

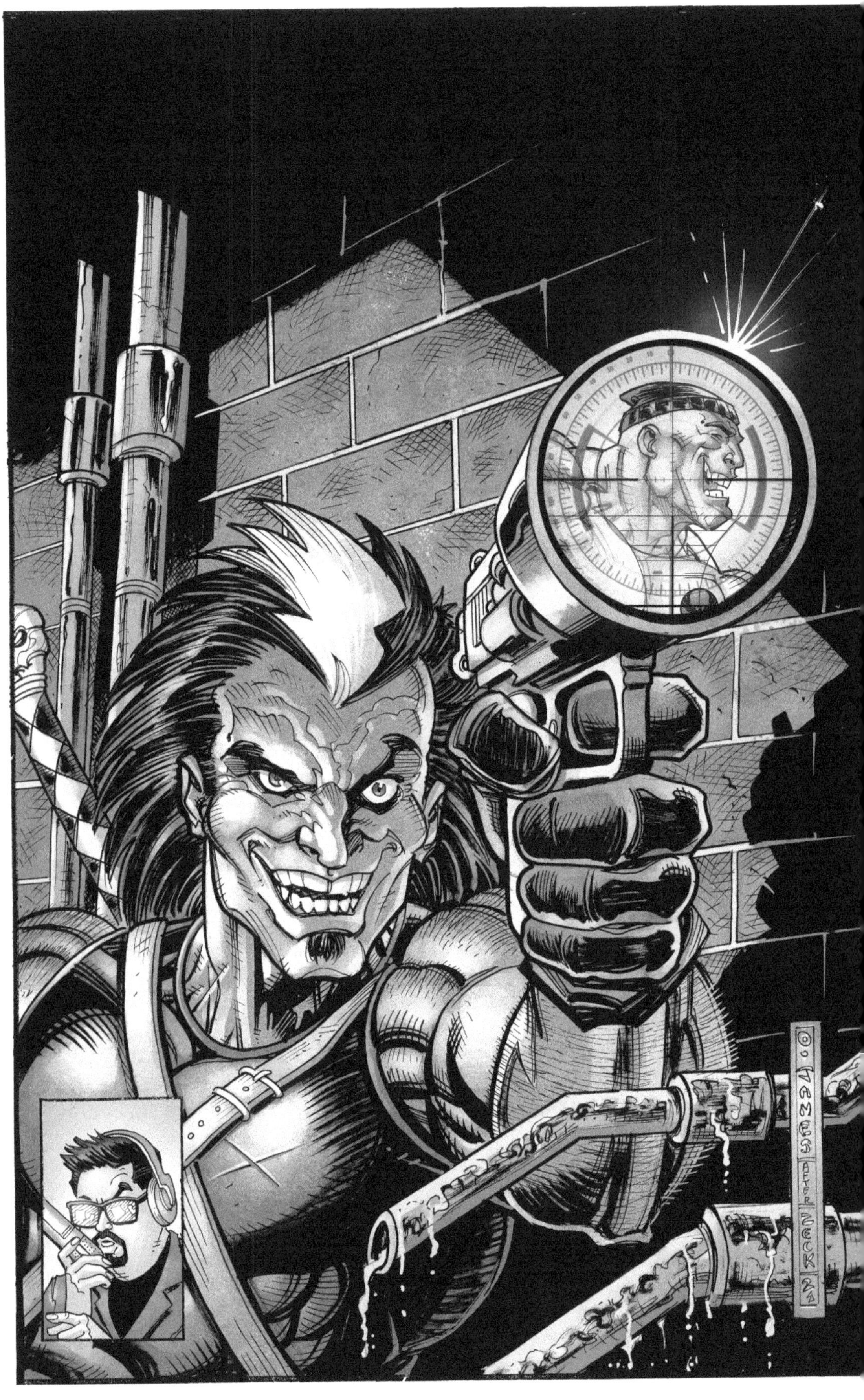
JAMES
AFTER
ZECK

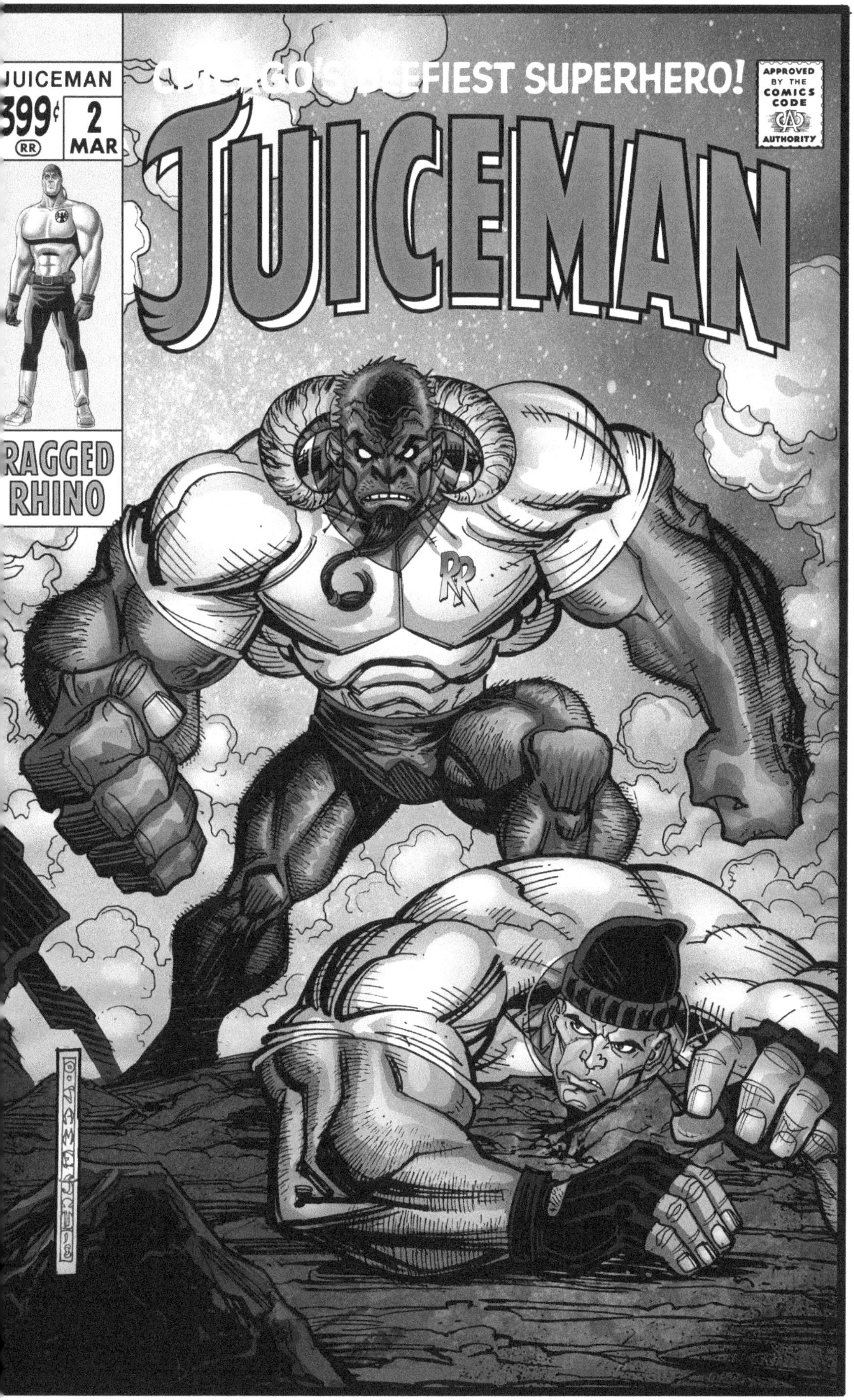

JUICEMAN
399¢
RR
2
MAR
SUPERHERO!
APPROVED BY THE COMICS CODE AUTHORITY
JUICEMAN
RAGGED RHINO
RR

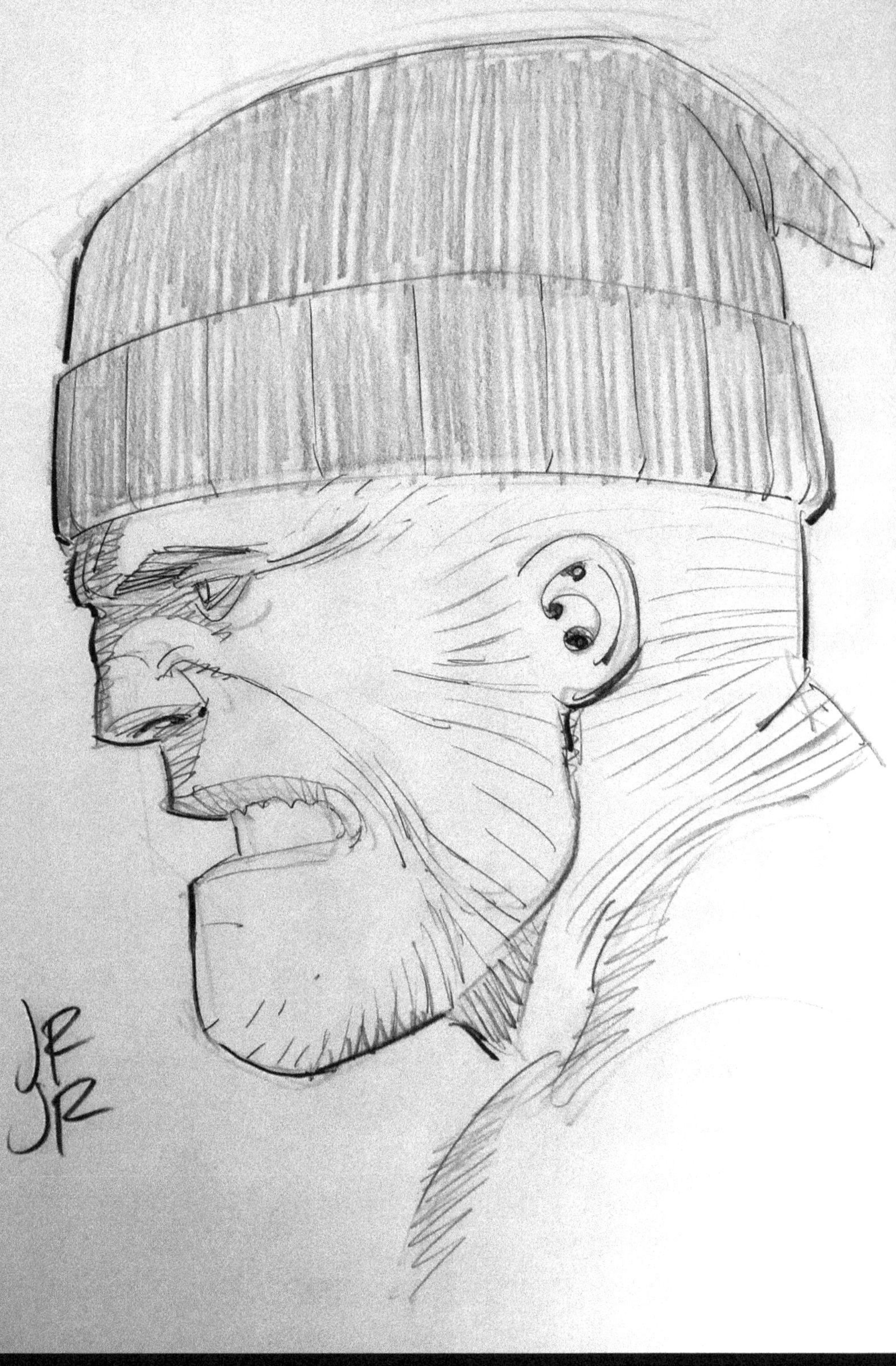
JR
JR

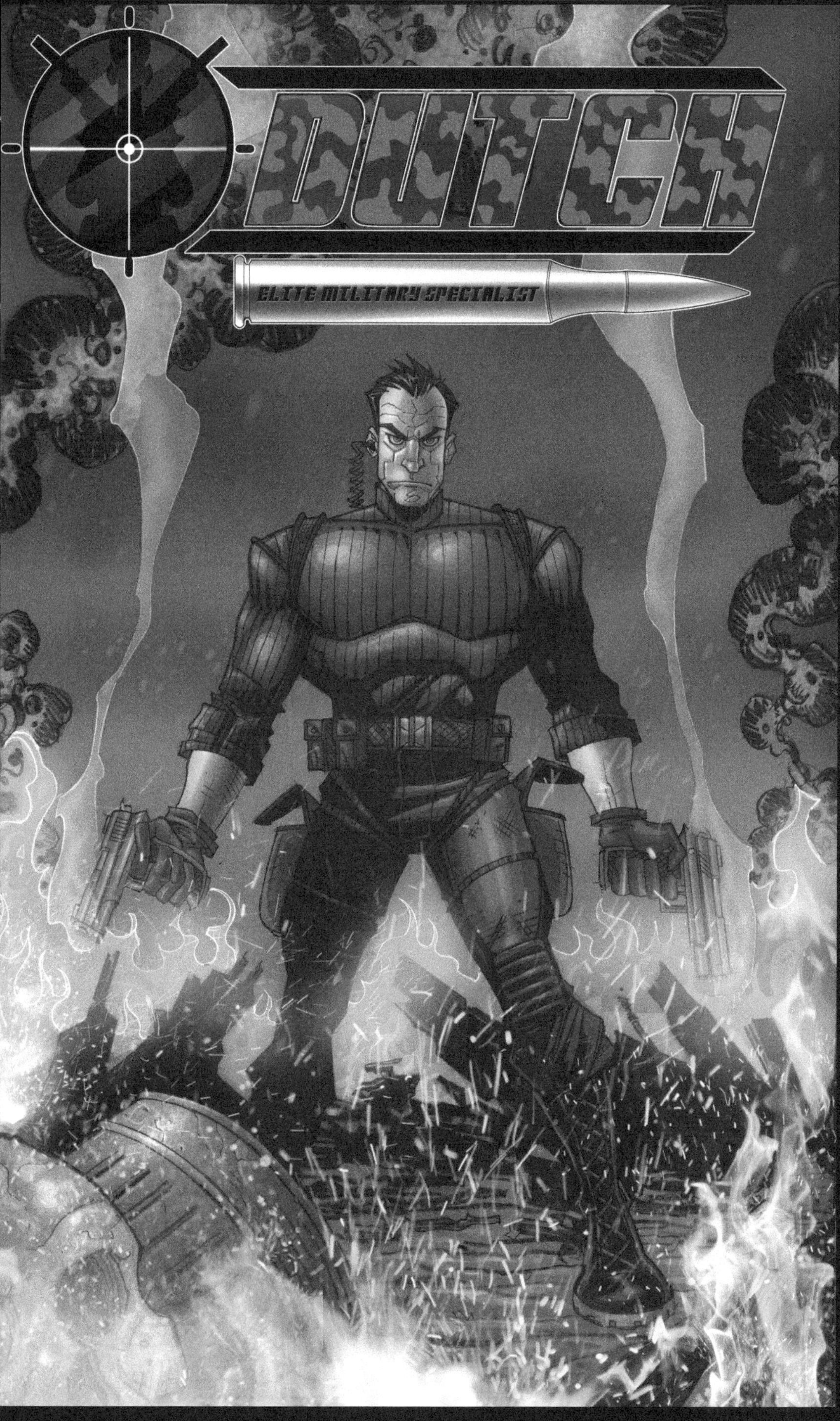
DUTCH
ELITE MILITARY SPECIALIST

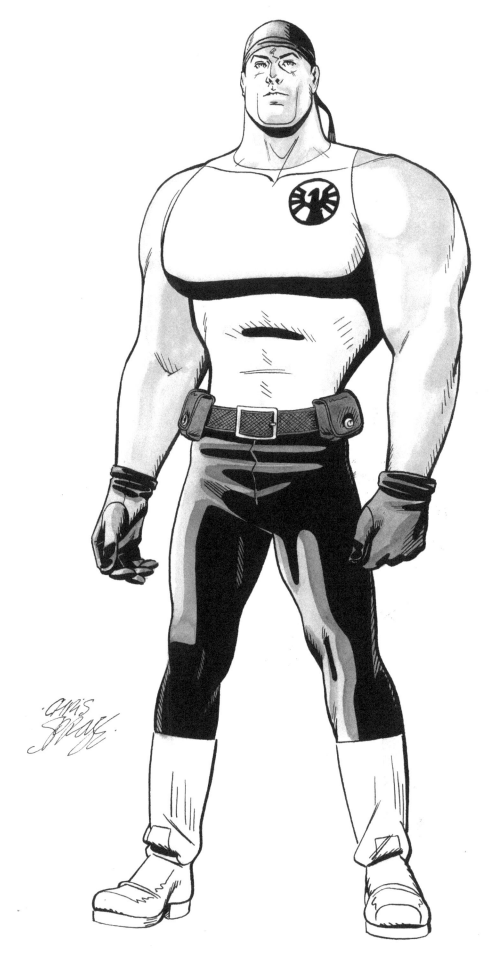

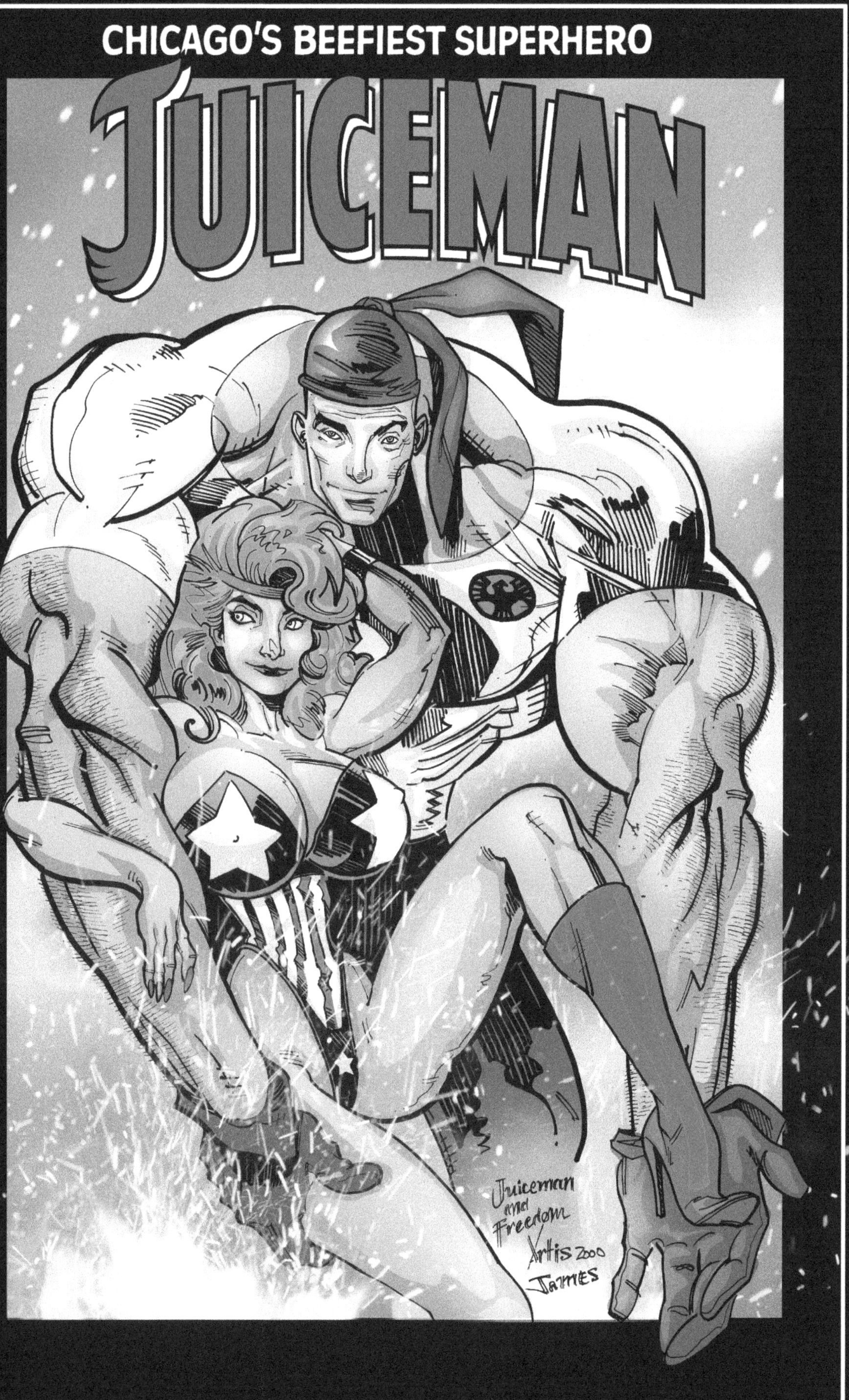
CHICAGO'S BEEFIEST SUPERHERO
JUICEMAN
Juiceman and Freedom
Artis 2000
James

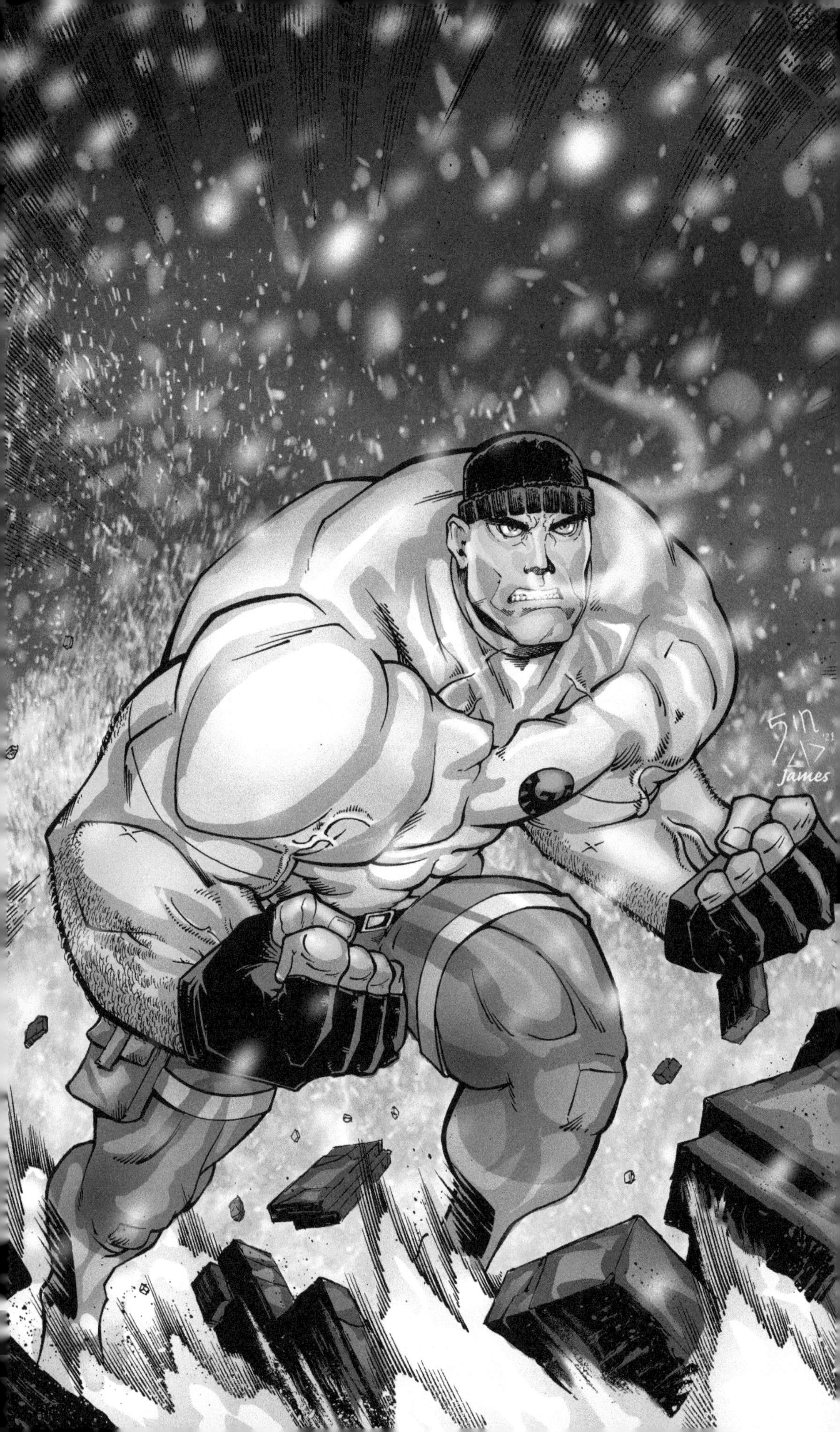
James

Lightning Source UK Ltd.
Milton Keynes UK
UKHW050640200223
417303UK00001B/2